21st-CENTURY CHURCH

By the same author:

The Ten Commandments and the Decline of the West
The Sermon on the Mount

21st-Century Church

Millennium Edition

ROB WARNER

KINGSWAY PUBLICATIONS
EASTBOURNE

First published 1993
This edition 1999

Co-published in South Africa with
SCB Publishers
Cornelis Struik House, 80 McKenzie Street
Cape Town 8001, South Africa
Reg no 04/02203/06

ISBN 0 85476 817 3

Published by
KINGSWAY PUBLICATIONS
Lottbridge Drove, Eastbourne, E. Sussex BN23 6NT.
E-mail: books@kingsway.co.uk

Designed and produced for the publishers by
Bookprint Creative Services, P.O. Box 827, BN21 3YJ, England.
Printed in Great Britain.

To James and Tom
our wonderful sons,
inheritors of the 21st century

Contents

Preface to the Millennium Edition

I have been delighted over the years to meet many leaders who have told me how much this book has come to mean to them. Some have even complained that they have read it so many times that their copy eventually became loose-leaf. Others have made a habit of giving their copy away on a regular basis. One American told me that his leadership team had studied the book before they planted a church and then built it around this vision.

Since the book was first published, I have had many opportunities to develop its themes at speaking engagements, especially those targeted at leaders. For three weeks in early 1999 I have been given the very great privilege of providing keynote addresses on the 21st-century church during the Evangelical Alliance tour of the UK. This seems to be a book whose time has come, and I was therefore eager to see this revised edition available at the dawn of the new millennium.

I have added, updated, clarified and refined much of the material throughout the book, as well as providing two additional chapters. One looks at post-modernity and the cultural captivity of Evangelicals, charismatics and various new church streams. The other reflects upon the lessons we need to learn from the amazing influence and success of Alpha, and its wider implications for church life and mission.

One practical detail was whether to adjust the references to Herne Hill Baptist throughout the text (the church where I was serving at the time of the first edition). I decided not to change them all to the past tense, because they indicate a work in progress – the continued task of making a church new and effective for contemporary mission while holding to the unchanging gospel. They have a continuing value as a snapshot of one experiment in reconnecting the church in two vital directions: back to the values and priorities of the New Testament and forward to reach effectively the generations of the new millennium.

In May 1998 I was lecturing two groups of leaders concerning the church in the 21st century. The Salvation Army leaders were attentive and stimulating company, asking searching and practical questions. The European Baptist national secretaries of evangelism were equally enthusiastic about the need to grasp the nettle of radical change for the sake of renewed effectiveness in mission. But then the French delegate asked an unexpected question: 'We accept the principles, Rob, but what are you doing about it?' I explained that in recent years I have had the privilege of speaking on these themes to many groups of leaders: local church leadership teams, national conferences for Baptists, Methodists and new churches, interdenominational regional training days for leaders, even a diocesan training day for Anglican churches and, not least, Spring Harvest and the first Spring Harvest leadership conference – *At Work Together*. All in all, I thought I was doing my bit to get the message across. Undeterred, the Frenchman persisted. 'That's all very well,' he explained, 'but we need someone like you to do it in practice. Give us a working model with values and methods that are transferable across the post-modern world!'

Like grit in the oyster, that provocation continued to niggle, and played a part in preparing the way for *Kairos* – Church from Scratch, which we launched in autumn 1998. It is too early to know whether we will be able to provide useful approaches for other churches, but our initial vision statement is included as an appendix to this new edition, to indicate one local exploration of what it means to be a church of the 21st century. There are two words in Greek that mean 'time'. *Chronos* is simple, chronological time, as expressed in the phrase 'What's the time?' *Kairos* speaks of timeliness: 'at just the right time', 'now is the time', 'for such a time as this'. It seems a good name for a 21st-century church. Like the French Baptist in my ministry, I hope this book might become creative grit in your life, producing the great pearl of new and effective ways of being church in the 21st century. Now is indeed the appointed time for radical, creative and urgent initiatives in our mission to the world.

Rob Warner
Kairos – Church from Scratch, Wimbledon
November 1998

Foreword to the First Edition

A few years ago I was invited to speak at a series of seminars which were part of the National Evangelical Anglican Celebration at Caister in Norfolk. At that time I was privileged to hear many speakers who addressed that distinguished gathering. One enduring memory was provided by Dr Robert Runcie, who was then Archbishop of Canterbury, when he issued a clarion call to the conference. While recognising the valuable contributions made by evangelicals within the Anglican communion, he highlighted one area that he regarded as a 'major' deficiency. Pointing out the absence of concentrated study in the area of ecclesiology, he urged a fresh impetus among Anglican evangelicals in their understanding of the nature and character of the church.

Some Anglican scholars have subsequently responded to this challenge. Yet I wonder what Dr Runcie's reaction would be to this book, written by an evangelical committed to renewal and church planting. I expect that the theme of *21st-Century Church* would meet with his approval. However, I suspect that its contents and stance may not prove equally appealing. For Rob Warner has not written a work of ecclesiastical scholarship, but instead has concentrated on addressing the issue of what it means to be a relevant church, capable of adapting to the requirements of life in the next millennium.

Any attempt to examine the nature and shape of church life necessary for the 21st century will be an unenviable task. Often evangelicals have concentrated on 'out there' issues. Books on prayer, evangelism and family life abound. Few have dared to attack the fundamental issue of life within the local church. We often forget that ecclesiology, our understanding of the church, is not an abstract discipline. Rather than considering theological propositions from a remote perspective, *21st-Century Church* takes us to the heart of the question, 'What kind of church do we want to be part of?'

By examining the practices we observe, Rob has ventured out on a daring journey. He highlights the irrelevance to secular society of many of the activities in which we engage and points out the redundant character of an archaic religiosity. But then he charts a course of fresh discovery. Rather than offering navigation from the safety of an academic institution, he offers insights drawn from direct experience in local church leadership. The result is a stimulating and invigorating book worthy of careful study and assessment. By reflecting the need for commitment to biblical scholarship and preaching, while advocating fresh means of relating these to contemporary society, a balanced evangelical approach is offered. Cultural relevance and doctrinal integrity are combined in a challenge to rethink traditional patterns of church life.

Not all Rob's ideas will work in every situation, however, but each merits consideration if we are to meet the challenge of the dawn of a new century. This does not mean that Rob

Warner's book is able to address everything. The absence of assessment of corporate church life, of deeper reflections on biblical understanding of 'church' and of the role of the church in the local community, all leave Rob plenty of room to write a sequel! However, by avoiding the danger of trying to cover too much ground he is able to concentrate on his real theme – how to live life as a local church.

Some people follow the axiom of 'if it ain't broke don't fix it'. There is much truth in that idea, and the church has managed to survive two thousand years without dying out. However, it is also true that when machinery looks as if it is becoming worn and liable to malfunction then change is necessary. The changes suggested in this volume do not threaten the life of the church; instead they offer new hope for the future.

Read on at your peril – you have been warned.

Clive Calver
London
October 1993

Preface to the First Edition

As we approach the 21st century, in a context of growing paganism and breathless cultural change, two crucial questions need to be asked by every local church:

- In biblical terms, what is a church meant to be and do?
- In practical terms, what changes must we bring about in order to bridge the gap to the modern world?

It would not have been possible for me to begin to explore these issues without the opportunities of ministry in the two churches I have served, Buckhurst Hill and Herne Hill Baptist churches. My thanks go to the members, congregations and leadership teams for their patience and encouragement which has meant so much. Particular thanks must also go to the late David Watson, under whose ministry in York I saw at first hand the attracting power of renewal in the local church; to Bob Moffett, who first prompted me to apply goal-setting and management principles to local church leadership; to Derek Tidball, who invited me to give a paper at a symposium on Gospel and Culture alongside his two other guest contributors, Lesslie Newbigin and Andrew Walker, and then encouraged me to take my ideas further; to Michael Green, with whom I spent some creative time during a World Evangelism conference in Brighton, teasing out some of my ideas about cultural engagement; to Mike Wheate, whose passion for world mission is tireless; to Penny Marsh, Herne Hill's director of evangelism and church planting, whose endeavours and expertise have taught me so much; to Jackie Lawrence, whose pastoral devotion and administrative skills keep our church on the road; to Edward England, who gave me some wonderful opportunities as a Christian book publisher and ever since has regularly encouraged me to make time to write; to the fellow members of my ministry support group, Peter Swaffield, John Taylor and Geoff Shattock, who prayed for me and believed in me as I wrote; to Heiner Rust, Reginaldo Kruklis and Stuart Christine, whose friendship and hospitality allowed me to discover more about church health, growth and planting in Germany and Brazil; to the four Brazilian seminaries in Sao Paulo and Rio de Janeiro, where I was able to test out my ideas with the students.

Above all my thanks must go to my dear wife, Claire, whose patient support while I have been writing has been magnificent, and to my sons, James and Thomas, who know how best to divert me into fun and games when I have worked more than long enough and to whom this book is dedicated.

Herne Hill
October 1993

PART ONE

BRIDGING THE GAP

1

Church on the Rocks

Have you ever wandered into a church, perhaps on holiday, sat quietly at the back and wondered how Christians could have become so out of touch with the vast majority of the population? Or maybe you have sometimes found yourself worrying closer to home: 'Help, I think my church is irrelevant!'

I remember once visiting three churches in a town, one Sunday after another. The Anglicans conducted their liturgy with great composure and solemnity in a time-honoured formal manner, attracting the upper middle-class élite of the town with hymns ancient and modern and classical music during the offertory. In his sermon, the rector warned his congregation of the dangers of excessive dependence upon the emotions. The Pentecostals shouted their hallelujahs and enjoyed exuberant, high-octane praise, in a style that appeared unchanged for generations, while the preacher warned his mainly unlearned congregation against the dangers of intellectualism. The Baptists had a middle-class, middle-aged, middle-of-the-road singing group, who sang safe and predictable melodies that would have been at home in the early fifties before the arrival of rock and roll.

These were effective churches by normal standards. They were reasonably strong in numbers, and wanted to make progress for Christ. The congregations all seemed fairly pleased with what was going on, which met their own needs well. What tore at my heart was a simple fact. Here was a town with several Bible-believing churches. They did things in different ways and respected one another, so their variety provided a positive advantage in trying to reach the people of the area. But the plain truth was that the vast majority of the local population remained entirely indifferent to the churches, untouched by their lives, unmoved by their message. For the insiders, it was good to belong to these churches. For the outsiders, they might just as well have existed on another planet.

The church in Britain and Europe is in a crisis of decline. Between 1975 and 1989 the churches of England lost 47,000 people each year. That was nearly 1,000 people leaving the church each week, and not all of them departed in coffins! In fact it seems that many churchgoers are losing the Sunday morning habit, and such recruitment as there is still leaves us with this massive shortfall.

The age profile of the church compared with the nation makes things worse. In Australia and the USA many churches are significantly greyer than the surrounding population. As for England, in 1989, 55 per cent of the adult population were under 45, while in the church just 45 per cent were under 45. Like many major cities around the world, London is younger than most of the country, with 58 per cent of adults under 45. London churches have 51 per cent of adults in this age group. At the same time, the least reached generation in England are those in their twenties, where a staggering 94 per cent have no real contact with the Christian church.

This means that during the next twenty years there will be more people dying in the church than in the nation, simply because there are more elderly people in churches. Therefore, unless something dramatic happens, the rate of decline of church attendance is likely to accelerate. Small wonder that *The Independent on Sunday* commented that the Christian era, 'with less than one tenth of the population attending church . . . can be said to be receding into history'.[1]

In Africa, Asia and Latin America the church is growing with mind-blowing speed. In Latin America, Evangelicals have been growing at 10 per cent per annum for forty years. In Africa, there were estimated in 1945 to be 20 million Christians. By 1978, over thirty years later, this had jumped to 70 million. By 1988, just one decade later, this figure had leaped to a remarkable 250 million. That is healthy growth by any standards!

Or take the case of a single church, the Deeper Life Bible Church of Lagos, led by William Kumuyi, which has grown rapidly to become one of the largest churches in the world. In 1973 there were fifteen members. In 1982 this had grown to 5,000. Today there are some 80,000 members, plus 40,000 children. More than 2,000 Deeper Life churches have been planted in over thirty African countries and more recently they have planted into Europe too. No wonder the Mission 2000 conference in Stuttgart in 1988 concluded: 'We rejoice in the unprecedented growth of the church . . .'

In the West there is a crisis of effectiveness. Indeed, some would say there is a crisis of survival, especially in the cities. So

---

[1] David Nicholson-Lord (20 June 1993).

is the church in terminal decline? Some local churches are dying, there can be no disputing the evidence. Some denominations may be spiralling to extinction. But there are also many churches reporting new signs of life, and many new church plants are appearing. As the Stuttgart conference stated, 'We believe that a new day of growth is possible in Europe.'

Take our church in South London as a fairly typical example. The membership in the mid-sixties was smaller than that in the mid-fifties. In the mid-seventies, we were smaller than in the mid-sixties. In the mid-eighties we were smaller than in the mid-seventies. However, by the early nineties the church was larger than it had ever been in its history. This is by no means an isolated example. Out of the ashes of the church as it has struggled along for many decades, there are hints of a new dawn. In town after town and city after city, new life, new confidence and new hope are emerging.

It is not enough to cite some thrilling stories of growth. I used to be a publisher, and my commercial experience taught me a vital principle: if a company is in crisis, it requires radical surgery or liquidation. I am convinced that the good news of Jesus Christ is infinitely more significant for the world than the success of any commercial organisation. I am therefore all the more convinced that a combination of blind optimism and papering over the cracks is no substitute for facing squarely the radical restructuring that is required by the church in the West. It is not simply a matter of asking what changes will be required for the church to be fit to communicate the gospel to the generations of the 21st century. The uncomfortable truth is that the church is not yet fit for today.

Ever since the collapse of the Soviet bloc, new souvenirs have filled the tourist sites of central and Eastern Europe: the badges, caps and coats of the enormous army of the Russian

Empire. An army that held half of Europe in bondage has been thrown on the scrap heap. The old equipment is now surplus to requirements. The church seems much the same to many people today. It is something they can do without, irrelevant to the world of the late 20th century and surplus to requirements. We need to put our feet in the shoes of outsiders, and view the church from their detached perspective. Instead of accepting the way we do things as normal or natural, we need a new way of seeing church life. Only then can we begin to understand the harsh truth that the greatest hindrance to the gospel today is often the church. I want to reflect on some of the key shaping influences of the modern world: office blocks and shopping malls, television, the women's movement, the growth of informality, marketing and open talk about sex.

The message of buildings

I was recently in Cairo and while I was there I visited a well-established church. The worship was vibrant and the preaching was clear. Indeed, the fact that a woman was preaching spoke volumes in a Muslim city about the liberating power of the Christian gospel. None the less, two things saddened me. First, the stained-glass windows contained pictures of Christ. Now I certainly have no hang-ups about stained glass, nor in principle to portrayals of Christ. Since God sent Christ in human form so that he could be seen and touched, I have never considered representation of Christ to be forbidden by the Old Testament ban on graven images. But Muslims take this command so seriously that all their art is abstract and geometrical. They won't have a representation of any human being in their mosques, let alone God. It seems to me that the Christians could live without the stained glass much more easily than passing Muslims could cope with it. To them it would be a great offence and a stumbling-block. And that is simply not necessary.

My second problem was with the furniture. It was beautiful. The pews were superbly carved from the finest quality wood. They would have looked wonderful in a traditional American church. And that was the problem! In mosques the floors are covered with carpets, but never pews. The pews looked foreign, indeed Western. But Muslims know only too well that the Western world is a sewer of immorality. They assume that the Western world is Christian, and therefore easily conclude that Christianity is morally degenerate. If Christians import the building styles and furniture of the West, an extra hurdle is created. Not the hurdle of the gospel itself, but the unnecessary hurdle of Westernisation. How often we still need to make it clear that in order to become Christians people don't have to become traditional Western churchgoers. In fact it is generally much better if that is exactly what they don't try to become!

The style and presentation of buildings is not just an issue in other parts of the world. It is a fundamental issue in the West. When the Anglican cathedral in Liverpool was opened some years ago, one newspaper observed, 'God likes Gothic.' The journalist seemed to mean that a building in an architectural style harking back to the Middle Ages felt suitably religious. It was somehow reassuring to be in a building removed from the everyday world. This reflects the kind of God many people feel it is safe to ignore. A God for the religious – quaint, nostalgic and completely out of touch with the real world of today.

Mock Gothic and modern Paris

The French are determined to make Paris a city with a future even more glorious than its past. New buildings are going up at a tremendous rate, for use by the government, in arts and education, and by major international companies. Some of the buildings have stirred great debate. Some will be reviled until they are torn down. Others are spectacular successes, and have been added to the tour bus routes. Because Paris is a city that is ambitious and confident about its future, the designs of the buildings, their decor and lighting, are vibrant, adventurous and bold. None is mock Gothic. The vitality of the living God is surely better expressed in the adventurous spirit of modern Paris than in our tired, safe and predictable church buildings.

Shopping today

The importance of the look of buildings is seen above all in the retailing revolution, for shopping has become a leading leisure activity in the Western world. The relentless construction of shopping malls is taking consumers out of town centres and old-style department stores into a new kind of shopping and leisure experience, with everything available under one roof. The choice is enormous, the convenience is considerable, the range of foods to consume between purchases is increasingly exotic. Descartes may have coined those immortal words: '*Cogito ergo sum*' ('I think therefore I am') and so argued that 'to think is to be', and Sartre concluded that 'to do is to be', but modern consumer society is driven by a more trivial pursuit. In today's world, 'to shop is to be' – '*Tesco ergo sum*'.

Shoppers require a shop not only to stock the right goods at the right price, but also to look right. Famous old stores on both sides of the Atlantic have failed to understand that you have to provide not only the right products, but also the right environment. As a result they have gone out of business, or come under new management that understands today's world. The malls and shops recognise that presentation is half the battle, because shopping today is no longer simply about products – it's about lifestyle. A few shops still survive on the old philosophy of pile 'em high and sell 'em cheap. But most shops are designed down to the last detail. It is not just the cardboard and plastic containers that are packaging; the shop itself has become packaging for the goods it sells. You may love or loathe the malls. Some people thrive on the ever higher standards of presentation and interior design. Others bemoan the fact that while the first impression is polished, there is no character in these places, no distinctive depth or style. If you've seen one mall, you've seen them all.

Whether you spend every free Saturday in the malls or you are reluctantly dragged there once a year for Christmas shopping, one thing is clear. People are becoming more visually aware in their shopping. We increasingly make judgements about the quality of the produce by the first impression made upon us by the shop itself. It is the same with offices and banks. More and more money is spent on presentation, conveying a visual message about the quality of the organisation and its products or services.

Now consider the typical church building. Most are visually illiterate in today's terms. Worn-out lino is partially covered by a cheap and tattered rug, of which the once violent colours have long since faded into drabness. Tired posters peel from poorly painted walls, advertising events that took place several weeks ago. Someone must have sold a job lot of bile green gloss paint to churches because the same wretched and dreary colour seems to adorn church doors and windows in every town. Church fabric committees certainly favour cheap lighting: bulbs that don't work and the harsh glare of bare fluorescent strips are the order of the day, when shops, offices and homes use increasingly subtle lighting effects.

Then there's the furniture. At one time most people sat on wood. It can look wonderful, and lasts for generations. However, most people today prefer something more comfortable at home and in the office. I am quite sure that when people sat on wooden chairs and benches at home it was perfectly natural to sit on an elongated bench in churches, but the world has changed. The pew no longer has a point of contact with the furniture of today's ideal home. The pew is alien, uncomfortable and certainly doesn't put outsiders at their ease, which more or less sums up their general reaction to churches and to God.

We live in an age where many consumers first assess a product by its package, and a retail outlet by its shop window and entrance. The whole experience of modern shopping creates this kind of visual responsiveness and sophistication. In such a world, where the look of a building indicates the quality of the goods or services, we have a grave problem. Run-down buildings suggest a second-rate product. A negative impression is being formed of our 'product' even before the believers are met and the message is preached. The threadbare appearance of our buildings suggests that we believe in a jumble sale god.

The accelerating pace of television

Even more than shopping, television has been a dominant shaping force of the modern world. We simply cannot begin to understand popular culture without considering the impact of this extraordinarily influential medium. Television devours time in almost every household. TV dinners have replaced the family evening meal together. We may not like what we see, but most of us just cannot help turning on to chill out.

A few react to TV's dominance by throwing out their TV and cutting themselves off. Though this may work as a form of self-purification, it is certainly not the way our society is going. Interactive entertainment and information systems are the way of the future. The box in the corner will not only have a huge range of channels available through the burgeoning satellite and cable networks of the digital revolution. It will also have a computer attached, providing a wide range of multimedia entertainment. The familiar alien-zapping of today's Gameboys will be accompanied by feature length films on DVD, in which the viewer will be able to take part, choosing between different story lines and endings. Many banking and shopping services will also be linked through the Internet to the same screen, so that many transactions will be completed from the comfort of home. Make no mistake about it, the impact of TV will keep on growing.

In order to understand how TV is changing the way we look at the world, it is illuminating to compare a documentary or drama made today with one from the sixties. At that time, documentaries tended to have a much more linear feel, developing their argument in a similar way to a book. Today, the theme is developed allusively, leaving gaps for the viewer to jump. Then, the documentary often presented an abstract thesis with visual accompaniment. Today, the general is told through the particular. That is, almost all television today tells a story, in which the issue or theme is experienced first hand through the plight of a particular individual.

At one time, directors would show clips of someone leaving home, getting into a car, making the journey and so on. Today, programme-makers can be confident that the viewer understands the medium, so swift scene changes are possible, relying on the viewer to fill in the narrative gaps. This is now the standard bill of fare for middle-brow programming. Today's popular story lines are multilayered and interleaved, weaving a fast-moving fabric of many different narrative threads.

Employing the sophisticated conventions of modern television does not make for more or less intelligent programmes, but it does make for a faster pace. It also encourages a lower tolerance for abstract propositions and a shorter concentration span. The main news programmes on the BBC are broken into accommodating morsels, as if built around advertising breaks. What is more, TV is almost universally allergic to the 'talking head'. Very few faces are shown for more than thirty seconds without some kind of changing visual stimulus, whether in the background or through cutting to film over which they continue to talk.

There is an aversion in most TV to presenting a single point of view. On almost any issue current affairs programmes, both light and highbrow, usually set up two experts or campaigners to debate an issue. Neither has time to develop an argument. No room is allowed for compromise. It is a kind of gladiatorial argument in which the verbal sword thrusts are crisp and striking aphorisms, sound-bites that have been carefully rehearsed in advance.

This lends an appearance of even-handedness, suggesting that the TV company is fully aware of what it means to live in a pluralistic world, where the market-place of opinions is enormously diverse. It also has the result of reducing serious debate to an entertainment in which the real winner is almost always the presenter. TV devours issues to serve its own end of successful ratings. Persuasive argument is replaced by the appearance, personality and rhetorical polish of a single sound-bite. Some of the great political debaters of the last century would never get on air today: too verbose, too ugly and too short. Worst of all for political triumph in the TV age, several of them had beards! Roll over Lincoln and Disraeli – there is no place for the grand old style in the entertainment age!

We may sum up some of the key aspects of television culture as follows:

- *A faster and snappier pace*, often with rapid changes of theme and mood.
- *Increased use of story-telling* in preference to abstract argument.
- *Decreased dependence on linear flow*, with a growing tendency to leave unseen the links between key scenes.
- *Increasing informality* – consider at one extreme the starchiness of fifties television. Note also that today's middle-aged guests on quiz shows often wear jumpers and open-necked shirts rather than the once mandatory jacket and tie.
- *Increasing participation*, whether on *Oprah*, programmes of political debate such as *Question Time*, or quiz shows. The old attitude of the formal lecture room expected a passive audience whose task was to sit quietly and imbibe the wisdom of the professionals on the platform. In the TV age this traditional style is in terminal decline. Now everyone expects the right to have their say.
- *Increasing visual impact*. Some of the highest production values on TV today are found in the top adverts: good to look at, with subtle camera angles and editing, obliqueness and humour, glamour and entertainment. Crude advertising gives a verbal hard sell. Sophisticated advertising recognises a simple principle: what enchants the eye is almost always more persuasive than what batters the ear.

Most of these trends are in themselves neutral. They represent a style of communication which is intrinsically neither better nor worse, but they do reflect the familiar conventions of the television age. This is the kind of communication with which the majority of people are most at home. Now consider the unspoken cultural conventions of most church services. Monday to Saturday we live in a world shaped by TV. A world imbued with prodigious pace, variety, colour, informality, fast-moving debates, a huge number of personal stories, and very few 'talking heads'. On Sunday mornings we enter an alternative world, in which one or two men (usually men) conduct a safe, predictable, slow-moving presentation, almost exclusively centred on 'talking heads'.

Some may find this a welcome escape from the TV age, but we are asking the outsider to make an enormous leap into an alien world. With acetates and Powerpoint, videos and banners, drama and dance, and the imaginative use of music and interviews, there is an enormous amount we can do to make creative contact with the world in which most people live. The fact that many churches find it hard to do so suggests that it is not really a high priority. The comfort of Christians usually matters more than communicating with the vast majority of the population. Many years ago Gavin Reid wrote about the 'gagging of God'. As the TV revolution not only continues to unfold but accelerates, the tragic truth in many churches is that with every passing year God and the gospel are more firmly gagged and bound – not by the persecutors of the faith, but by the failure of the church to adapt to a new world of communication.

When I studied English Literature at university I had to spend time learning Anglo-Saxon, the ancient language from which English eventually grew. To distribute leaflets in London today written in Anglo-Saxon or Latin would be completely futile; we would be trying to communicate in a dead language. As communication to the inhabitants of the

TV age, some of our Sunday services are just as pointless. To put it starkly, we are boring people to hell.

The women's movement

It may seem strange to include an ideology alongside shopping malls and television, but that is the kind of world in which we live. The women's movement has provided an influential and compelling critique of Western society. It has come in from the cold and entered mainstream and popular thinking. While radical feminism will always remain on the margins, the essential analysis of sexual equality and sexual discrimination at home and at work has become the received wisdom of late 20th-century society. Many battles have been won in principle, even though the implications are yet to be worked out in practice, both in the workplace and in the home. As leading Labour politician Harriet Harman concluded in *The Century Gap*:

> Women have left the twentieth century behind. To the majority of young women of all backgrounds today the role of lifelong, full-time, dependent housewife is neither an option nor an ideal . . . the vast majority of men are still living by the old twentieth-century-breadwinner-dependent-housewife model, with all the assumptions about control and values that this entails.[1]

There are still relatively few women in senior business positions, but it is no longer tenable to suggest that women are not up to the job. There are still far fewer women in politics than there should be, but across the world women are making an increasing impact. Golda Meir and Indira Gandhi proved

---

[1] *The Century Gap*, pp. 1, 25.

to be two of the most powerful heads of state of the post-war years. Margaret Thatcher made her uniquely forceful mark upon Britain and the world, and proved more successful at winning elections than any previous party leader this century. When I first wrote this chapter, Kim Campbell had just become the first female prime minister of Canada, and Tansu Ciller had achieved the same in Turkey. This latter case was the much more surprising, given that Turkey is a Muslim country and that Ciller had declared an intention to promote equality for women as well as improve Turkey's human rights record. It is a sign of new times that the leader of the pro-fundamentalist Turkish Welfare Party stated, 'The coming of a woman to power is not important. The important thing is to see how she runs the country.'[1] Maybe there will even be a woman President of the United States within a generation.

In television, women are no longer a rarity as news presenters. Their presence has come to be expected, and it is increasingly common to have the news anchored by two women, where once only men were seen. While some early women reporters were chosen more to decorate the studio than bring journalistic incisiveness, women are now appointed according to ability. The playing field is becoming more level. It is true that there remain a number of professions and workplaces where women are conspicuously absent. Inevitably there is also a fossilised sexism among the dinosaurs of the establishment, notably among those deprived of contact with women on an equal basis as a result of a so-called 'privileged education' – through a single sex school, a single sex college and a practically single sex profession. But the

---

[1] *Newsweek* (28 June 1993).

basic climate of opinion has shifted radically and irreversibly. You can no longer get away with dismissing career women with snide and patronising remarks. What is more, each new generation is more acutely aware not only of overt sexual discrimination, but also of unconsciously sexist attitudes, assumptions and language.

Women are still excluded from senior positions in many fields of work, resulting in the experience of a 'glass ceiling', an invisible restriction on their opportunities. In the late nineties, it has been suggested that new values emerging in the workplace are likely to result in the shattering of the glass ceiling. Every era has its own preferred qualities for success at work. Today new qualities are coming to the fore: team-working, juggling roles, co-operation and collaboration. It has been suggested that women more often excel at these qualities and that their approach to leadership is more co-operative and less authoritarian. If there is any truth in these claims, in future it may even be the men who are struggling to learn new ways of working in order to succeed in their career.

So what of the church in this new world of sexual equality? In Britain, the Anglican debate about the ordination of women seems to have been going on for ever. Even now, when the final votes have been taken, the debate appears to be gathering fresh pace and vehemence, with great resistance to the prospect of women bishops. The impression to many outsiders is that, when even a political party as wary of change as the Tories has been able to appoint a woman leader, the church can barely stomach the idea of women being treated as men's equals.

The history of the church regretfully includes a catalogue of misogyny and discrimination from some of its finest champions. Augustine and Luther were two of the greatest leaders and thinkers of the Western church. Both experienced dramatic conversion as a result of reading the book of Romans. The writings of both have profoundly enriched historical theology, not least in their studies of the human condition, the nature of salvation and the doctrine of the church. Sadly both exhibited a lamentable, but no less typical, disregard for women. While Augustine expressed doubt that women were made in the image of God, Luther attempted to derive from their physique the conclusion that a woman's rightful place is in the home:

> Men have broad shoulders and narrow hips, and accordingly they possess intelligence. Women have narrow shoulders and broad hips. Women ought to stay at home; the way they were created indicates this, for they have broad hips and a wide fundament to sit upon, keep house and bear and raise the children.[1]

If we consider local churches today, the old jibe often remains true: that the church is an organisation run by men and made up of women. In many churches, two-thirds of the congregation are women, with few women in any leadership role and even fewer in any kind of platform ministry. I first observed intense sexism among Christians as a teenager. It indicated a distinct worldview, not so much Christian but rather an obsolete pre-war perspective. At each year's AGM in the Anglican church where I was converted, one bone of contention was bound to be raised: whether women could become sidesmen. Every year the same old man would rise to his feet and explain that he had been brought up to believe that a man's place was to show a lady to her seat, and he could not bring himself to believe that anything else was becoming in a civilised world. One year a member of our church won the Tunbridge Wells

---

[1] *Table Talk* (1531).

poetry reading competition. The rest of the congregation was naturally delighted. But the champion of public reading was unable to contribute to Sunday services. Unfortunately the victor was a young woman, and, as the PCC's representative patiently explained to the youth group, it is a fact universally acknowledged that the acoustic of ancient church buildings makes it impossible to hear a woman's voice. Try telling that to Dame Judi Dench or Baroness Thatcher, let alone Tina Turner or Celine Dion!

Things have improved a great deal since those days, but reactionary churches have sought to emulate Henry Ford, when he explained that you could have any colour car you wanted, so long as it was black. Women in chauvinist churches can engage in any ministry for which they are gifted, so long as it is making coffee or working with children. The lost opportunities are gargantuan. The Bible presents an attitude to women radically different from traditional Western society. The 'wife of noble character' in Proverbs 31 bears no comparison with the Victorian ideal of the 'little wife at home', whose wealth became her husband's and who was stripped of just about all initiative save in deciding the menu for dinner. The Old Testament ideal for womanhood had wealth of her own, ran a business from home, and engaged in trading and land purchases without consulting her husband.

In the Roman Empire, the early church proved to be a radical alternative society. Disdain was the prevailing attitude to women. They were unschooled, glorified servants at home, and generally had no religious function except as temple prostitutes. In the marriage relationship, speaking to men who had been used to treating their wives as those who must obey, Paul gave the instruction to love your wife just as Christ loved the church. So far so good – unthreatening to any husband of the Roman Empire. Then Paul defined this new kind of love – 'and gave himself up for her' (Ephesians 5:25). This was an absolute bombshell to 1st-century husbands! In the Empire a wife gave herself up for the well-being of her husband and master. In the church, Paul argues that the self-giving of Christ now requires husbands to give of themselves in like manner for their wives. An entirely radical and even subversive concept of mutuality in marriage arose among the first Christians.

As to the life of the church, when the Holy Spirit came upon the believers for the first time, the same baptism of power came upon women as well as men, and Peter drew attention to this when he quoted from the prophet Joel: 'I will pour out my Spirit on all people. Your sons and daughters will prophesy' (Acts 2:17). Among the women who received and used the gift of prophecy were the four daughters of the evangelist Philip (Acts 21:9). Lydia hosted a new church plant (Acts 16:15), Priscilla seems to have taken the lead in training a key young leader (Acts 18:26), Junias – probably a woman's name – is described as an 'apostle' (Romans 16:7), and Phoebe and other women served as deacons (Romans 16:1; 1 Timothy 3:11). The evidence is plain that the early Christians believed in and encouraged practical expression of the liberation of women in Christ in ways that were quite extraordinary to the world of the Roman Empire.

The apostle Paul observed that the three fundamental patterns of discrimination in human society are racial, economic and sexual. His glorious assertion is that faith in Christ has the power to annul these divisions and bring about a new world order: 'There is neither Jew nor Greek, slave nor free, male nor female, for you are all one in Christ Jesus' (Galatians 3:28). What a tragedy that over the centuries the institutional church has accommodated to the prevailing values of society and become far removed from the first Christians' alternative way of living.

Sexual discrimination in the church is unjust to individual gifted women. It is unjust to half the human race, given neither opportunity nor real dignity. It is unjust to the whole church, because everyone misses out if half the human race are suppressed. And it is unjust to the world, which is led to draw the conclusion that if the church is an accurate reflection of the gospel, then the gospel itself is sexist, and has no relevance to a post-modern, post-sexist society. If we have the courage to get back to our roots, and the courage to engage with society today, where the abilities of women have been well proven and deep-rooted discrimination has been unmasked, the church has the potential again to be a community of equality and liberation. But all too often the judgement of the world remains accurate: the church has been and frequently continues to be a sexist institution.

An informal society

Our three remaining factors make a less dramatic impact. But each of them shapes today's world in such ways as to create new hurdles for the church. Britain has long been a country where respected men dress up in strange, archaic clothes to conduct their public duties. But times are changing. Even in Britain there is now a serious debate as to whether judges should abandon their traditional wigs and fancy dress. Banks are working hard to abandon their old formal, fustian ways. Some twenty years ago there was a British advertising campaign stressing that bank managers really are approachable and accessible to ordinary customers, by showing a warm and friendly individual waiting patiently in a wardrobe until you requested help with your finances. It was not the most subtle or convincing of adverts, and some real bank managers at the time complained that it brought their serious-minded profession into frivolous disrepute. Just go into a bank today and see how much the conventions have shifted: staff in major banks now wear lapel badges giving their first name only.

In the States, the presidential press conference is a striking example of a new world order. Presidents are now expected to face tough questions and not simply be given an open platform to trumpet their successes. In Britain, Sir Robin Day is generally credited with abandoning the old forelock-tugging servitude of political journalists. Today his successors show no sycophancy before politicians' slippery evasions.

Meanwhile, there are still churches where first names are never mentioned in the notices. Collecting the offering has the formal precision of a military exercise, and communion is distributed with the co-ordinated stiffness and unreality of a synchronised swimming team. No one is ever allowed to be out of step as communion is dispensed. There is of course one striking difference: a synchronised swimming team operates with fixed grins, while in some churches the obligatory fixed expression is a good deal less cheerful.

I remember visiting a church in a university town where more graduates were gathered in the congregation than anywhere except a university senior common room. The minister was the only one of them to wear his hood and gown. But why? In previous generations, the minister was often the only graduate in a local church; in some the only person who could read. Today's society is more educated, more informal, more egalitarian. One solution would be for everyone to wear their robes of office and uniforms to Sunday services. But that is just not true to today's world. In most sections of British society, traditional 'Sunday best' has been replaced by weekend casual. When outsiders visit a church these days, more often than not they don't dress up; they come as they are. It's about time, not merely in what the minister wears, but more importantly in the whole feel of the event, that the church entered today's informal and egalitarian world.

A society immersed in marketing

When our children were young they were always trying to persuade Claire and me to take them to McDonald's, even though I kept trying to explain that I prefer Chinese. But when I'm out of town and want a quick bite or a coffee, there is something reassuring about the Golden Arches. You can always recognise the decor. You know they won't keep you waiting. And you know they are proud of standards you can trust. As a result, I've had a Big Mac in many cities. They may not be haute cuisine, but they are always reliable, and they certainly know how to promote themselves.

I recently spoke with a publisher who had just received the sequel to a best-seller. He believed in the book, he anticipated considerable profits, and he considered his expensive marketing strategy a necessary investment. In today's world, if you believe in your product, you will invest in marketing it.

There is no doubt that junk mail is a major growth industry of the late 20th century and one of my favourite senders of junk mail is Pizza Hut. Every six weeks or so, there is another full colour leaflet through our door. Whether you've never tasted fast food in your life or you're a pizza junkie, they want to do everything in their power to ensure that you know they have an outlet in your area. They don't distribute one leaflet when they open and then leave market growth to word of mouth. The flow of leaflets keeps on coming to make sure that when you think pizza, you'll think Pizza Hut.

Every day a new bombardment for savings and loans, pensions, insurance and charity appeals is thrust through our letter-box. The standards of presentation are ever higher. Personalised letters and full colour leaflets have become *de rigeur*. The promotions are targeted so that you increasingly receive advertising geared to the kind of person the direct mail computer has decided you must be; not just the product but the marketing approach is customised to maximise response.

Those spending the money know there will be a limited response rate. But they believe in their product and the opportunity of extending their market. As a result, they consider the investment worthwhile. What is more, they know the only way to compete in unsolicited direct mail is to maintain high standards of writing and design.

So how does the church compete in the arena of mass marketing and direct mail – a world of high investment, professional journalism, full colour, clear corporate identity, consumer targeting, and high profile campaigns that you just can't miss? The news is hardly good. Day-glo posters, duplicated sheets from a manual typewriter, and a well-meaning but rambling Christmas letter from the vicar just don't cut any ice. If we are not prepared to set high standards, encourage creativity and unusual angles, explore targeting strategies, and spend significant money on sustained promotional campaigns, we simply will not be heard amid the clamouring voices of today's market-place. The duplicated list of festival services on poor quality paper only reinforces a common prejudice: the church is less relevant and matters less than home delivered pizza.

A sexually explicit society

In 1957, renowned conductor Sir Malcolm Sargent was blamed for rowdyism at the last night of the proms. The enthusiastic audience not only threw pennies at the orchestra, but also what the British newspapers referred to as 'streamers of excessive width'. In fact, the promenaders were throwing toilet rolls, but it was quite impossible for the press to say so directly back in the prim and proper world of the fifties.

Today there is non-stop talk about sex in the media. Sexual crises fill the problem pages, unusual sexual appetite and the quest for sexual fulfilment are constantly discussed. Sex talk is no longer something mainly for furtive teenagers or drunken sportsmen. What was once the province of *Playboy* magazine has become a major theme in women's magazines, whose covers trumpet without a hint of embarrassment the latest research into adultery, sexual fantasy and the female orgasm.

Meanwhile the grim reaper, AIDS, continues to take its remorseless toll. No one can be sure how many are HIV-positive. No one can be sure whether AIDS really will prove to be a latter-day global plague. But the infection and death count is growing ever higher, and in some parts of the world the incidence is already nothing less than catastrophic. The World Health Organisation estimated in 1993 that 14 million people had contracted HIV since the beginning of the epidemic and more than 2 million had developed AIDS. On present trends both numbers have tripled by now. In Africa, the main group of victims is not made up of homosexuals or drug addicts, but heterosexuals with many partners. In the United States, AIDS is now the second highest cause of death among men aged 25 to 44, and the rate of infection is now increasing fastest in poor urban communities, particularly among young blacks.[1]

What about the church in this age of almost constant sex talk? The church should be able, in accordance with the Bible, to celebrate sex as a gift of God and not treat it as something dirty. The church is well placed to talk frankly, as does the Bible, about sexual intimacy and fulfilment. The church could declare the limits on sexual activity which God has given in the Bible, and explain that without such restrictions the gift of sex can become overpowering and traumatic, leaving broken lives in the wake of casual use and abuse. On the whole, however, the church has preferred to keep silent about sex. In many churches sexuality and sexual ethics are never preached about or explored frankly in discussion groups.

As to AIDS, Christians have taken some extremely significant initiatives. Our church has been pleased to support the Mildmay Hospital in London, a Christian foundation which has become a centre to provide specialist care for those dying of AIDS. Sadly not all Christians have taken this view, and Mildmay has received letters from some church leaders rebuking them for providing such care. We need to grasp that whatever the reasons for infection, those dying of AIDS have become in our society what those with leprosy have been in the past. They are treated as untouchables, to whom Christians have a special responsibility to show God's love, providing an opportunity to die with dignity in a caring environment. We also support the Christian charity ACET (AIDS Care and Education Trust). ACET provides regular courses to train volunteers to work as home helps for AIDS sufferers. Naturally such courses need to address the means of

---

[1] *Newsweek* (21 June 1993).

contracting HIV, the means of protection and the symptoms of AIDS. Sadly the trainers have to acknowledge that in many churches it would not be possible to present such information with the necessary directness.

We live in an age which talks more about 'having sex' than 'making love'. An age which is sex-obsessed, in which many people end up feeling deeply inadequate about their sex lives in the light of the exaggerations of the popular magazines. An age in which virginity is looked down on as if it were a sexual disease to be eliminated as soon as possible. An age which longs for intimacy, but has forgotten how to achieve relationships that last. An age in which it is difficult to give yourself completely, because next month the relationship might be over. An age which doesn't yet know how to cope with the spectre of AIDS. If only we had the courage to speak frankly, we could show God's better way. But church has become the last place where sex is talked about. Many churches are like an ageing maiden aunt, blushing at the slightest hint of sexuality, preferring to pretend the world would be a less indelicate place if we weren't sexual beings at all.

Facing the task

We have come to the end of our initial investigation of formative factors in the modern world. Their collective impact is to increase considerably the church's credibility gap. We wouldn't thank a doctor who prescribed a pain-killer when we needed radical surgery. In the same way, if we are serious about taking the good news of Christ to today's world, we must face squarely the vast chasm of disconnectedness between the church and an unchurched society.

Before I visited Brazil I thought these pressing issues might be restricted to the West. I soon discovered that Brazilian children watch the same TV programmes as my children, and that the same pop music and feature films are enjoyed. As *Newsweek* has observed, 'MTV has created its own generation, reaching more than 200 million households in some eighty countries.'[1] One Brazilian complained to me about a sea change in their society: 'I made my own toys and entertained myself, whereas the children of today want everything bought for them.' The fascinating thing was that these words were spoken by a man of my age, but I could remember my father using almost exactly the same words when I was a child. In short, the tidal wave of post-modernity which has fallen upon the West and brought almost breathless change, is now sweeping through the middle classes around the world, bringing an even faster rate of change in the developing countries. A new culture of post-modernity is emerging worldwide. And this emerging worldview finds traditional church profoundly alien.

In the light of the enormity of the task and the decline of the institutional church, this chapter closes with a simple but stark proposition:

> *The modern world will not be reached effectively*
> *by traditional forms of church.*

---

[1] *Newsweek* (27 September 1993).

2

Rejecting the Church

Objections to Christianity

In the first chapter we identified several shaping trends in the modern world. In order to face up to the rejection of the church by the West we now need to consider some of the standard objections to the church that are regularly heard.

The church is only for the middle classes

A strange mutation has overtaken the church. A movement which was originally strong among the poor has found it hard to make a mark among the modern urban poor of the West. This criticism of the church is certainly accurate in part. Some of the most lively and effective churches are exclusively middle class and find it hard to reach beyond that world. But the criticism may also reflect a view of churchgoing that is increasingly out of date. For as long as attending church was the respectable thing to do on a Sunday morning, people dressed in their Sunday best and trooped out for a public ritual without the need for inner personal conviction. Such an approach to faith is foretold and warned against in the New Testament as 'having a form of godliness but denying its power' (2 Timothy 3:5).

This nominal Christianity of outward conformity held its tightest grip on the middle classes. Now the grip has slackened, those with a living faith can rejoice with relief that Christianity is once more widely understood to be a matter of personal conviction and not merely the automatic religious inheritance of the bourgeoisie. In fact, despite the frequent failures and indifference in some quarters, the latest survey of church attendance actually indicates that there is more evidence of new life and growth in inner London than in the smarter outer suburbs.

I am middle class, and I make no apology for it. It is a given of my life, and neither a reason to look down on anyone else, nor something to be treated as an impediment. Like most people, I relax and communicate most easily with people from a similar background. But the mission of the church cannot and must not be restricted to a middle-class comfort zone. The church which erects boundary walls of class consciousness is no more than a cosy club.

The church is for elderly women

George Carey was accused of ageism when he compared the church to an old lady sucking at toothless gums. There are far too many churches where a dozen old ladies make up the congregation. Of course, not all churches are like this. In our church we found that the age distribution of the congregation matches closely the age profile of the local population, and that the largest single generation are those in their twenties. For some outsiders this is mind-blowing, so firmly established is the assumption that you have to be old and female to be found in any church.

I have nothing against old ladies, but common sense says that while such a group may attract other ageing women, it is unlikely to have the vitality to attract, let alone retain, younger generations. In practice this is plainly the case, and many churches are dying in slow motion – too far gone for change and waiting for inevitable extinction.

Two factors have brought many churches to this end. First, it reflects a church style which suited women born into a generation where they were passive and men were active. Such generations of women attended churches where the only active participant each Sunday was the minister. Today, women are encouraged to be just as assertive and active as men, with the result that few younger women are content to sit back in a passive role, whether or not they pursue a career outside the home. A church style based on a passive, ageing and female congregation indicates a church without a future.

Secondly, it reflects an inability to keep up with the times. Churches are no different from other voluntary organisations. In a world of rapid change, all such organisations can struggle to maintain recruitment, because they are unable or unwilling to sustain the necessary rate of change. But here's the bottom line: keep up to date, or become obsolete.

We live in a world which is obsessed with youthfulness, and where every organisation must keep changing to avoid going to the wall. In this context a natural and stark assumption is made about any movement that is ageing and unchanging. It is almost certain that it is past its prime and quite possibly in terminal decline.

The church is only after your money

It is a rule of life in some churches that whenever more than a dozen people meet together there has to be another whip round. When Willow Creek Community Church, one of the fastest growing churches in the United States, carried out a neighbourhood survey they found that this was a major image problem for the church. Some churches are like pickpockets: if you're near one, you had better hold tight to your wallet.

At worst, willing churchgoers knock on doors while shaking a collecting tin, explaining without realising the absurdity, 'We believe in an almighty God who supplies all our needs, and please could we have a donation to help mend the church roof.' Some even imply that the local community has a duty to cough up for the church. We need to face a simple principle: every local church should be self-supporting, unless in a very poor area, and also aim to provide money for evangelism and community care, relief and development, at home and overseas. What is more, all this money should come from the bank accounts of believers.

Collecting money at special social and evangelistic events should surely be avoided like the plague. Otherwise the guest may wonder whether the only reason they were invited was to help out with the church debt. On Sundays I encourage churches to provide an explanation to visitors that there is no obligation or expectation that they will hand over any money for the offering. As to the active church members, let them give on Sundays if they must, but offering bags tend to encourage a 'loose change' mentality. That is, giving to God out of whatever happens to remain in your pocket at the end of the week. This is not what the apostle Paul had in mind when he advised the Corinthians to 'excel in this grace of giving' (2 Corinthians 8:7). We live in an age when more and more people pay fuel bills, subscriptions and other major and regular expenses by direct debit. If we are serious about giving by believers, and serious about neutralising this common objection to the gospel, isn't it time that most Christians started giving 'serious money' and paying by direct debit?

Congregations are tiny and churches are empty

Some church buildings in Britain are an affront to God. They were built by wealthy industrialists, not for the glory of Christ, but to demonstrate the success and power of the industrialist. They have never been full, warm or useful, and they would be better pulled down. Other churches were built at the heart of a community, but shifts in population have resulted in a building far away from where most people now live. I used to worship at a village Anglican church which had been built next to the country house of the Lord of the Manor, who had made sure that the rest of the village was kept well out of sight on the other side of the valley. Over the last century or so, the main village has grown ever larger as part of the London commuting area. Now the old parish church is cut off from the village, not only by a valley, but also by a motorway. Not even the Lord of the Manor lives nearby any more, because the old family has died out.

It is of course true that many churches have seen better days, but not all churches are small today, and some are larger than ever. For example, in 1991 our church building was comfortably full and we were able to extend the seating capacity from 240 to 350. In February 1992 we moved back in, and a year later we had to start a second morning service because the church had grown to fill the new capacity.

One comparison I make is with supermarkets and corner shops. Throughout the developed world there is a trend for food shopping to be done at a one-stop major outlet, often out of town with its own car park, etc. Urban and suburban people – and that means most of us – are used to the convenience of going somewhere big and thriving for regular shopping. Most people expect churches to be more like a corner shop: maybe friendly, probably a bit run down, but somewhere only to fall back on in an emergency.

I am not saying that only big is beautiful. Of course not! Different sized churches meet different needs. Large churches and small churches should complement not criticise each other, working in a partnership of mutual respect to proclaim the same gospel. But in our society many people assume that all churches are small, struggling and on the way out. There is a tremendous pre-evangelistic impact in seeing a Sunday service with standing room only. The size of a church never converted anyone, but if someone has assumed that every church is tiny and weak, the sight of a thriving and growing congregation can make the walls of their prejudice begin to crack.

Churches use old language

Verily, verily, saith I unto you, of base falseness doth this reek! I remember attending a graduation ceremony at Oxford University, where the entire event was conducted in Latin. When the majestic rhetorical flourishes of the mother tongue of this great seat of learning were at last complete, a final phrase was added: 'Please sit down!' In that phrase all the pomposity of the proceedings exploded, since it revealed that almost none of the students had understood a word that had gone before! Some churches are not dissimilar.

There have been tremendous advances in the last few decades in this area. Despite the snootiness of some arty circles, the AV has been swept away, and the RSV, which held the fort for a generation, has begun to follow it into general disuse. Out of the profusion of new Bible translations the Good News and the NIV now dominate the market and they look set to continue to do so.

As a publisher I was pleased to publish not only the NIV

but also *Hymns for Today's Church*, which sought to modernise sensitively the wording of traditional hymns, so that they might still enhance contemporary worship rather than fall into the oblivion reserved for archaic and obsolete words. I remember talking to Michael Baughen, the consulting editor of the project, about the revolution of the last few decades, before which the Authorised Version was the standard Bible of the English speaking world. It had stood for so long many never dreamed it would be so completely superseded. Few Anglicans as recently as the sixties would have guessed that *The Book of Common Prayer* was so near the end of its life as the standard book for parish worship.

Of course, there are still churches where prophecy is not considered valid unless it approximates to Elizabethan English, as if the living God preferred communicating to us via Shakespeare rather than direct. In other churches prayer develops its own archaisms and circumlocutions which urgently need to be severed from the bough. There is the sincere prayer: 'We really do pray that we'll really . . .' There is the just prayer: 'We do just pray that we'll just . . .' And then there is the sincere and just prayer: 'We really do just pray that we'll really just . . .' Some insist on praying for 'travelling mercies', which have always sounded to me like a group of minor cherubs hovering over the wheels of a car, when I would prefer simply to pray for a safe journey. Others still pray for someone 'laid aside on a bed of sickness', when I prefer to pray that someone who is sick will get better. These are surely forms of speaking in tongues that certainly would not be commended by the apostle Paul.

If we are getting better at avoiding such talk, it is still worth asking why it is done. It is partly nostalgia, recalling the so-called good old days by talking like them. It is partly conformity, picking up the unspoken rules of how to pray in a particular church and doing the same without really knowing why. And it is partly a false spirituality, assuming that the living God, who in fact is always ahead of rather than behind the times, is so removed from the everyday and modern world that he would not wish his ears to be sullied by anything more up to date than the Queen's English (Elizabeth I variety). It sometimes amuses me to hear someone who is perfectly capable of holding a lively conversation in today's English reduced to stumbling incoherence by trying to speak mock-Shakespearian to God. Such folly is dying, and the sooner it dies the better – for Christians and outsiders alike!

Church is boring

In a recent Gallup survey, the clear majority in every age group under 50 found traditional church worship boring. What is more, those in their fifties are commonly an absent generation from churches, so we find that traditional worship is accessible largely to those who have retired, plus those who have grown up in the Christian sub-culture and are therefore accustomed to it. This complaint is partly due to the failure to adapt to the television age, which we explored in Chapter 1. TV has reduced attention spans, which makes preaching an even more demanding skill. It also makes leading in prayer a difficult task. I remember Richard Foster speaking about the low boredom threshold in public prayer: 'If I pray aloud for one minute my congregation prays with me. If I pray for two minutes they pray for me. If I pray for three minutes they pray against me!' As to silence in prayer, in most churches on Sunday mornings there will be some people who find silence wonderful, and others whose entire life is surrounded by sound – usually the sound of pop music. This suggests that silence usually needs to be handled like plutonium: with great care and in small doses.

I don't want to pretend that church can't be boring. For some years I tried to persuade myself that the reason for my boredom in church could only be some kind of major spiritual problem. I assumed that everyone around me was really enjoying the service, even if they were too discreet to show it. Eventually I made a simple discovery. Most of them were just as bored as I was, but thought that church was meant to be that way.

My sons are much more direct than I am. They attend church almost every Sunday, and are used to Christian music tapes playing in our home and car as well as all the other kinds of music we like. (At the moment they have just discovered the Beach Boys, which is very nostalgic for me.) With a dad who leads a church they are hardly rank outsiders, unexposed to worship, but when a traditional church service comes on the radio they groan in unison, 'Oh Dad, turn it off. It's so boring!' I have come to the conclusion that all too often they are absolutely right.

Our worship of the living God is not meant to be a dull, cold, starchy, immaculately ordered performance. The Greek word translated as 'worship' literally means 'I come towards to kiss'. When I return home from a trip overseas, I don't expect a formal handshake from each family member. I hug my wife warmly, I swing my boys around in exuberance, and we all fend off our excitable Labrador as best we can. There surely ought to be rather more enthusiasm than many of us tend to muster when we worship the living God. There is no excuse for churchgoers to wait in line for communion with even less evidence of joy or expectancy than those in a dole queue.

If we are going to reach the vast majority of people in the modern world, and if we are to rediscover the overflowing joy the first Christians knew when the Spirit came, our worship needs to be a lot less like an exquisite classical concert, and a lot more like Wembley on the afternoon of the FA Cup Final. I happen to love classical music, but the reason Radio 3 has about 3 per cent of the radio market is that the vast majority of people find such music inaccessible and, let's face it, boring. What we have seen in the last twenty years is the rediscovery of an old principle: the music of church worship needs to be shaped by the prevailing styles of popular music in the surrounding culture. A vibrant church doesn't have to exclude the music of Bach or Handel, but the dominant style today needs to be much closer to pop and rock.

Suppose somebody tells his friend that he will never buy another CD because he bought one once and it was boring. His friend's reply is natural: 'Don't be daft. You're missing out on so much! You owe it to yourself to try some more music. But not by the same band.' If someone says that church is boring, tell them that you find some churches boring too, and then invite them to yours . . . if you dare!

Church is only for religious people

While some religious people are admirably caring, the unchurched make common assumptions about us. The only thing that really matters to many is the service we provide – the job club, the playgroup or the lunch for the elderly. The religious dimension is not thought to be in any way intrinsic to the caring initiative, but rather is considered an optional extra. Church initiatives can seem like social work with a religious gloss. This suspicion is reinforced by the regular appearance on TV of senior churchmen who don't appear to believe anything at all. They speak with a great deal of subtlety and complexity, pulling rank on their interviewer with Latinate theological jargon. But the impression conveyed is often a deeply held agnosticism in deeply religious garb.

I attended the seminars of a professor of theology at Oxford, whose brilliant analytical mind ruthlessly tore into the fanciful speculations of modern and historical theology. I admired the rigour with which he dissected groundless and specious flights of theological fancy. However, while his rigorousness was a necessary antiseptic for the bacteria of idle speculation, there was never any hint of personal faith in Christ. At the end of his seminars, come what may, he would attend a service at the cathedral. It is quite possible that this indicated a real depth of personal faith. But it could equally reinforce the impression of many outsiders that church leaders don't believe any more than the man in the street; they're just more religious!

It is plainly the case that some people are 'religious' in this sense. They enjoy attending church on Sunday mornings, when others would prefer to be washing the car, having a lie in, or reading the paper over a cup of freshly ground coffee. The Christian faith can then be compared to a conservatory. Just as some people choose to add a conservatory to a perfectly adequate house because they happen to have a fondness for the sun, others add a religious extension to their life. If you are not that partial to the sun, a conservatory is not something to waste time considering. If you are not religious, and a traditional church service is a turn off, it seems in the same way that you need never make the effort to consider Christianity seriously. Like it or not, this is the world in which we live. Many people have taken half a glance at church, considered it to be boring, unattractive or irrelevant, and have then swept everything away in the phrase, 'I am not religious.'

I suspect the roots of this problem are found in Platonism.

Plato taught a dualism between the material and the ideal. In much Western Christianity this shaped a division between the secular and the sacred. Marriage, for example, was for the secular, while celibacy was for the spiritual. Life was increasingly divided between secular work and leisure on the one hand, and spiritual worship and prayer on the other. Believers, apart perhaps from the priests, monks and nuns, inhabited two distinct worlds, and life was increasingly divided into secular and spiritual compartments.

This understanding of life has nothing to do with the Bible nor with the Hebraic mindset. Central to Jesus' teaching on the kingdom of God is the fact that the dynamic rule and presence of God comes right into the everyday world. Central to the coming of the Holy Spirit, after Jesus' death and resurrection, is the revelation that God is not locked up inside certain buildings or only conjured up and made available through certain religious rites or ceremonies. On the contrary, God is ever present and available, with the result that the material and the spiritual enfold one another. Christian faith is not something locked away in a compartment marked, 'Likes churchgoing. Only use on Sundays.' Faith that is truly living can touch and energise every dimension of life.

This unbiblical dualism is deep-rooted in the Western world. It has caused immense confusion to Christians for many centuries. But in the modern world this misconception has taken a new twist. If the spiritual dimension is locked up in a separate compartment, and has no impact, relevance or point of contact with the everyday world, then maybe the simplest thing is to ignore it completely and throw away the key. Under the impact of secular materialism, 'being religious' is thought to be an optional extra. And for most people, Christianity has become surplus to requirements. Not something carefully considered and rejected, but something that doesn't warrant serious consideration at all. From a Hebraic perspective, it is reasonable to anticipate a revolt of the human spirit against the life-constricting narrowness of materialism. Indeed, I believe we are seeing the beginnings of that uprising whenever we hear the cry, 'There must be more to life than this!'

Here is a great irony. The Western church adopted a dualistic worldview and passed this on to our society, and now the 'secular' compartment has declared independence. Having split life all too neatly into two distinct compartments, the church must now learn how to communicate with a world that no longer has any time for traditional religious trappings. It is no good trying to convince people that old time religion is fun after all. We need to demonstrate the life-enriching impact of Jesus Christ in the busy and complex, hopeful and tragic, grimy and ambivalent material world of the every-day. We need to be able to show that the kingdom of God and the Spirit of God have indeed come, and are among us, not merely on Sunday mornings but in every moment and dimension of modern life.

The power of relativism

The objections we have been facing are not all fair. You may feel that most don't apply to your church at all. But whether or not these objections are an accurate description of the church in the West, they certainly depict how many outsiders perceive us. Such perceptions are critical when it comes to our effective communication of the gospel. The conclusion that the church is archaic and remote has led to increasing rejection of the institution. Church is not somewhere most people expect to go, other than for a funeral. The number of infant baptisms and church weddings has declined enormously in the last two generations. While those in their fifties are more often reasonably polite about the church, though declining ever to put in an appearance, those in their teens and twenties are more direct. You don't have to go far to hear someone say, 'Church? What would I want to go there for?' Or even, 'I wouldn't be seen dead there!'

As well as rejection of the institution, considered culturally alien, we also face a rejection of our fundamental thought forms. The modern world is increasingly cosmopolitan and multi-ethnic. Every day, particularly through the media, we encounter a market-place of diverse values, convictions and belief systems. Our society is now accustomed to being pluralistic. Out of the seed-bed of pluralism grows not only a healthy and welcome emphasis on tolerance and mutual respect, but also something more insidious. Relativism insists not merely that all should be respected, but that there is no such thing as absolute truth or a definitive revelation of God. This is, of course, a self-contradiction. In order to carry the authority that it claims for itself, relativism would have to be the very kind of absolute truth it seeks to preclude. Relativism is a bindweed which seeks to crush the life and truth out of the gospel.

Christianity should always have been a ready champion of tolerance, respect, and the need for minority groups to be protected against prejudice and exploitation. Christians today readily defend the rights of members of other world religions to be able to worship together freely. But Christianity cannot be melted down into a soup of relativism. The bones of absolute truth refuse to dissolve. The uniqueness of Christ as the incarnate Son of God, the uniqueness of his all-sufficient atoning death, his definitive revelation of the Father, the supreme authority of the Scriptures – all these and more are fundamental Christian convictions which relativism cannot absorb or swallow.

What is more, as Stephen Carter has argued in his provocative study, *The Culture of Disbelief*,[1] America's liberal élites are steadily imposing a 'public secularism'. The media and the universities increasingly invite us to conform to the view that religion should be considered as an exclusively and merely private matter. We are asked to treat 'God as a hobby', privately engaging, probably eccentric, and certainly of no relevance in the public arena of politics, economics and law. This trend is apparent and growing more assertive today throughout the post-modern world.

This relativism extends to ethics as well as religious convictions. It is assumed that there are no moral absolutes and that no one has the right to impose their moral values on anyone else. What matters is not conformity, but finding what works best for you personally. In short, a morality that is individualistic, tentative and highly pragmatic. While there are dimensions of morality where the Bible gives Christians liberty to draw divergent conclusions, there are certain irreducible moral absolutes on which Christians must take a stand. For example, by no means all Christians would insist that abortion is always wrong, but we do all insist on the sanctity of life, and the need to protect the rights and health of both the unborn child and the expectant mother.

As the population of the developed world grows grey, and a smaller workforce supports ever larger generations of the retired, the next great moral debate will almost certainly centre upon euthanasia. Christians can be found on both sides of the debate about whether to turn off the life support system of someone in a permanent vegetative state, but we will unite in insisting upon the sanctity of life against any

---

[1] Basic Books, 1993.

attempt, however well meaning, to impose a maximum age, whether statutory or 'recommended and voluntary' upon the elderly. Because we hold to certain moral absolutes, Christians will prove to be an annoying irritant in an increasingly relativistic age.

What is more, because we believe that Christianity is not a religion born of human wisdom and insight, but a saving revelation from the living God, Christians not only respect others, we also wish to convert them. Relativism is pragmatic and says, 'I am glad that works for you, but something else works for me.' The apostle Peter, on the contrary, was determinedly evangelistic and proclaimed Christ to everyone, without apology or hesitation: 'Salvation is found in no-one else, for there is *no other name* under heaven given to men by which we must be saved' (Acts 4:12 italics mine). When the world rejects the institution of the church as something archaic and irrelevant, we need to ask searching questions of ourselves concerning what aspects of the traditional church are expendable or even obsolete. But when the world rejects the very concept of a Saviour, it is impossible to be true to Christ and also accommodate such a conviction. We are surrounded by people who blithely assume that no one can believe in anything exclusive or absolute any more. Of course, when we explain patiently that in fact we do hold non-relativistic convictions, many will write us off quickly with the easy jibe that we cannot be other than 'fundamentalists'. Christian orthodoxy is a long way from the narrow world of fundamentalism, but cannot be assimilated within the mindset of relativism.

Contented ignorance

A growing number of people in the West are sublimely ignorant of the Christian faith and the Bible. And they are quite content in their ignorance. They know that the church shows little or no evidence of relevance to the modern world, so they have rejected the institution. They know that Christianity does not conform to the values of a hedonistic and relativistic age, so they have rejected its basic thought forms. And having rejected the institution of the church and embraced relativism, most people have simply presumed that the Christian message is irrelevant. This prevailing assumption needs to be understood. None of us has the time to consider carefully every idea or conviction championed by the many minority groups of the modern world. Therefore, there are some preliminary questions to raise before we make the effort to ask, 'Is it reasonable?' We need to determine, 'Is it worth considering?' And to do that we need to ask, 'Is it plausible?' In other words, we have to determine whether something is attractive, intriguing or sufficiently credible to warrant further investigation.

If the church is doing its job well, it establishes a platform of plausibility for the gospel. That is certainly what happened on the Day of Pentecost in Acts 2, when outsiders demanded to know what had got into these people. The technical term for this pre-evangelistic task is that the church has the potential and responsibility to be a hermeneutical community. That is, if we are authentic to the gospel and engaged with our culture, we become a bridge over which our contemporaries can walk in order to explore the gospel for themselves.

The downside of this principle is profoundly grave, for a culturally remote church does the opposite. Such a church conveys the impression that the gospel itself is implausible, irrelevant and not worth considering. Perceived irrelevance in the institution leads to the presumed irrelevance of the message. That is certainly the assumption of those who brush aside any leaflet or invitation with the dismissal, 'I am just not interested in Christianity!' Where there is no plausibility, no apparent contact with the 'real world of today', some look back on a period of compulsory attendance at Sunday school like a convict serving a prison sentence. The church seems out of touch, out of date, and as soon as possible, they're out of there!

John Stott is said once to have seen a graffiti slogan that declared, 'Jesus, yes! Church, no!' During the greedy eighties many people were effectively saying, 'Money, yes! Jesus, no!' It seems to me that today a steadily growing number of people are expressing dissatisfaction with mere materialism and are beginning to say, 'Spiritual reality, yes! Church, no!' That is, 'Do you seriously suggest that we'll find spiritual reality for today in a Christian church?'

Here then is my second proposition:

The church has often become the greatest hindrance to effective communication of the gospel.

3

Bridging the Gap I–
Jesus and the Apostles

I was working at home and thought I heard a tap dripping. Having checked the bathroom and found nothing, I examined the hot water tank. Where one of the pipes emerged there was a slow but steady leak. At first I thought the problem was where a pipe was joined to the tank, but more careful examination revealed that the tank itself had begun to crack. We had been very fortunate, for the tank was so old it might well have burst later that day. If I had been working in the office, I would have come home to a flooded house. Had I noticed the problem but treated it lightly, there would have been no saving our home from a sudden and destructive deluge.

It is vital that we face the enormity of our task. It is simply not the case that the church merely has to do better what it is already doing or patch up a few minor problems in order to ensure a great advance. We are not in a situation where a little more prayer, a little more spiritual warfare, a little more door to door, or a little more care in the community will do the trick. We have allowed a chasm to open between the surrounding culture and the internal church culture. Today in the West, no less than among unreached people groups in the remotest parts of Africa, we need to learn to be a missionary church. And in order to become effective missionaries, we need to bridge the gap between the gospel and the world of the people around us. If Jesus and the apostles made strenuous efforts to live and communicate the gospel in ways that bridged the gap in their generation, it is simply not good enough today to pray for revival while changing nothing in the church.

In order to grapple with our responsibility, we need first to examine the precedents in the New Testament. Is cross-cultural mission something new, invented by theoretical missiologists with time on their hands, or is it integral to the gospel?

The supreme communicator

Jesus himself demonstrated the need to bridge the gap. He didn't come to earth as some kind of disembodied manifestation, but was incarnate in human flesh. His incarnation was not merely a matter of the outward appearance of physicality, but he took on specific flesh in space and time. He embraced in his own incarnate life the particular context, including its limitations, of a Galilean peasant in the time of the Roman Empire. He didn't receive a classical education, nor study the Greek philosophers and poets, nor travel to the great cities of the ancient world. Nor did he discourse on the value of antibiotics, the theory of relativity or particle physics. Of course not! To talk of things that had no point of contact with the thought world of his day would have been no better than to talk gibberish, and Christ chose to be self-limited in his incarnation. In short, Jesus knew the intellectual and cultural restrictions of a manual worker of his day. He didn't claim to bring an answer to every question that might be addressed in the history of science or philosophy. Rather, he addressed the deepest human aspiration and need: to know personally the dynamic presence of the love and rule of God.

This accommodation to the cultural context of a specific time, place and people is seen at every level of Jesus' proclamation. First, in the language used. The very idea of divine revelation in human language requires a massive accommodation: words are made to carry a transcendent burden, and are stretched to the very limits of their meaning. What is more, the Son of the living God communicated eternal and absolute truth not in one of the great, sophisticated, literary languages of the world, but in the peasant dialect of Aramaic, the minor and provincial language, from the perspective of the highbrows of the Roman Empire, of the unschooled Jews.

Secondly, we see cultural relevance in Jesus' parables. Any public speaker will use illustrations drawn from life, yet few have the ability to make a world live and breathe in the stories they tell. Jesus' stories teem with the life of ancient Galilee. Even today, if you walk beside the Sea of Galilee, you recognise how Jesus' parables capture the life of his peasant world: the shepherds in the hills, the sower in his field, the woman cleaning her house. His parables encapsulate the familiar details of everyday life in that locality, keenly observed and made to live again in words. For some, his stories must have brought back to mind a similar experience. He may even have pointed out someone nearby actually performing the very task with which his story began.

Jesus was one of the greatest story-tellers of all time. He understood the world in which he lived, and knew how to communicate its vitality and values. But he was far more than an entertainer. The parables capture the imagination and then intrigue the mind. There is an element of mystery and enigma. The world of the parables is so concrete, definite and specific, and yet they always point beyond that world, to a higher dimension of reality. Confucius was the great teacher of better behaviour; Jesus Christ taught that his own life and teaching represented not merely a good example, but the inauguration of the breakthrough of the rule and presence of God. The parables, in all their earthy detail and vitality, carry this transcendent implication: in and through Jesus, the rule of heaven has come down to earth.

Thirdly, we see Jesus responding to his context in the phrases that shaped his proclamation, notably 'the kingdom of God' and 'the Son of Man'. For Jesus' original audiences, both were resonant with echoes of familiar Old Testament scriptures and longings. To take 'the kingdom of God', the Jews would have recognised immediately a phrase that drew on their triumphant period under David and Solomon, when the kingdom was wealthy and renowned, its borders secure. Through later and harder eras the great Messianic hope had grown, namely the promise declared by the prophets that God would send a son of David who would be greater than David; a king who would more than restore the glory of Israel.

To these historical and prophetic hopes the immediate context lent additional pertinence, for Israel was once again subject to an empire, held fast under the iron grip of Rome. Furthermore, King Herod was hated by many as a pretender king, despite his ambitious building projects, most notable of all the rebuilding of the temple in Jerusalem. He had married into the Hasmonean royal family, and later killed them off to preserve his own power base, which explains his paranoia when the wise men made mention of a new king of the true line of David. Faced with such a king, ruthless with the Jews and yet little more than a puppet before the Romans, it is

small wonder that there was still much life in the old longing
for a Son of David to come and restore the kingdom.

In drawing upon this resonant heritage of hope and longing, Jesus communicated good news in ways people could
understand. But he wasn't imprisoned by his chosen
language. While many Jews anticipated a sword-wielding
hero, Jesus explicitly repudiated military force as a way of
accomplishing his purposes. He sharpened a tension within
the kingdom hope, presenting a kingdom which has come
into being in the present, and yet still looking forward to its
future consummation. He spoke of the kingdom in such ways
as to point not to a socio-political reality – that is, a newly
independent nation state of Israel – but rather to introduce a
new dimension of living which could be entered by faith, not
automatically by birthright. Above all, as Jesus spoke of the
kingdom, he was inviting people to come to a decision about
himself. He presented himself as the great mediator, the one
who brought the kingdom of God and made it possible for us
to come under God's ruling presence.

Jesus' teaching built bridges to ordinary Galileans, for he
understood their world and knew how to be relevant to them.
His miracles too can be understood in this light, as a demonstration of the love and power of God which reaches out to
address the felt needs of the crowd. But the bridge-building
doesn't lead to the one-way traffic of demand free relevance.
While the need for relevance shaped his message, the demands
of the gospel were always explicit and never compromised.
The Gospel writers' summaries of Jesus' teaching always
return to the word 'repent'. He met people on their home
turf, but what he brought to them there, in ways they could
understand and relate to, were the invitations and demands of
the living God.

What we see in the teaching of Jesus is a fundamental

principle of verbal communication. That is, effective communication requires that the speaker and hearer share a common mode of discourse. This remains true even when Jesus chose to make that shared language do things it had never done before, making the picture language of his parables the vehicle for transcendent truth.

We can also identify a fundamental principle regarding the gospel, namely that even Jesus needed to communicate the gospel in a specific cultural context. In fact we can go further and state that while the gospel is not culture-bound, tied ineluctably to one cultural context and rendered inaccessible to those for whom that culture is alien, the gospel must always be communicated within a particular cultural context. In short, language and culture are the necessary vehicles of the eternal gospel. There is no such thing as the gospel in a culture free form.

Breaking the mould

Even as Jesus met his hearers where they were, in his dialect, his stories and his terminology, the first Christians soon faced a similar problem. It was one thing to proclaim the good news to their own people, but how were they to implement Jesus' command to speak to the Gentile world? For some this was not much of an issue. The gospel and Jewish culture were seen as a package deal and indissolubly meshed – you couldn't have one without the other. If any Gentiles wished to put their faith in the Jewish Messiah, they would also have to convert to Judaism, accepting male circumcision, Jewish food laws and the rest.

Fortunately, this school of thought did not win the day. The Holy Spirit provoked a searching debate by giving the gift of tongues to Samaritan and Gentile converts, which served to demonstrate a new equality in Christ, without regard to being Jewish by ancestry. The Jerusalem Council finally ruled against the package deal approach, and gave liberty for Gentiles to work out their own distinctive ways of living as disciples (Acts 15:1–31).

Such a decision was not without considerable heart-searching and pain. For some believers, this ruling represented a betrayal of their own Jewish roots, and this led to the first great schism of the church. We don't know how many of these Judaisers there were, but Paul's letters give ample evidence that they remained a thorn in his side, for he continued to have to argue vigorously against their influence. It seems that wherever he travelled proclaiming the gospel, the Judaisers were sure to follow, seeking to impose Jewish ritual law on his earnest and sometimes only too amenable new converts.

What then of the apostolic mission to the Gentiles? They didn't simply duplicate Jesus' message, retelling his parables and his teaching about the kingdom of God. Rather, they emulated his methods, holding fast to his principles while finding new language and thought forms which would be expressive in the Gentile context. There have been times when churches have become guardians of a dying culture, their liturgy preserving a language which has ceased to be the common currency of the people. We have seen this with Latin, and also with the Coptic language, which is now only used in the services of the ancient Coptic Church. The first Christians' motivation was missionary not linguistic, and they were prepared to abandon the language spoken by Jesus so that the Greek speaking world might have a real opportunity to believe in his name.

To be sure, in the context of Greek speaking proclamation and worship they did retain a few Aramaic phrases, but the battle for worship in the language of the Gentiles had already been won. The most notable term they imported into Greek speaking worship was 'Abba', the intimate term for Father still used by Jewish children today. In this instance, the new name for God which Jesus himself introduced and regularly used was evidently retained because it was so expressive of the miracle of adoption, through faith in Christ, as the children of the living God (Romans 8:15; Galatians 4:6).

One natural question arises when we move from Jesus' proclamation among the Jews to the apostolic proclamation among the Gentiles. Whatever happened to the kingdom of God? Clearly this term was at the heart of Jesus' preaching, and just as clearly it was not at the heart of the preaching of the apostles. We must surely reject the suggestion that the apostles fundamentally distorted the message of Jesus, and can identify several reasons for this shift of emphasis.

First, Jesus himself never gave a direct definition for 'the kingdom of God'. It was a suggestive term for his Jewish audience, evoking a rich context of Messianic expectations. Deliberately enigmatic it served as a pointer beyond itself to the dynamic rule of God breaking in to space and time. It was designed not to introduce a concept for theoretical deliberation, but rather to signify a momentous event that demanded personal response, whether of faith or rejection. For Gentiles, this same phrase was a much more difficult peg on which to hang the gospel. Without its cultural and biblical context, the phrase lost its suggestiveness and would risk seeming too hazy and unfocused.

Secondly, the phrase may have brought risks of excessive and unnecessary danger. Christians were rapidly under suspicion for lack of loyalty to the Empire, and for forming some kind of secret society. It was one thing for a religious teacher in a remote corner of the Empire to speak of 'God's kingdom'. It was quite another for a movement which was rapidly spreading among the influential cities of the Empire to speak of an alternative kingdom. Such talk may therefore have been avoided to prevent the Romans suspecting Christians of sedition. It could easily have seemed that the Christians were conspiring to establish a political, this-earthly kingdom, in opposition to the Roman Empire.

Thirdly, Jesus' proclamation of the coming of the kingdom of God was almost certainly understood to be fulfilled in his own death and resurrection. While Matthew, Mark and Luke record at length Jesus' preaching of the kingdom, the Gospels they wrote ultimately concentrate not on Jesus' words or miracles, but upon his death and resurrection. The last week of Jesus' life takes about a third of the length of the Gospels, and nothing else is given nearly so much attention. The enigma and mystery of Jesus' teaching was replaced by the confident and direct proclamation of Jesus' death on the cross as the decisive turning point in human history. While Jesus proclaimed the kingdom, the apostles proclaimed the risen Christ as King.

Integral to this mission to the Gentiles was the harnessing of new thought forms to express an unchanging message. In the prologue to his Gospel, John develops the concept of Logos, which had its origins in Greek philosophy and had gradually entered the world of the Hellenistic Jews. The term 'Logos' indicated not only the word spoken, as in the creation narrative in Genesis – 'And God said . . . and it was so' – but also the conceptual word in the mind, and the rational principle which governs the cosmos. It was a term familiar to any thinking and educated Gentile of the 1st century. John therefore uses a Gentile mode of discourse in such a way as to make a strong point of contact with the thought forms of the culture of the Empire. He bridges the gap in order to speak clearly, comprehensibly and creatively of the unchanging Christ.

Once the conceptual bridge has been built, John introduces an element which is distinctly Christian and radically discordant for the Gentile world. He reflects with intelligence and sophistication upon the function of the Logos in the creation of the world, but suddenly makes a quite extraordinary proposal: 'The Logos became flesh and made his dwelling among us' (John 1:14). Any self-respecting educated Greek speaker would be familiar with the concept of the Logos, and he would also be quite clear that if two things couldn't conceivably mix, being more mutually exclusive than oil and water, they were surely the governing and unchanging rational principle of the cosmos and paltry human flesh, being material and mortal, and therefore always subject to decay. For some, the very suggestion was absurd, even repellent. However, John presents this astonishing fusion not as a philosophical conundrum, but as an observed event in space and time (John 1:14; 1 John 1:1).

John is direct and unyielding. He begins within the culture of his hearers, builds a bridge of familiarity to establish a real point of contact, and then introduces the radical newness of the gospel. Therefore we can see in John the studious avoidance of two equal and opposite errors. On the one hand he doesn't proclaim the gospel in such distinctly Jewish terminology as to become incomprehensible and alien to Gentiles. On the other he avoids so accommodating the gospel that its very essence is dissipated and lost in the process of cross-cultural communication. John is acutely aware of two principles which must be held in tension: the need for communication which begins with the vehicle of the language and thought forms of the 'target audience'; and yet the need to ensure that such thought forms do not hijack the gospel by distorting or even excluding its very core.

We see the same creative tension in the apostle Paul. He was well read in the poetry of the civilised world, for example quoting Epimenides and Aratus when preaching to the Athenians, and citing to the Corinthians a poet, Menander, who would have been well known to them (Acts 17:28; 1 Corinthians 15:33). While he quoted the wisdom of poets, he asserted unhesitatingly the supreme authority of the Scriptures (2 Timothy 3:16–17). In his evangelism, Paul once commended the Athenians for building an altar to the unknown God, explaining that the living God has indeed been unknown among them but that he is now revealed in Christ crucified (Acts 17:23). As for the Ephesians, he denounced their idolatry and dismissed their superstitions as not gods at all, which resulted in a public bonfire of scrolls. It also led to a riot that endangered his life, brought about by the prospect of a collapse in the market for silver shrines used in the particularly sordid Ephesian cult of Artemis, the many-breasted fertility goddess served in that city by many prostitute priestesses (Acts 19:17–41). Paul is at home in the culture of the Empire, but he is also sufficiently detached to provide a searching critique. While he communicates within the framework of this culture, he speaks without hesitation against the moral depravity and wrong thinking of the Roman world, both in society (Romans 1:18–32) and also whenever it infects the church.

This creative process of being culturally relevant and yet culturally critical is seen supremely in the early Christian confession, 'Jesus is Lord' (Romans 10:9; 1 Corinthians 12:3; 2 Corinthians 4:5; Philippians 2:11). Those who knew their Jewish Scriptures in the Greek version known as the Septuagint, would recognise immediately the word which had been used to translate the name of God: Yahweh. It is notoriously difficult to decide which term is most appropriate when translating the name of God, but this word had been chosen, and appeared in the Septuagint no fewer than 6,000 times. The apostle Paul speaks of the title 'Lord' as the name above all names (Philippians 2:9), which plainly indicates that he recognises that it signifies God himself. What is more, he quotes Old Testament passages which speak of God as 'Lord', and then refers them to 'the Lord Jesus Christ', thus expressly asserting the divinity of Christ.

This same word had a rich web of meaning in the Greek speaking world. Its non-religious use signified 'master' and it was a token of respect in polite conversation, rather like the English 'sir'. In the religious context, 'Lord' was often used of various pagan gods. And in the political world it was used of 'the Lord Caesar'. 'Caesar is Lord' gradually developed a religious as well as political dimension, and Caesar worship became a standard test of loyalty within the Empire.

In this complex cultural context the simple phrase 'Jesus is Lord' plainly had points of contact with both the Jewish and the Greek worlds. For the Jews, the term built a bridge in reaffirming biblical belief in the one and only Lord God. And yet, to the shock of many Jews, this confession emphatically extended this lordship to Jesus Christ, as the only Son of the living God. The Jews were therefore confronted in this phrase with explicit insistence on the incarnation. For the Greeks, the familiar term claimed divinity for Jesus, but in such a way as to claim exclusivity and reject wholesale their pantheon of gods. And for the rulers of the Empire, the confession pointed to the inevitability of a head-on clash. Caesar and Jesus represented two mutually exclusive claims of ultimate allegiance. The one thing the Empire demanded from its subjects but could never expect from the Christian movement was absolute loyalty.

Here, then, is a further proposition:

> *The church which is true to Jesus and the apostles*
> *will always be ready to change its outward forms,*
> *without compromising the essential gospel,*
> *in order to reach into new cultures.*

4

Bridging the Gap II–
The Missionary Task

The first time I visited the States I was taken aback at my first all-American business lunch. I had always been accustomed to the British habit of eating with a knife and fork, holding onto both until the end of the meal. For the first time in my life I was surrounded in smart and fairly expensive restaurants by business people who cut up their food, put their knife down on the plate, then transferred the fork to their right hand in order to consume the meal. If I had eaten this way at home as a young child, let alone in a restaurant, I would have been told to eat 'properly'. There is, of course, no right and wrong way to eat with a knife and fork, but the power of culture tells us that 'the way we do things round here' is the right way for everyone to behave.

We have seen that Jesus knew how to be culturally relevant and yet called people to repentance. We have also seen that the apostles needed to translate the good news in order to communicate effectively into the Gentile world of the Roman Empire. That was by no means the end of the difficult but crucial task of cross-cultural transfer of the unchanging gospel of Christ. Much of the Western missionary movement exported two sets of values to the countries being added to European empires. They did indeed take the gospel, and all too many died early for the sake of mission to the world. But most also took Western civilisation, with the assumption that Western values were a consequence of or even integral to the gospel. Many missionaries proclaimed soap as well as Scripture, and taught allegiance to the monarch back home as well as allegiance to Christ. It is the very nature of a cultural context to appear self-evidently appropriate and fitting, both as a way of seeing the world and as a means of expressing the gospel.

Hudson Taylor was a pioneer in rejecting this monocultural approach to world mission. After a frustrating start to his missionary career he drew the conclusion that the gospel could not be taken successfully to the Chinese so long as it was still presented within European trappings. As a result, Taylor took the revolutionary steps of abandoning Western clothing, growing his hair Chinese style, living among the Chinese and eating Chinese food (not, presumably, from a take away).

For some of his fellow missionaries, securely isolated in their European compound, this was the last straw as far as this misguided and over-zealous young man was concerned. They considered the abandonment of British ways to be a betrayal of Western civilisation, a betrayal of the Chinese who owed it to themselves to Westernise, and a gross dishonour to Christ and his gospel. With the benefit of hindsight we now realise it was they who were betraying the gospel, by taking for granted the rightness of the culture in which they had grown up and where they instinctively belonged. It is all too easy to assume that your own culture, whether in terms of society or in terms of the sub-culture of a denomination or local church, is both superior to all others and the only natural and altogether adequate expression of the gospel of Christ.

Denominational and cultural imperialism

In order to explore further the need to bridge the gap – that is, the appropriate enculturation of the gospel – we must first recognise a pair of constraints that can totally paralyse the church. *Denominational imperialism* assumes that a single and definitive church order can be read off the pages of the New Testament and applied to the church in every generation and culture. The New Testament is assumed to provide not merely the authoritative guiding principles, but also the definitive blueprint for church structure and life. We therefore turn to someone from another denomination and say, with ecumenical graciousness, 'You worship God in your way, and we'll worship him in his way.'

Like men staring down a well and seeing their own faces reflected below, the founders and advocates of each new denomination stare into the Bible and all too often find their own structures to be the exclusive, legitimate pattern for the apostolic church. Those who disagree have frequently been assumed to lack intelligence, integrity or spiritual illumination – that is, if you are not 'one of us' you can only be stupid, compromised or lacking in spiritual anointing. The pervasive assumptions of denominational imperialism have regularly resulted in the founding of new churches. Indeed, evangelical Protestantism has proved particularly vulnerable to fragmentation as a result. Such misplaced dogmatism is by no means the sole preserve of some of the more recent new denominations, formerly known as house churches. It was just as much the spur to the founders of many of the older denominations. The result of denominational imperialism is the imposition of fixed and inflexible requirements, whereas the New Testament reveals liberty, variety and pragmatic flexibility in church life and order.

What of those denominations which have long since outgrown the first flush of youthful enthusiasm? In time denominational imperialism mutates into its secondary form. Traditions become set in bronze and stone. Yesterday's pragmatic solution to an immediate problem becomes today's immovable essential of denominational identity. Historical accidents become non-negotiable fixtures, at times enshrined with a permanency neither intended nor foreseen by the original pioneers. As a result, old denominations and local churches often find it hard to give room for experiment and new ways, and easily see such initiatives as a threat to the traditions rather than a positive and necessary way to revitalise the church. The truth is that no church order should ever be absolutised, for each reflects dialogue and experimentation within a particular cultural context.

Cultural imperialism is still more pervasive and insidious. We have already cited the 19th-century missionary movement's twofold zeal to evangelise and to civilise. Even today, it remains true that 'many western missionaries still consider the cultural wrapper of their home Christianity an integral part of the gospel'.[1] The 1978 Willowbank Report on Gospel and Culture summed up the unconscious cultural conditioning of the Western missionary movement, which the writers described as a 'mono-cultural export system':

> The tendency was to produce almost exact replicas. Gothic architecture, prayer book liturgies, clerical dress, musical instruments,

---

[1] J. Loewen, 'The Gospel: its content and communication', *Down to Earth*, p. 124.

hymns and tunes, decision-making processes, synods and committees, superintendents and archdeacons – all were exported and
unimaginatively introduced into the new mission-founded
churches . . . all this was based on the false assumptions that
the Bible gave specific instructions about such matters and that
the home churches' pattern of government, worship, ministry,
and life were themselves exemplary.[1]

Rene Padilla has condemned the emasculation of the gospel
which results when the church has grown inflexible and
culturally remote:

> . . . in many parts of the world Christianity is regarded as an
> ethnic religion – the white man's religion. The Gospel has a
> foreign sound, or no sound at all, in relation to many of the
> dreams and anxieties, problems and questions, values and
> customs of people. The Word of God is reduced to a message
> that touches life only on a tangent.[2]

Cultural relevance and cultural engagement

An Anglican vicar told me about an unforgettable visit to
South Africa, where he had spoken at a Zulu service. The
set liturgy was *The Book of Common Prayer* and the hymnal
was *Hymns Ancient and Modern*. Although the feel was more
lively, the form of worship was an exact replica of any traditional English parish church. After the final blessing the congregation finally had their own say, and what followed was a
tremendous flow of spontaneous worship using the rhythms
and melodies of the Zulu people. Only then did the Zulu
Christians have the freedom and opportunity to get real with

---

[1] *Down to Earth*, p. 329.
[2] 'Hermeneutics and Culture', *Down to Earth*, p. 77.

God. My Anglican friend wept inwardly that such vibrant faith was confined within the unyielding straitjacket of a 17th-century English service. It was as if the original missionaries had borrowed the Starship Enterprise in order to beam up a rural parish church in England and beam it down, nothing changed at all, among the Zulus.

Modern thinking on world mission stands square against such an approach. In previous eras the aim of missionaries was often to found churches in the image of their home culture and denomination. Now the emphasis is on missionaries assisting in the planting of indigenous churches. An indigenous church is designed to draw upon its setting in order to be both culturally relevant and culturally specific. That is, the national and local context matters profoundly, and is part of what determines the character and style of a truly indigenous church.

This same concept needs to be applied in the West as church-planting initiatives gather pace. It is absolutely vital that we have a clear concept of what we are trying to plant. Otherwise we may end up cloning existing churches, with all their cultural irrelevance intact. We need to be alert to the hazards of denominational imperialism, which takes for granted the innate rightness and permanence of the model of the sending church as the blueprint for all future plants.

We also need to reject the 'McDonald's mentality', which turns church planting into a franchise operation. On this basis, once the corporate style has been determined, every new branch is established on an identical basis and is a replica of every other branch. If the church is meant to be indigenous, every church plant must have the freedom to respond in a unique way to the local community it seeks to serve and reach.

There are limits to indigenisation. Just as a totally alien

church sub-culture is a profound error, a totally indigenised church has betrayed itself and the gospel, as Kierkegaard protested so vigorously. The church must have enough in common with its context to be palatable, but must also retain the 'offence of the gospel' which in any context will remain hard to swallow without real repentance.

A total subservience to the demands and values of a cultural context, even when that context goes by the name of Christendom, actually represents a disastrous failure for the church, regardless of its popularity or its socio-political influence. The church that sells out to cultural conformity has performed a reverse miracle, turning the wine of the gospel into the water of religious respectability.

Recent missiological thought has explored the helpful model of dynamic equivalence, drawing on modern principles of translation. For various examinations I have had to produce rather wooden and laboured literal translations from Latin and Greek, French and Middle English. Such translations may convey some superficial fragments of the sense of the original, but a great deal is lost in the process. This kind of travesty of real translation is often inflicted upon English speakers in the instruction manuals for Japanese electrical goods. No one would doubt that effort has gone into the translation, but the Japanese idiom has been carried over so literally that the result cannot remotely be recognised as the language of any among the English speaking peoples!

Far from such wooden literalness, a dynamic equivalence translation seeks an equivalence of response rather than an identical linguistic form. That is, you identify the response evoked by the words in the original language, and then you attempt to find a means of expression that brings about as close a response as possible in your translation. As the poet and translator Robert Graves wrote about his own translation of Suetonius, 'the genius of Latin and the genius of English being so dissimilar . . . a literal rendering would be almost unreadable. For English readers Suetonius' sentences, and sometimes even groups of sentences, must often be turned inside out.'

A schoolboy's attempted word for word correspondence results in far less than an authentic translation. Not only poetry is lost in literal translation, but also much essential meaning. The forms, therefore – the words, metaphors and syntax – must be considered subservient to the meaning they convey. In the case of the Bible, the words and metaphors, the sentence structure and idioms are understood to be vehicles of the gospel rather than gospel themselves. Dynamic equivalence is a guiding principle of almost every modern Bible translation.

On this basis, a 'dynamic equivalence church' would be profoundly mistaken simply to replicate the forms of the sending church. Rather, the intention will be to produce an equivalent impact to the original church in a quite different cultural context. Chuck Kraft sums up the priorities of such a model: 'A dynamic equivalence church (1) conveys to its members truly Christian meanings, (2) responds to the felt needs of its society, producing within it an impact for Christ equivalent to that which the first century church produced in its society, and (3) appropriates cultural forms that are as nearly indigenous as possible.'[1]

In the case of translation, if the external forms of an alien culture are retained literally, not only does the original meaning fail to be conveyed, but that meaning will quite inevitably be distorted. Similarly, in cross-cultural church planting, if the

---

[1] 'The Church in Culture', *Down to Earth*, p. 224.

external forms of a church from a different culture are retained, the resultant church life will inevitably be a distortion of the life of the mother church. Conservatism in the matter of external forms, in both translation and in church planting, has the entirely unintentional impact of a betrayal or even a parody of the original meaning and purpose.

The apostolic task of the church requires that we learn to become bridge-building communities. We must learn to live out and express the gospel in ways that are culturally specific to our particular context. The commonly used term is 'cultural relevance'. However, we have also identified the limits to indigenisation, recognising that the church must not become subservient to its context, watering down the essential gospel or becoming syncretistic, absorbing uncritically cultural and religious influences. The examples of Jesus and the apostles demonstrate the need not only to build a bridge to the world around us, but also to face our world with both the hope and the demands of the gospel. The 'fit' of the gospel to their cultures was more like a bridle to a horse than a glove to a hand, providing new direction and not merely warmth and comfort. It therefore seems advisable to speak not merely of *cultural relevance*, but more precisely of the need to be *culturally engaged*.

Cultural engagement and the modern world

We have argued that many of our contemporaries have been repelled not so much by the offence of the gospel, but rather by the archaic and remote sub-culture of the church. Church as we generally know it does indeed have a 'foreign sound', in Padilla's phrase. For an increasing number the church has no audible voice at all, and our message is simply not getting through. Issues of cross-cultural mission therefore cannot be restricted to the non-Western world. In the post-modern setting, cross-cultural mission begins at home.

Though this task is urgent, it would be foolish to assume that cross-cultural mission in the modern world is straight-forward, let alone free from mistakes and conflict. The pro-liferation of new, culturally specific churches is in part an indictment of the inability of the older churches to evolve speedily and sufficiently in order to relate convincingly to our world at the turn of the century. In much experiment in worship and church order, there is surely an urgent quest for Christian expression that is genuinely contemporary. That doesn't validate every product of this quest, but in a period of cultural upheaval, such experiment is both necessary and inevitable, even if some misguided Christians welcome all uncritically or dismiss all wholesale.

The theological task – exploring and articulating the gospel within a particular cultural context – is always both necessary and unfinished. Even so the ecclesiological task – being the church within a particular cultural context – is equally necessary and unfinished. Sadly, some who enthu-siastically endorse and engage in the theological task prove unyieldingly diehard when considering change in the church. It is quite possible to be creative in mind but reactionary in churchmanship. Schillebeecx speaks with pungency into all traditionalist churches and historic denominations: '. . . the fact that at a particular moment a wave of alternative prac-tices is sweeping over the church throughout the world indicates that the existing church order has lost a structure of credibility and at some points is in urgent need of being revised'.[1]

---

[1] *The Church with a Human Face*, p. 258.

The death of permanence

With every passing year we are living at a faster pace. Values and ways of living are continuously on the move. We face not only a technological but also a cultural rate of change that is accelerating. Toffler well described this 'death of permanence' and the consequent 'future shock':

> . . . if the last 50,000 years of man's existence were divided into lifetimes of approximately sixty-two years each, there have been about 800 such lifetimes. Of these 800, fully 650 were spent in caves. Only during the last seventy lifetimes has it been possible to communicate effectively from one lifetime to another – as writing made it possible to do. Only during the last six lifetimes did masses of men ever see a printed word. Only during the last four has it been possible to measure time with any precision. Only in the last two has anyone anywhere used an electric motor. And the overwhelming majority of all the material goods we use in daily life today have been developed within the present, the 800th, lifetime.[1]

In Toffler's words, the present lifetime 'marks a sharp break with all past human experience'. We are moving beyond the period of 'built-in obsolescence'. Today, new technology is outmoded long before it breaks down. In the computer industry, with ever broadening impact on daily living, by the time a product is launched on the market, the next generation of hardware is already in prototype. To put it more personally, as a fifties baby, I can remember our first car, first TV, first colour TV, first automatic washing machine, first fridge, first freezer, first hi-fi, first video, first microwave, etc. My experience of everyday living has been built on the

---

[1] *Future Shock*, p. 22.

basis of change that is both continuous and accelerating. Sometimes the pace may seem bewilderingly fast, but continuous change is actually one of the constant factors in my total experience of life.

The apostolic task of bridging the gap is a continuing and unavoidable responsibility in the mission of the church, which has to be taken up anew in every generation. It is also, in our context, a responsibility that requires from us an accelerating rate of change. The mission responsibility of the church requires that we keep pace with the rate and nature of change in the culture we seek to reach. The trouble is that in most churches the mechanisms of change and adaptability were established in an age when the culture changed much more slowly. Many churches view change like chemotherapy. We can cope with a limited dosage so long as we're persuaded it is absolutely necessary. As soon as possible we want to settle back into our old, accustomed ways.

Even new churches can struggle to keep up, and face the predictable lament of teenagers that their approach is increasingly out of touch. I am quite convinced that one of the consequences of the world in which we live is that a number of single generation churches will spring into life. They will initially bridge a cultural gap with great effectiveness, but will then find themselves unable to sustain the necessary momentum to attract a second or third generation of adult members. As a result, another new church is likely to be needed in the same locality just a few years later. I am not commending such a strategy, but rather conclude that it will prove practically inevitable, unless we can rid ourselves of our habitual inability to provide rapid responses to cultural change.

Churches with a long history and tradition are beginning to face the harsh market forces of modern life. It is not only businesses that go to the wall because they fail to change and keep up to date. Those churches which refuse to incarnate the gospel in terms accessible to the outsider are condemned to evolve into museums; time capsules which lovingly commemorate dead traditions. Adrift from the contemporary world while holding fast to the security of yesterday, for the remnant of insiders they will become ghettos of consolation, one short step from extinction.

Reaching the vast majority

At the Pan African Assembly in 1976, Chuck Kraft called for a clear-sighted fresh cultural engagement: 'I have nothing against those who as part of their Christian devotion to God choose to follow God according to the patterns of Europeanised African culture. These are truly God's people . . . But my heart yearns for the other 300 million . . . who will not Westernise in order to become Christian.'[1]

There is a similarly critical and urgent need for clear-sighted cultural engagement by the church in the West. We live in a society where a growing number have long since rejected the traditional church, with the appalling assumption that the all too apparent irrelevance of the church is a reasonable basis on which to predicate the irrelevance of the gospel. I therefore suggest we need to echo Kraft:

> *We have nothing against those who as part of their*
> *Christian devotion serve*
> *Christ according to the patterns of traditional*
> *Western culture.*

---

[1] *Together in One Place*, p. 85.

These are truly God's people . . .
But our hearts yearn for the 90 per cent of today's Westerners
who simply will not traditionalise in order to
become Christian.

5

Objections to Cultural Engagement

The same objections frequently arise in any discussion of cultural engagement. It is therefore essential that we consider them before developing our argument any further.

Our ways are right, so we shouldn't change them

In any culture, from the minor details to the major issues of life, we grow up with a set of customs which, because they become so familiar, we assume to be absolutely correct and universally applicable. In our own culture we 'do what comes naturally', and then assume that what is natural for us must be right for everyone. Within the walls of their sub-culture, traditional churches have been 'doing what comes naturally'. And because the familiar ways come naturally, Christians easily assume that such ways must be right in every time and place. Some churches have expressly instructed members concerning the authority of their unchanging traditions and denominational identity as principles that are non-negotiable. As a result, many Christians tend to confuse 'what comes naturally' in their particular church with the essential gospel. They therefore begin to fear that to change such things would risk betraying the gospel itself.

Consider hats. I know a group of women who spent years in a Christian sub-culture where women were encouraged to wear hats to church 'as a good witness'. Everyone else, it was explained, will know where you are going and that you are a believer if you wear a hat on Sunday mornings. Now I don't personally care whether a woman wears a hat on Sunday or any other day of the week. So far as I am concerned it is entirely a matter of personal choice. What is more, for most Westerners, the only thing a hat on Sunday morning means is that the wearer likes hats! A problem only arises if the Christian woman who wears a hat judges another Christian woman to be a 'bad witness' simply because her head is bare on Sundays.

The more you are used to your sub-culture, the more you are likely to take for granted the rightness of how your church does things. As a result, if someone speaks of the need for change and for engagement with the surrounding non-Christian culture, first reactions are likely to be strong. You may feel threatened, or angry, or even betrayed. You may feel that the old ways are not understood or appreciated any more. The more you feel you are 'doing what comes naturally' for Christians in your church, the more you risk assuming that your church has got everything right. It is only a short step to assume that outsiders not only need to become Christians, but they also need to learn to fit in with the tried and tested ways of your church.

The truth is that there are countless different expressions of the gospel in styles of worship and structures of church life. The one thing none of us should ever presume to say is that the style of our church is God's definitive last word for every culture and generation. The church that commits itself to standing with the culture of yesteryear has made a reassuring choice for the remaining insiders. But it can hardly then complain about a new church springing up to meet the needs of those who see no good reason why joining a church should require a cultural shift akin to passing through a time warp. And that is true whether our church was founded in 1070, 1870 or 1970!

Don't water down the gospel

The essential gospel is unchanging. Christ has died, is risen and will come again. Hallelujah! We need to be absolutely clear that cultural engagement has nothing to do with adjusting the gospel itself, with the misguided intention of making it more palatable or easier to believe. The utter failure of modern liberalism to grow strong churches through new conversions demonstrates the simple fact that if you tamper with the heart of the gospel, you end up with nothing worth believing in. Such an approach is guaranteed to fail.

One leading liberal wrote in the early sixties that modern people who are used to turning on electric light bulbs at the flick of a switch no longer find it possible to believe in a God who intervenes to bring supernatural healing. I found this suggestion absurd when I first read it, and just as absurd today. If anything, the rise of New Age religion indicates that our culture is becoming more open to the spiritual dimension and to supernatural mysteries rather than rejecting all such possibilities out of hand. Absurd though it is, some churchmen today appear to believe less than their non-Christian neighbours.

What we need to ensure is a clear-sighted distinction between the gospel itself and the forms of church life. I was

fascinated on a recent preaching trip to Poland to see the
farmers reaping with hand scythes and gathering the crops
with horses and carts. It was such a shock to see a pre-
industrial harvest in the continent of Europe. The Polish
peasant farmers had no choice, of course, for communism
had robbed them of benefits we have taken for granted for
many years. Imagine that a Polish farmer inherited a huge
farm in the States, and emigrated as soon as he could to
enjoy the good life. You visit him at harvest time and discover that while other farmers are hiring huge combine
harvesters, he is busy hiring every horse in the state. 'Why
do you want so many horses?' you enquire patiently. 'Well,'
he explains, 'it wouldn't be a proper harvest without horses
and carts.'

Just as such a farmer would have confused the means of
transportation with the end of getting in the harvest successfully, we need to understand afresh that the church is the
vehicle for the gospel, not the gospel itself. When the vehicle
is rust-holed and weary, it is time to get a new model. Any
methods, any structures grow out of date. Embodiments of
the gospel which serve well in one era become obstacles to the
gospel in the next. We are not watering down the gospel
when we change the church. The gospel absolutely requires
such change from us.

When I was in Poland, a phone call came through one day
to the church where I was staying. Normally the tap water was
safe, as long as it was boiled. On this particular day there had
been an emergency announcement: acute and deadly contamination meant the water had become totally undrinkable. We
readily accept that the gospel can be polluted by the immorality of a godless age, but the gospel is also contaminated
when we confuse eternal truths with dying and dead traditions. Traditionalism doesn't intend to water down the

gospel, but such contamination can leave the gospel so un-palatable as to become almost undrinkable. We need to ask some fundamental questions. What are the principles which are non-negotiable and must not be changed? What are the non-essential practices which have become alien in today's world and need to be retired speedily?

Some strong churches haven't changed

A sustained period of numerical decline is likely to lead not only to nostalgia, but a tendency to 'shore up the ruins', holding fast to the forms that served well in the past. As a result, a church in decline can become ever more isolated as a sub-cultural remnant, increasingly lacking a plausibility structure through points of cultural contact with wider society. This can be a particular problem not only for elderly congregations, holding fast to the familiar externals of religion in a world of accelerating change, but also for conservative Evangelicals. If the strength of evangelicalism is the unreadiness to be swayed by passing fashions in academic theology, the Achilles' heel is not merely an uncritical theological conservatism, but also an uncritical cultural conservatism. In the desire to preserve the unchanging essence of the gospel, it has been a frequent failing of Evangelicals to confuse gospel and form. As a result, antiquated forms of religion are mummified and greatly obscure the message of divine grace.

This unreadiness to accept that the disentanglement of gospel and church, rather than being an act of appeasement or compromise, is fundamental to the churches' task of incarnating the gospel, is exemplified by Martyn Lloyd-Jones. A supremely gifted preacher, and undoubtedly the foremost mid-century evangelical free churchman, Lloyd-Jones was always more admired for the tenacity of his convictions than the breadth of his sympathies. It seems he was utterly persuaded that the only valid model of Christian worship involved the minister leading worship, praying at length and preaching at greater length.

Contrast this with today, when more and more churches are influenced by the following trends: informality, expectancy in worship, participation rather than passivity, openness to manifestations of God in worship, the ministries of healing and prophecy, a desire for closer and more expressive loving fellowship, the use of contemporary songs which speak of an intimate love relationship with God, and a readiness to use the performing arts in public worship.

Lloyd-Jones' dismissal of experiment in worship by fellow Evangelicals seems to have been summed up in a derogatory epithet – 'entertainment'. No doubt some experiment has always been no more than that, but Lloyd-Jones could not apparently conceive of an evangelical defence, say of the performing arts, on biblical grounds. (It would not appear that the argument from cultural context would have found a sympathetic hearing.) Lloyd-Jones' cultural inelasticity deprived the radio and television audiences of his preaching. Only in Wales was it thought possible to broadcast his eloquent but uncompromisingly lengthy sermons.

Lloyd-Jones' biographer, Iain Murray, voices the same inclusive conservatism when he observes with considerable disquiet:

There was also the development of a feeling – soon to sweep all before it – that a main hindrance to the church effectively reaching the world lay in her out-of-date Bible version and in her forms of worship which had changed so little in centuries. The climate of thought – not uninfluenced by the secular world – was swinging against all things 'traditional' and 'old fashioned'.[1]

I am passionately concerned to see a recovery of biblical preaching, and I would say without hesitation that our debt to Lloyd-Jones is immense. He was the Churchill of mid 20th-century preaching, a supremely gifted individual, a colossus of the pulpit. But it simply will not do to suggest that all we need is a thousand ministers to lead churches with the methods of Lloyd-Jones. For a start, a century only sees a handful of men so immensely gifted. More than that, Lloyd-Jones' ministry marked the end of an era. The gospel that he proclaimed must still be proclaimed with equal vigour and clarity. None the less, his world pre-dated the rise of modern popular culture and the age of television. He inhabited a world that has gone, and will never come back.

This is by no means the first time a distinctive Christian era has come to an end. The age of the church of Jerusalem began to fade as soon as the mission to the Gentiles gathered speed. Very soon Jewish Christians began to be outnumbered, and their influence on the prevailing culture of the church in-evitably waned. Or consider the great American awakening. Jonathan Edwards saw revival break out when he preached without a microphone, by the light of a candle, reading his sermon word for word from his quill scripted text. Micro-phones have arrived in force, word processors have replaced most quills, and few churches are now lit by candlelight. Maybe it is the historical gap which makes it easier for us not to confuse such externals with revival itself.

A further example often cited in defence of church as a

---

[1] *D. Martyn Lloyd-Jones – The Fight of Faith*, p. 313.

change-free zone is the church under communism. I recall one senior church leader telling me about the Russian Baptist churches, packed for every service and thoroughly traditional in approach. 'These churches,' he explained with great conviction, throwing his ace into the argument, 'haven't needed to change a thing!' The complicating factor here is that the church took on a distinctive role in the communist era. Since communism was seen as a totalitarian intruder, the church became a vehicle for preserving an old culture, under assault from the novelties of an imposed communist culture that few really wanted. Now that communism has collapsed through its own inefficiencies and corruption, the church is no longer the place of conservation for pre-communist Russian culture. Russian Christians are now needing to come to terms with a new climate, in which they face similar pressures to the Western church. We need to face reality as we enter the 21st century. Almost invariably those churches that resist cultural engagement are nostalgic. Their best days are behind them. They are on the slide.

I don't like change

While some are so accustomed to change that they enjoy it, most of us dislike change at least some of the time. I felt greatly aggrieved when my new driving licence arrived through the post. Ever since passing my test I had been irrationally fond of the green licence. Suddenly this perfectly good document was replaced by a lurid pink computer printout. Still more I disliked my new passport. There was something special about the old, outsize, dark blue British passport. It had a sense of history, of a nation with a proud past. As you queued at passport control it was easy to feel superior towards those without one, as if they must have secretly longed to be British. When the new passport arrived, all such absurd, post-imperialistic fantasies were shattered for ever. The new passport is not only smaller, and red rather than blue, it is also merely the UK version of the standardised passport of the European Community!

We referred earlier to 'future shock', Toffler's memorable phrase to describe a common reaction to an overdose of rapid change in the technological society. The accelerating changes of new technology are now accompanied by growing fears of ecological doom. The major cities of the world are becoming increasingly dangerous places to live, with an urban under-class excluded from the growing prosperity of those living in the wealthier, outer suburbs. In this context, it may well be that 'future shock' will evolve into 'future dread'. Great leaps forward in computing and technology have been paralleled by a great increase in alienation, broken relationships and even despair.

For all the downside of a society on a roller-coaster of change, there is no way out. Short of moving to a desert island, change is inescapable and inevitable. It is the world in which we live, so we need to get as used to it as we can. A culture of continuous change makes us feel insecure. Like a sailor charting his course through unknown waters by the north star, we navigate the uncharted waters of our rapidly changing world by finding some fixed points we can rely on. In this human quest for security, some people look to a church that doesn't change. It is not just believers. I have met people who have no intention of ever darkening the door of a church who feel very strongly that the church should never change. In a world where everything is new, it is comforting to know that a few things in life will always stay the same.

The trouble is that we have got it all wrong. It is not the

church that never changes, but God. We are never invited in the Bible to find our security in an ancient institution 'as it was in the beginning, is now and shall be for ever'. On the contrary, our security is in the unchanging God. What is more, the living God's intention is not to leave us just as we are, but to keep on changing us into the likeness of Christ (2 Corinthians 3:18). This applies not only to individual believers, but also to the church. In the book of Acts the church was for ever needing to catch up with the changes the Holy Spirit continually introduced to their life and mission.

If we are to get beyond initial resistance to the very idea of change, we need to understand the dynamics of change. Any organisation, whether a business, a club or a church, will have the following personality types represented in roughly these proportions.

First, there is the radical element, some 5 to 10 per cent who have already thought about most changes long before the leaders say anything public. Their immediate reaction to a proposed change is likely to be, 'At last! The leaders have finally caught up with the need for a change that has been staring us in the face for ages.'

Secondly, there is the early majority, the 40 per cent or so who readily come in line behind a proposed change that is timely. They had not thought of the change before it was mentioned, but they are confident in the leaders and readily support their new ideas.

Thirdly, there is the late majority, another 40 per cent or so, who are instinctively cautious. They are not opposed to the idea of change, but they need time to think about it and they want to make sure it really makes sense, cautious of being carried away on a tide of enthusiasm or fashion. Their first reaction is likely to be, 'We need more time.' They tend to overstate all the things that could go wrong if the changes are implemented. If they are given the time they need, they tend to come round.

Fourthly, there are the diehards, again making up some 5 to 10 per cent. Before they knew what change was being suggested, they already knew that they were against it. As a matter of instinct more than principle they are opposed to the very idea of change. David Watson once met a churchwarden who fell neatly into this last category.

'I've been a churchwarden here for twenty-five years.'

'You must have seen a lot of changes in that time.'

'Yes, and I've resisted every single one of them!'

If leaders don't understand the dynamics of change, they run the risk of responding badly to the third and fourth groups. They may be tempted to dismiss out of hand the worries of the cautious, assuring them that their fears are groundless since the leaders would never have proposed anything foolhardy. Unfortunately, if the cautious feel pressured they tend to become increasingly nervous about the likely impact of the changes. Give them time and gentle, persuasive reassurance and they have a habit of coming round to support the proposed change.

Just as an impatient leader may alienate the cautious, highly pastoral leaders may concentrate their efforts upon the diehards. Unfortunately, an entrenched and determined diehard does not have the slightest intention of changing their mind. They still need loving, but we need to recognise that they are extremely unlikely to be persuaded. Even years after a change has taken place, diehards have been known to still be complaining about it.

If the cautious are pressured, they may begin to fear that the diehards are right after all. If the cautious are won over, an overwhelming majority will support the new venture. Diehards tend to make their choices after a decision has been made. Some are won round by an overwhelming majority. Some move elsewhere. A few are tempted to sit on the back row and scowl doggedly for the next ten or twenty years . . .

A second dimension of the dynamics of change is just as vital to grasp. For the traditionalists, time is the payment which earns trust, and trust is the basis for giving permission or eventually approval for any subsequent change. For the postmodernists who have entered into the cultural experience of our day, change is the normal experience of life. For this second type of person, change needs to be delivered in order for the trust to grow which will allow them to give leaders time in a job. Not that change once delivered can then simply be institutionalised. On the contrary, such people increasingly embrace the truth that constant change is here to stay.

These equal and mutually contradictory attitudes can be drawn as follows:

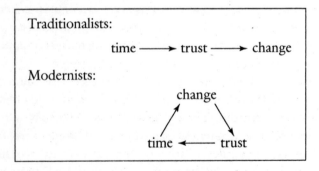

Traditionalists:

time ⟶ trust ⟶ change

Modernists:

change

time ⟵ trust

Those in the first group hope to put off change. They don't like the idea of it and keep their fingers crossed that once it has happened things will settle down again. The second diagram is represented as a cycle to reflect the dynamism of continuous change. Neither group is 'right' over against the other; they simply reflect different cultural perspectives. Both outlooks have weaknesses, and both outlooks are a fact of life today. But the willing embrace of the dynamism of change is inevitably becoming ever more prevalent.

When these attitudes collide we can all too easily begin to sling insults at one another, two favourites among Christians being 'dead' and 'irreverent'. We surely need to learn that all that is traditional is not intrinsically dead. Equally, all that is contemporary is not necessarily irreverent just because it wasn't done that way in years gone by. Only as we begin to understand the dynamics of change can we begin to implement and manage change effectively, working to minimise the fallout, even if some is inevitable.

The church should first make insiders comfortable

I heard recently about the most comfortable church in Britain. Several decades ago it was a large church, with a reputation for success. When leading American evangelists visited the country, this church was a natural port of call. Over the years, slowly and imperceptibly the church got older and smaller. They got out of the habit of expecting visitors at services. They forgot about mission altogether. Now there are fewer than thirty members left. They have all known one another for decades. Their church life never struggles with change, because nothing ever changes. The insiders are very comfortable together. Far too comfortable to risk any strangers rocking the boat! Sadly it is all too true that churches can become so concerned with the needs of the insiders that mission grinds to a halt. A small, exclusive voluntary group which happens to be a church is no less of a self-absorbed clique than any other cosy club.

Other churches have a fortress mentality. The believers huddle together, taking refuge from the terrible world outside. Every waking moment not spent at work is spent at church events, almost for fear that someone might mix with non-Christians socially, which would have dread or even fatal consequences. Once every few years the fortress church might have a mission. The drawbridge is let down warily, and the Christians head out nervously into the surrounding area. They hope to round up a few locals who will be dragged back into the fortress. As soon as possible the drawbridge is raised and the portcullis plummets back into place. Secure in their refuge once again, the Christians breathe a collective sigh of relief. Safe at last!

Consider the apostle Paul's account of how easy and comfortable his life became as a Christian:

> Five times I received from the Jews the forty lashes minus one. Three times I was beaten with rods, once I was stoned, three times I was shipwrecked, I spent a night and a day in the open sea, I have been constantly on the move. I have been in danger from rivers, in danger from bandits, in danger from my own countrymen, in danger from Gentiles; in danger in the city, in danger in the country, in danger at sea; and in danger from false brothers. I have laboured and toiled and have often gone without sleep; I have known hunger and thirst and have often gone without food; I have been cold and naked. Besides everything else, I face daily the pressure of my concern for all the churches. (2 Corinthians 11:24–28)

The reason he could put up with all of this was quite simple. For Paul, mission to the world was infinitely more important than his own creature comforts.

Being a Christian is not usually meant to feel like being a marine or a member of the SAS. We are not crack troops whose only task is to obey orders with a grim stare, fixed and determined. The church really is meant to be a place of belonging and enjoyment, as we live for Christ together. We need to know that we are loved and cared for. We need to be given every opportunity to grow as disciples. But the church that will not make time for outsiders until all the insiders are comfortable will discover a simple truth. If the comfort of Christians is an all-consuming priority, the time for mission will never come. There will always be someone pleading, 'We're just not ready yet.'

When a church begins to look outwards in mission, six words can sometimes be heard which are a kiss of death for personal spiritual vitality: 'What is in it for me?' The first law of Christian growth is that if you want to receive, you need to give. If you want to find a church with a high proportion of fulfilled and flourishing Christians, look for a church that makes mission, not the comfort of Christians, the number one priority.

This approach could threaten our denominational identity

The English Church Census makes vital reading for Christian leaders today. Such comprehensive figures are not available for many countries, but the evidence speaks beyond one nation to raise questions about global trends in the Christian church. No survey can claim total accuracy, but MARC Europe has provided us with the most definitive snapshot of church health we could hope for. What the survey confirms is that the church in England is changing fast. At every level old assumptions no longer apply. Denominational identities are shifting significantly, and we need a clear understanding of the changing face of the church.

The impact of the Free Churches

Some establishment commentators convey the impression that the Free Churches can be consigned to the ash heap of history, and that the future of the church in England is essentially Anglican and Roman Catholic. Nothing could be further from the truth. In 1975, churchgoers divided unequally between these three sectors: the Free Churches with 30 per cent were slightly weaker than the Anglicans with 32 per cent, while the Roman Catholics were much larger at 38 per cent. By 1989, only the Free Churches had grown numerically, with the result that the Anglicans were then the smallest sector at 31 per cent and the Free Churches (34 per cent) were not much smaller than the Roman Catholics (35 per cent).

In the light of growth trends and age distribution, the survey projects the size of churches in the year 2000. Without a dramatic shift of fortune, only the Free Churches are likely to enjoy overall growth this decade. That means by the year 2000 the Anglicans will remain the smallest sector, their share of churchgoers shrinking to 30 per cent; the Catholic decline will continue, reducing their share to 32 per cent; and the Free Churches will consolidate their ascendancy, growing to 38 per cent of the total number of churchgoers. A major shift of identity already seems to be emerging among the English churches.

How evangelical are the denominations?

The Anglicans live up to their reputation as a broad church: 12 per cent Anglo-Catholic, 18 per cent liberal, 18 per cent evangelical, the rest low, broad or catholic. Among the Free Churches 56 per cent are evangelical, but the proportion varies widely. Methodists are 33 per cent evangelical and 16 per cent liberal, but their essential identity is found among those who are low and broad (47 per cent). The URC have the fewest Evangelicals (24 per cent) and the highest concentration of liberals (37 per cent); they are also the Free Church experiencing the most severe decline. These two factors are not unrelated. As to the Baptists, the only historical denomination that is reporting slight growth, just 5 per cent declared themselves to be liberals, and 10 per cent are low and broad. Some 84 per cent of Baptists identify themselves as evangelical. The other believer baptising groupings, the Pentecostals and new churches, are of course almost entirely evangelical.

The character of the Free Churches

We should not think of the Free Churches as a fixed and predictable grouping, whose identity was defined immutably in times past. The shifting centre of gravity of English Christians is magnified in the changing face of the Free Churches. In 1975 the Methodists (454,000) were the largest group, followed by the Baptists (193,000), the Independents (167,000) and the URC (150,000). By 1989, Methodists had declined markedly, but were still the largest group (396,000), while the surge of growth among Independents (293,000) overtook moderate Baptist growth (199,000) and the Pentecostals (95,200) were not far behind the URC (114,000), the fourth largest group.

Over the past decade, the Methodists and URC, sometimes described as the establishment of the traditional Free Churches, have continued their sorry decline. We move ever nearer to MARC Europe's estimate that by 2000 the largest group will be the Independents (397,000), who will have overtaken the Methodists (352,000), while the Baptists and Pentecostals continue to grow (205,000 and 119,000), and the URC drop to 91,000. If the Free Churches are becoming numerically dominant today, then this is because the face of the Free Churches is changing: that face is increasingly Independent, Baptist or Pentecostal. Indeed, recent evidence of churches missed by the survey indicates still greater strength among Independents and Pentecostals, most of whom are both evangelical and charismatic.

The new Evangelicals

As the face of the church changes, the only group that have been enjoying consistent growth are the Evangelicals. The evangelical proportion of all churchgoers, including Roman Catholics, is now 27 per cent and rising. Among Evangelicals too the ground is shifting. MARC Europe identified three groupings, although the borders between them are inevitably blurred. In 1985, the smallest group was mainstream Evangelicals (257,000) with broad Evangelicals second (349,000) and charismatic Evangelicals leading the way (395,000). By 1989, mainstream Evangelicals had grown slightly (262,000), broad Evangelicals had declined (340,000) and charismatic Evangelicals had surged ahead (425,000).

In percentage terms, charismatics were 39 per cent of all Evangelicals in 1985 and 41 per cent in 1989. On current trends, by the year 2000, 24 per cent will be mainstream Evangelicals, broad Evangelicals will decline from 35 per cent in 1985 to just 29 per cent and charismatics will increase to 47 per cent. No attempt to pretend that either Evangelicals or charismatics can be marginalised or ignored will have any credibility in the coming years.

Post-denominationalism

In the light of this evidence we have to conclude that denominationalism as we have known it is already on the move. The frequency with which people move house today contributes hugely to another dimension of change. The anecdotal evidence, from church after church, is that Evangelicals are no longer choosing a new church by denomination. Rather, they are looking for spiritual vitality, measured above all by the style of worship and preaching.

This means that the so-called 'laity' (the word means 'people' and in the New Testament the entire church is the *laos*, the people of God) are a long way ahead of the professional ministers. Christians are in fact already showing a high degree of involvement in a non-institutional ecumenism. Indeed it bypasses the institutions altogether, for these Christians are identifying with one another not along denominational lines, but according to the cross-denominational common currency of evangelicalism. The inevitable result is that such Christians, once they have moved house a couple of times and as a result moved denomination a couple of times, no longer have any kind of denominational identity at all. They increasingly describe themselves not as Anglicans or Methodists, Baptists or new church, but as Christians who play an active part in their local live church.

The urgent need for cultural engagement adds a further dimension to the process of dissolution of the old-style denominations as watertight compartments. We are running out of members of the 'Once an Anglican, always an Anglican' school. What cultural engagement does is to weaken further the grip of a sub-culture, by asking whether some of the trappings of denominationalism are really necessary or relevant any more. In principle, of course, cultural engagement doesn't preclude the strengthening of denominations. It is quite possible that we are entering an era without precedent in the West, where historic denominations end up strengthened and vibrant as a result of a fresh exploration of biblical foundations and creative implementation of cultural engagement. On the other hand, we may be at the beginning of an era of fundamental regrouping among Christians, in which some of the older denominational structures are found to be increasingly obsolete and gradually wither away. After all, the less strongly you identify with an organisation, the less money you provide for its support. Only time will tell which way the wind is blowing.

One thing is sure: cultural engagement is based on the priority of mission in the life of the church. This implies that neither the success nor even the survival of a denomination is the primary objective. It seems reasonable to observe that if your primary objective is that your denomination retains its historic identity and forms, a struggle is all but inevitable with the conflicting priority of cultural engagement. But if we are serious about the gospel we must also be serious about cultural engagement. What we long to see is not the mere survival of a particular denomination, but the effective re-evangelisation of the Western world.

As a publisher I once asked the editor of one leading religious newspaper about his ambition. 'To keep the paper going till I retire,' was his reply. Such bleak survivalism, with no attempt to extend the market, is hardly a recipe for advance. But it appears to be the ambition not merely of one journalist, but of a number of leading churchmen. Blessed are those who expect little, for their disappointments shall also be modest!

Like a house in Venice that has stood firm for many hundreds of years but is now beginning to slip into a canal, signs of new and unpredictable movements, both slippage and rebuilding, are in evidence across the structures of the denominations, old and new alike. Don't blame cultural engagement. The realignment of Bible believing Christians is already well under way.

I don't like all these gimmicks

The movie *Sister Act*, starring Whoopi Goldberg, amusingly sends up Maggie Smith's Mother Superior, whose faith is locked inside the music of yesteryear. When Whoopi gives the choir some Tamla Motown and Soul, the crowds flock in. It is certainly true that the church urgently needs to break free from cultural captivity, but since the movie came from Hollywood it is hardly surprising that the new-style religion on offer was no more than a glittering surface. The nuns begin to sing up tempo in a contemporary style, but there is no real content to their performances. In the same way, if we become enslaved to the preferences of post-modernity or to numerical growth as an end in itself, the gospel will begin to slip between our fingers until we have nothing left to offer except religious recreation. Contemporary techniques without biblical truth will drift towards the trivial. The gospel should never be boring, but it makes demands upon us that can never be reduced to mere entertainment. We need to bridge the gap and yet hold fast to the unchanging gospel.

A friend of mine still winces when he recalls the first Sunday he introduced dance to a church. The woman who danced was professionally trained and performed well. But to the objector who lay in wait before the evening service, her ability was immaterial.

'Now you've tried to bring in that kind of thing, I want you out of here,' was the warm welcome.

'Well, bless you anyway,' my friend rather lamely replied.

'I don't want your blessing,' came the retort. 'I just want you out of here!'

Despite the curious venom which the performing arts can provoke among the more puritanical, we need to insist that they can by no means be dismissed with the pejorative term 'gimmick'. Christians ought to have a high view of the arts, including the performing arts. Men and women are made in the image of a creator God. Human creativity is a reflection of divine creativity, and to express our creativity is in itself a form of worship before our creative God. Art is not merely 'redeemable' if used in the context of evangelism. Art needs no justification.

As to dance and drama, the value of both is well established in the Old Testament. David danced before the ark of the covenant, leading the people in worship. It seems that he recognised a dimension of worship that could not be expressed in his music or poetry, but only through the use of the body in a dance of praise (2 Samuel 6:14). To be sure, even David's dancing was despised by Michal, but his retort indicates how wrong she was to value conventional dignity above celebratory worship: 'I will celebrate before the Lord. I will become even more undignified than this . . .' (2 Samuel 6:21–22).

As to dramatic enactment, this was used frequently by the prophets to convey their message. Isaiah walked stripped and barefoot for three years as a sign of the coming Assyrian defeat and humiliation of Egypt and Cush (Isaiah 20:2–5). Jeremiah smashed a pot in full public view as a sign of the disaster coming upon Jerusalem: 'This is what the Lord Almighty says: I will smash this nation and this city just as this potter's jar is smashed and cannot be repaired' (Jeremiah 19:1–13). Ezekiel gave public performance to a series of prophetic enactments. He packed his bags by day and left the city at dusk, using a hole he had dug through the city wall, as a sign that the Jews would be taken into exile as captives. Then he trembled while eating and shuddered in fear as he drank, as signs of the anxiety and despair of the years of exile (Ezekiel 12:3–20). What gives the performing arts a particular strength today is the fact that we live in the age of television. When the most familiar forms of everyday communication are visual, dance and drama enhance our effective communication enormously.

In affirming the enormous value of dance and drama I don't deny for one moment that they can be trivialised and reduced to being 'gimmicks'. Some use them without the necessary discipline of thorough rehearsal, or without a critical eye to discard items of poor quality or taste. Even worse, some try to copy vibrant churches by singing all the right songs and using all the right techniques of communication, but it is mere imitation. Without a clear grasp of the gospel, and without the indwelling power of the Holy Spirit, such efforts may be well intentioned, but they remain full of sound and fury, signifying nothing.

I argued earlier that we need to recast our worship services in the light of popular television programmes. However, to move beyond cultural relevance to a fully apostolic approach of cultural engagement, we need to provide a critique of the downside of the impact of television. In this way we can not only learn from this means of communication, but also endeavour to transcend its limitations. Indeed, any concern about 'gimmicks' and trivialisation in the modern church is ultimately linked not merely to the place of the performing arts, but to this wider context of the impact and nature of modern television, and the kinds of communication it promotes.

Neil Postman, Professor of Communication Arts and Sciences at New York University, has produced a telling polemic. The essential problem with television, he argues, is not in the realm of light entertainment, where its vacuity pretends to be nothing else. The problem is where television presents itself as a medium for serious discourse, whether in education or news, politics or religion.[1]

The medium of TV so constrains the message, to adapt Mcluhan's axiom, that the kind of content valued in a print-based culture is in danger of extinction. The logical development of a linear argument is replaced by the 'sound-bite' – a slogan memorable enough to make the news headlines (although the rapacity of television is such that the shelf-life of most sound-bites is a single day). Intelligent debate is replaced by a verbal duel, in which the sparring gladiators have just a minute to present their case and refute their opponent. The real focus may seem to be the audience rating of the programme and the presenter's star quality rather than the issue to hand. Persuasion is replaced by entertainment, which elicits a shallow response susceptible to being overturned not by better argument, but by more enjoyable entertainment. Ideas are replaced by glamour, so physical appearance is increasingly determinative not only of political preferment (at least in the United States!) but also of the perceived plausibility of both an argument and an individual on television. Today's newsreaders are more often favoured by the public for their good looks than their sagacity.

The critical faculty and the development of cogent personal convictions are being subverted, in Postman's memorable title, by 'amusing ourselves to death'. He cites Huxley's scenario in *Brave New World* as precariously reminiscent of the television age: 'They did not know what they were laughing about and why they had stopped thinking.'

There is much talk today about a lack of interest in doctrine

---

[1] *Amusing Ourselves to Death*, passim.

among Evangelicals and a failure to take seriously the discipline of reading the Bible or the Christian classics of
doctrine and spirituality. The primary origin of this attitude
is not hard to find, but it is not any particular movement
within the church. Like everyone else, we are being dumbed
down by the one-eyed god in the corner of nearly every living
room. We have failed to accommodate in appropriate ways to
the forms of our culture, thus making our message more alien
and remote. At the same time our culture's unseen grip has
shaped our ways of seeing, thus making our own grasp of the
gospel more superficial and pragmatic.

Malcolm Muggeridge offered an extreme response and
solution. He declared television to be an intrinsically menda-
cious and distorting medium. With characteristic caustic wit he
warned, 'The camera always lies.' Then he announced that
television had once for all been evicted from his home. Most
of us find that position unacceptably extreme and one sided.
Television is an inescapable shaping force in the lives of almost
everyone in the modern world. If we find television to be
ambiguous in its potential and influence, then we simply cannot afford to ignore either its creative or its negative impact,
both upon our communication methods and upon the values
of our age. Rarely can the urgency of addressing our twin task
have been so acute. We need to establish a fresh and creative
enculturation of our church forms, and with equal vigour we
need to resist the emasculation of our gospel content. In all of
this, the double faced opportunist with whom we must battle,
yet from whom we must learn, is television.

It's OK as a means to an end

Some readily embrace the idea of cultural engagement as a
strategy for initial recruitment. However, once the converts

have 'signed up', it is assumed that they should be inducted into the regular services as soon as possible. The underlying assumption is that the old, accustomed ways are right and proper. As a result, all that is required is a temporary measure which eases the transfer of outsiders into an unchanging church. I have heard this view expressed both of seeker services and youth services. The real task of the church is considered to be sustaining business as usual. Cultural engagement is merely window dressing for a successful recruitment drive. Reach them through whatever means you like, the argument goes, so long as they end up at our unchanged regular service!

I recall one church where the monthly family service made a real effort, with help from Scripture Union materials, to relate to the world of young families. Every first Sunday of the month, without fail, the church was absolutely packed. On the other Sunday mornings they reverted to straight down the line *Book of Common Prayer*. Unaccountably, the vast majority who thronged the church on the first Sunday discovered compelling commitments in their diary to prevent their attendance for the rest of the month. As a strategy for recruitment to a traditional service this family service failed abysmally. It was a hugely successful first port of call, achieving genuine cultural engagement. But it desperately required a form of service on the other Sundays that connected with it. The regular Sunday morning congregation were simply fooling themselves into believing that such an event could recruit into their service. The points of contact between the two kinds of service were almost non-existent.

As new converts are added to churches today, a familiar tension begins to surface. Those established within the old sub-culture simply cannot understand why their ways of living out the gospel should not be retained and passed on wholesale. It is considered to be a package deal. Receive Christ and you get the church thrown in as well! Those who become Christians from within today's cultural context see no reason why they should buy into an archaic sub-culture. And they generally have no desire to do so. Cultural engagement cannot work effectively as a covert strategy to assist the survival of the traditional church. The truth is that if a church takes cultural engagement seriously, and really gets involved, the life of that church will break free from the moorings of set ways and traditions and will never be the same again.

I'm convinced in theory, but our church just couldn't take it

There is an ambiguity in this response. It could be a convenient way of dodging the issue, along these familiar lines: 'It's an interesting idea, but it would never work here!' None the less, this kind of reaction is certainly not always evasive. I have met a number of leaders who are quite genuinely supportive in principle. They understand the vital need to find new ways to relate to our world even as the apostles did to the Gentile world of the Roman Empire. But they are also realists. In some churches the congregation would block such a move. In others they just couldn't cope with the radical differences required. In still others, it is the minister who couldn't cope, either with the high level of risk and uncertainty, or with the possibility of flak from the more outspoken members of the existing congregation.

Many years ago I drove an old VW Beetle with 100,000 miles on the clock. When the engine was finally dying there was no point in spending time touching up the paintwork. I needed a new engine or a new car. When the missionary task is so vast, and the traditional churches have been declining so fast, surely this is a time for bold initiatives. We simply cannot afford to tinker around with the details of existing structures any more. We live in a society in urgent need of the gospel of Jesus Christ. But the gospel needs to be presented in ways 21st-century generations can readily understand, so they can have a real opportunity to respond.

I have a simple suggestion to make to leaders and churches that accept the need in principle for cultural engagement, but are reluctant to run the gauntlet of experimentation within an existing service. Why not seek carte blanche a totally experimental, alternative service at a different time of day? Or even on a different day of the week. Only those with the vision for it need get involved. If you are convinced of the need for new initiatives, and your present congregation really couldn't take it, how about developing a new, pioneering congregation in your church during the next year?

Having worked through this minefield of objections and concerns, we close with a further proposition:

New initiatives in cross-cultural mission are essential if we have any real intention of reaching the modern world with the unchanging gospel of Christ.

PART TWO

RETURNING TO ROOTS

The Church in the New Testament

6

People with Vision

Understanding the world we seek to reach is only half the battle. We must also keep a firm hold on the foundations of the Christian faith. The church is designed to be a bridge between the culture of today and the Bible, but to serve as an effective bridge we must have firm foundations both in today's world and in the faith. The church which has foundations in the Bible, but lives on its own sub-cultural island, is like a bridge which fails to cross the full width of the river. If you want such a church to help you with the gospel, you first have to make your own way to their island, wading into the stream.

Other churches are built into today's culture, but have lost touch with the foundations of the faith. Cut adrift from biblical Christianity these churches lose both the gospel and their own cutting edge as they gradually come to represent modern caring values with a religious face. Such churches eventually cease to build bridges to Christian faith at all.

In order to return to our roots, we need to explore the priorities and self-understanding of the church of the New

121

Testament, and this will be our concern in the next four chapters.

In spring 1992 I was at a gathering of European church leaders where some British and German leaders began to speak enthusiastically about European church-planting initiatives. Confusion soon clouded the discussion. It became apparent that for some delegates the word 'church' immediately brought to mind a Gothic pile, complete with a choir, pews and priests. The idea of multiplying such edifices was bewildering: how could the Germans and British begin to implement or finance such a project?

In *Through the Looking Glass*, Lewis Carroll presented Alice with a fundamental problem of communication: '"When I use a word," Humpty Dumpty said in a rather scornful tone, "it means just what I choose it to mean – neither more nor less."' It is quite impossible to use the word 'church' without most people assuming that they know exactly what you mean. The trouble is that it means entirely different things to different people. For some it has strong connotations of old-fashioned irrelevance. For others it is a word which speaks of conflict or rejection. Above all, for many believers, the word 'church' signifies the particular institution or denomination with which they are most familiar. If we want to explore the best ways to be the 21st-century church we need to strip away the accretions of denominational identity and Christian history in order to recover the biblical essentials of the apostolic churches.

I am certainly not suggesting that there is a blueprint for church life in the New Testament. In fact there is considerable liberty for each group of believers to develop their own way of being church. There are, however, some guiding principles and priorities that we neglect at our peril.

People first

The early church was not the kind of organisation where the institution is of greater concern than the people. Nor was it an impersonal machine, where all that mattered was to get the job done. Nor was it like the church in a novel by Anthony Trollope – a clergy-dominated edifice where neither the laity nor the unconverted appears to matter a great deal. The first Christians made a real priority of Jesus' new commandment, 'Love one another. As I have loved you, so you must love one another' (John 13:34).

We see this love in action in Luke's summary of the commitments of the first church in Jerusalem. Not only did they devote themselves to the apostles' teaching, to the breaking of bread and to prayer, they also devoted themselves to the fellowship (Acts 2:42). Luke identifies three ways in which the fellowship was strengthened: regular contact, open homes and sharing their possessions.

As to contact, the first Christians met together daily in the temple courts. This doesn't necessarily mean that every Christian was present every day, but it does indicate they knew where to find one another and they made a real effort to be there. You didn't meet Christians by 'going to church', and then keep to yourself for the rest of the week. They were your brothers and sisters, so you made a priority of spending time with them.

We are doubly reluctant to have too many meetings in churches today. We know that many people are under pressure, because we live in a crazy economy where increasing numbers are unemployed while those still with jobs are obliged to devote more and more hours to work. Some careers are like bottomless pits; the more you put in, the more is demanded of you. We also recognise that a church event every night is no good for anyone. Far from strengthening ourselves, we are weakened in our witness if Christians hide away in holy huddles every hour they are not at work.

So how did the first Christians get away with it? In part they lived in a less pressured society, freed from the time-consuming nightmares of modern commuting. The most important factor is the place where they met, for they didn't huddle away in a private building, but met in the temple courts, the natural public meeting place for the people of Jerusalem. As a result, their devotion to the fellowship would naturally spill over into witness. Where do people meet together in your local community? Maybe some of your church could begin to 'devote themselves to the fellowship' there.

As to homes, the first Christians' homes were not castles with the drawbridge up and the portcullis down. They weren't locked into fortresses behind security systems, chains and burglar alarms. They had an open home approach, where other believers were always welcome and they didn't have to make an appointment a month ahead in the diary. Modern life, especially in cities, cuts people off behind the defences of their front door. We have much to learn about open homes.

Their homes were also where they broke bread together. This is hardly surprising, since the Passover meal from which Jesus derived the Lord's Supper is a family meal. There is something very wonderful about breaking bread at home, whether in a home group, with friends or family.

As to possessions, their radicalism was simple. If someone was in need, the wealthy released money by selling their possessions or even their land (Acts 4:32–35). This wasn't compulsory. The apostles didn't come round to take an inventory and then force you to hand over your favourite things. Instead, the believers shared everything on a voluntary basis. It is hardly an accident that after describing this miraculous generosity Luke reports in the very next verse that the apostles continued to testify 'with great power' (Acts 4:33).

If we are serious about taking good news to the poor we need to learn a great deal more about this radical generosity. In the West, possessiveness is drummed into us every day, and much of life is devoted to accumulating extra possessions. To be sure, many churches have a 'fellowship fund' from which the leaders can provide gifts for the needy, and there are times when such a fund is quite literally a Godsend. But such a fund is a long way from the voluntary shared ownership of these first believers in their supreme devotion to the fellowship. Few modern churches have dared to follow their example: 'No-one claimed that any of his possessions was his own, but they shared everything they had' (Acts 4:32).

For all this admirable devotion to the fellowship, things still went wrong. The widows among the Grecian Jews began to be overlooked in the distribution of food, and felt marginalised by the Hebraic Jews (Acts 6:1). There is probably a hint of racism here, however unconscious. These widows certainly felt left out, neglected by the church and the apostles.

The response of the Twelve showed great wisdom. They didn't try to shrug off the complaint, despite the many other demands upon them. They accepted that the complaint was justified, and took responsibility to come up with a solution. Even so, they declined to deliver the solution themselves (Acts 6:2–4). Less wise leaders would either have delayed responding to the justified complaint, or rushed round to every Grecian widow personally, providing an apostolic fast food delivery service. The apostles addressed the need, but guarded the specific focus of their own ministries.

During this difficult period people were the priority in several ways. First, others were prepared to stand up for the widows rather than leave them to look after themselves. Secondly, the apostles took the complaint on board, and made sure they wouldn't be neglected in future. Thirdly, the whole church was involved in the solution, for the apostles didn't hand pick seven men, but instead invited all the believers to participate in the selection (Acts 6:3, 5–6).

There was not a hint of hunger for power in the apostles, nor were they leaders who viewed the people as mere pawns or pew fodder. Leaders and new converts alike were devoted to the fellowship, for here was a church where every believer mattered, because they all knew that every individual was loved by God. Are we prepared to rediscover this alternative way of living for the 21st-century church?

One of the common difficulties churches face today is how to reach the large numbers who don't consider themselves in need of help from the church, whose lives are going quite well, who are comfortably well off, and who don't consider themselves to be religious. On the whole, churches are better at providing groups for the elderly and for young mums with pre-school children, or help for the bereaved or depressed. What will bridge the gap to the materially fortunate and spiritually indifferent? The answer is surely the power of love.

The greedy eighties saw the rich getting richer and the poor getting poorer in many industrialised nations. Ethnic divisions are intensifying across Europe, with a growing number of race attacks in Britain, France and Germany and the horrors of ethnic cleansing in Bosnia. Neighbourliness is a lost art of relationship in many urban settings. Community and belonging, taken for granted a couple of generations ago, are all but forgotten experiences. Modern marriages are brittle and have a limited life expectancy. Everyone is looking for love, but few know how to find it.

In a world of social fragmentation, where relationships are falling apart, the church has a duty and an opportunity to create alternative communities of love, where dividing barriers are broken down, and where all believers can belong as brothers and sisters in Christ. In an increasingly lonely world, churches can become a sign of hope. Our relationships can make Christian faith more attractive and plausible, pointing beyond ourselves to the good news of Christ. Only as communities of love, depending on the outpouring of super-natural love by the Holy Spirit, can we begin to walk in the power of the first Christians.

Mission to the world

There is a driving motivation thrusting forward Luke's account of the early church. Peter takes the lead among the Jerusalem apostles in proclaiming the good news, and Luke delights in recording the proclamation and the resultant con-versions. Philip begins his ministry as a server at tables, but is soon thrust out into evangelism. Barnabas is a great encour-ager, but his warm-hearted concern for believers doesn't distract him from the priority of reaching others with the gospel. Paul receives his commission to be the apostle to the Gentiles, and the second half of Luke's book traces his missionary journeys. The task of mission, however, is not left to the evangelists and apostles alone. When the church in Jerusalem is scattered under persecution, the ordinary believ-ers do their bit, gossiping the gospel informally wherever they settle (Acts 8:4). Witnessing to friends is quite different to public proclamation, but it is every bit as vital.

Luke could have given potted biographies of the leaders of the church in Jerusalem, providing a history of the early church as an institution. Out of the several thousand conversions he reports, he could have selected those with the most sordid backgrounds in order to provide an anthology of sensational testimonies. Instead, Luke's chosen focus and his selection of material is determined by the command of the risen Christ, with which he introduces his history: 'But you will receive power when the Holy Spirit comes on you; and you will be my witnesses in Jerusalem, and in all Judea and Samaria, and to the ends of the earth' (Acts 1:8). This command provides both a focus and a structure to Luke's history. As the history unfolds he presents the proclamation in Jerusalem (Acts 1:1 – 6:7), attention shifts to Palestine and Samaria (Acts 6:8 – 9:31), then to Antioch (Acts 9:32 – 12:4), Asia Minor (Acts 12:25 – 16:5), Europe (Acts 16:6 – 28:10) and finally Rome (Acts 28:11–31).

Luke's choice of focus is by no means arbitrary or eccentric. The centrality of mission to the world is emphasised towards the end of all four Gospels (Matthew 28:18–20; Mark 16:15–16; Luke 24:47–49; John 20:21–23). Matthew in particular emphasises world mission as the decisive final instruction of the risen Christ, making the Great Commission the definitive climax of his Gospel:

Then Jesus came to them and said, 'All authority in heaven and on earth has been given to me. Therefore go and make disciples of all nations, baptising them in the name of the Father and of the Son and of the Holy Spirit, and teaching them to obey everything I have commanded you. And surely I am with you always, to the very end of the age.' (Matthew 28:18–20)

The reason why Luke is passionate about conversions is plain to see. The primary task given by Christ to the apostolic church is mission to the world. As a result, Luke is keen to report numerical church growth. Some 3,000 were baptised on the Day of Pentecost (Acts 2:41), and then the Lord 'added to their number daily' (Acts 2:47). Despite persecution there were soon 5,000 believers (Acts 4:4), and still more continued to be added (Acts 5:14). A chapter later Luke reports that their numbers 'increased rapidly, and a large number of priests became obedient to the faith' (Acts 6:7).

If we want to be committed to church growth that is truly biblical we cannot afford to lose Luke's emphasis, for the numerical growth that matters most is always conversion growth. It is good to hear reports of churches that are growing, but sometimes the main factor is transfer growth. We have become better at recycling saints than saving sinners. There may, of course, be a necessary period of strategic preparation when believers are drawn together to become a vibrant church in their local community, but the acid test is what happens next. Does the church settle down for the comfort of Christians? Or do the believers who have been drawn together now commit themselves to the priority of evangelism for conversion growth?

It is not just weak and dying churches that put all their energy into looking after the believers. Some large churches, with a reputation for life, are also at risk of pouring their resources and energy into believer maintenance and endless administration, with mission receiving whatever scraps remain. This is not the kind of church priority that Luke records and celebrates.

'Evangelism' has nearly as many different connotations as 'church'. For some it is a dirty word, bringing to mind a particular brand of brashness or manipulation which they despise. For others, the word provokes a sense of failure and guilt. They don't really know what they should be doing, but the one thing they know is that they're not doing it! We need to take the sting of fear out of evangelism. We are not all called to be high-profile evangelists, but we are all called to be witnesses. We are not failed witnesses if those we speak to are not converted on the spot. But we are failed witnesses if we never mention Christ at all. The person who never speaks about anything except Christ is not a wise witness; he is probably a religious bore! But it is no witness at all if we become undercover Christians, hiding away our faith from friends and colleagues, as if we were ashamed of the gospel.

Our lives are a witness before we even open our mouths. But since Jesus needed to speak to explain his life and miracles, how much more do we need to add words of explanation to the flawed witness of our lives. Just letting someone know I'm a believer is a witness, or explaining how I became a Christian and what difference it has made in my life, or lending them a Christian book or video, or inviting them to a special event. I am totally convinced that churches need a programme of evangelistic events – guest services and suppers, concerts and open-air presentations, occasional missions and regular literature distribution – but none of this will begin to be effective without the personal witness of friendly words.

The first task of the apostolic church is much bigger than friendship evangelism in our own locality, for the risen Christ has commissioned his disciples to nothing less than mission to the world. While Luke takes evident pleasure in reporting church growth in Jerusalem, there is no suggestion that growing one strong church is enough, and so Luke soon turns to the wider picture. The church at Antioch became pivotal for world mission. The turning point came with a prophecy, as a result of which this church released two of its outstanding and hand-picked leaders (Acts 13:1–3). The church didn't simply commission Paul and Barnabas and then forget them. They stayed in touch, and were an active home base, encouraging return visits and report back sessions (Acts 14:26–28).

World mission is a responsibility which has slipped from the agenda of the Western church, and the number of missionaries we send has continued to decline for several generations. It is wonderful to see the growing numbers of African, Asian and Latin American missionaries around the world, but the Western church has a continuing responsibility too. It is thrilling to see the growth of Tearfund, World Vision and other initiatives to bring relief and development to the two-thirds world. Unfortunately, in some local churches this giving has been at the expense of giving to missionary societies committed to direct evangelism. The two strands of mission need never be thought of as in competition, let alone conflict. They work together like the two blades of a pair of scissors. Together they express the mission of Jesus, doing the works of the kingdom as expressions of God's compassionate love, and declaring the words of the kingdom that many may repent and be saved.

In each local church the world mission budget needs to have a balance between these two dimensions of missionary work. If your church doesn't have such a budget, then seek to have one introduced as soon as possible. What is more, it would be wise to agree a percentage of the total budget which will be set aside for world mission. About 20 per cent seems a reasonable target. If your church engages in an expensive building project, how about setting aside 10 per cent of the total cost as an additional gift for world mission?

World mission requires more than our money. We saw that at Antioch the church needed to release its best people and support them in prayer. Likewise, every church has a duty to pray that new missionaries will be sent out on a regular basis. School-leavers and students can be encouraged to go for short-term experience with groups like OM, YWAM and Oasis. Doctors can go short term with a number of medical missions to give a break to medics working overseas. Those who have taken early retirement can also make an invaluable contribution, whether in direct evangelism or in a support role, as grandparents or administrators for a team. Above all, we must not lose sight of the fact that some people need to be called to long-term service overseas, for world mission simply cannot be accomplished by short-termers alone.

In our church we reached a point a few years ago when our overseas missionaries were all returning home for various reasons. My colleague, Mike Wheate, and I called the church to pray that we would be a sending church. Within six months Mike received an invitation to work overseas and since then we have seen several new missionaries sent out each year. As I write I know about the following new missionaries whom we expect to send out during the next nine months: one couple will go to Africa with MAF, a broadcaster will begin work in the Pacific islands, a nurse working with drug addicts will go to Amsterdam, two women will complete their training at All Nations College and begin work overseas. In addition we expect a number to give time as short-term volunteers. We also hope to experiment with weeks of mission abroad to assist the evangelism of other city churches in Europe. If you pray that Christ will make you a world church and a sending church, be prepared for your prayer to be taken seriously! Your church will never be the same, and nor will your world mission budget!

We should never thank God for our missionaries and then work on the assumption that they are different from us, and it must be easy for them to work in locations and conditions that we would find unbearable. Missionaries are ordinary human beings just like you and me, and they struggle with the same kind of hopes and fears as the rest of us. They just happen to have been called by God to the frontline of world mission. They not only need our prayers, but our love and continuing friendship through letters, gifts, magazine subscriptions and even visits. We are in it together. Neither Jesus nor Luke presents world mission as an assignment for the missionaries alone. World mission is the risen Christ's great adventure of faith for the 21st-century church.

The challenge of world mission needs to be kept before every church in regular and imaginative ways. There needs to be a prominent and high quality world mission display, preferably in the main room where the church meets. Home groups can also be asked to adopt missionaries from the fellowship. Above all we must not lose sight of our shared responsibility. World mission is not something for missionaries to get on with alone. Every Christian is called to be a world Christian.

Worship

Some may have already begun to object that the first priority of the church is not mission but worship. Before the believers began to witness on the streets, they were caught up in Spirit-inspired worship. Indeed worship proved a springboard to witness, since their joyful praise in tongues intrigued the crowds in Jerusalem. New Testament worship has several distinctive characteristics. It is an overflowing, even spontaneous response to the glory of Christ and the goodness of the Father – not something that needs to be explained and commanded before it can begin. Futhermore, in contrast to his instructions about waiting for the Spirit before starting out in witness, Jesus did nothing to discourage worship before the coming of the Spirit, even though the outpouring at Pentecost clearly took worship into new dimensions.

The priority of worship can certainly be derived from the first part of the summary of the law which Jesus endorsed: to love God with all your heart, soul and mind (Matthew 22:35–40). Worship is a natural expression of this all-embracing love for God, both personal and corporate. In short, worship is a principle of creation. Since the whole earth declares the glory of God (Isaiah 6:3), we can draw the conclusion that worship is the first calling of all created beings. As a calling of love, worship will continue beyond death, for heaven is above all a place radiant with worship, surpassing everything we know of worship in this world. Of course, worship is not restricted to church gatherings. Rightly understood it becomes a way of life in the service of the living God (Romans 12:1).

In fact the summary of the law can also be applied to witness, for we take the gospel to the ends of the earth in obedience to Jesus, who said, 'If you love me, you will obey what I command' (John 14:15). Furthermore, while witness is not the sum of loving our neighbours as ourselves, it remains integral to fulfilling the second part of the summary of the law. If we fail to communicate to others the merciful love of God, then we fail in a double duty of love, both to Christ and to our neighbours. Witness is thus a principle of the new creation, and the first duty of all who are born again. Witness is a task with an end in sight, for when the gospel has been preached to all peoples, Christ will return (Matthew 24:14). Witness, like worship, is by no means restricted to church events, but is rather a way of life in the service of Christ and his gospel.

As the believers discovered at Pentecost, worship and witness are meant to enrich one another. Witness without worship will lose its way and become a treadmill of duty without joy. Worship without witness turns in on itself and becomes self-indulgent. True worship is not about what I get out of it, but is centred on the glory of Christ. When we are truly Christ-centred in the eternal calling of worship, Christ himself also inspires us by the Holy Spirit to fulfil the first duty of every believer in this life: witness to the world. Worship is going to be infinitely richer beyond the grave, but this life is the only time when we can fulfil the command to witness. Matthew's account of the Great Commission bonds together worship and witness. Before he gives his command, Christ welcomes his followers' worship, and we have described this spontaneous response as their first calling. But worship alone is not enough, and so in the light of their ready acknow-ledgement of his lordship he gives them their missionary marching orders.

The seeker services of Willow Creek Community Church have received a great deal of attention. Some are deeply dis-turbed by the suggestion that Sunday services should be built around the needs of outsiders, with Christians making the effort to gather midweek to address the spiritual needs unmet on Sundays. Others struggle with the concept of setting aside every Sunday morning for enquirers, but are prepared to concede the possibility of such seeker-centredness on a more occasional basis. We need to insist that seeker sensitivity is nothing new. Though it may seem extraordinary to those accustomed to Sunday worship which is blithely indifferent to outsiders, the very first time that Christians experienced Pentecost empowered worship, the event was shaped by the Spirit according to the needs of unbelievers.

When the Christians were caught up in an intensity of worship they had never known before, they were neither safe behind locked doors nor using a sub-cultural devotional terminology that no one else could understand. The Spirit drove them out onto the streets in praise and he also gave them not the tongues of angels but the tongues of men – specifically the languages of those visiting Jerusalem for the feast. In the very heights of worship, the believers were still communicating with outsiders, because the Spirit insisted on bridging the gap, by making the believers both visible and intelligible. As Hahn expressed it in his classic study of worship in the New Testament, 'Worship has by nature a missionary function.'[1]

When the apostle Paul instructed the Corinthians on the use of spiritual gifts in public meetings, he urged them to be aware of the outsider. This need not be considered an unusually Pauline emphasis, derived from his passionate zeal for evangelism. He had learned the lesson of Pentecost. The Holy Spirit who releases us into depths of worship is also the missionary Spirit. Even as he inspires our worship, the Spirit shapes our worship to be an effective and provo-cative witness. It is a great fallacy to suggest that if we are seeker sensitive there should be no manifestations of the Holy Spirit. Whitefield and Wesley repeatedly saw dramatic manifestations as they preached, including intense weeping, people crying out in spiritual torment, and the kind of spontaneous swooning that today would commonly be called 'falling under the power of the Spirit'. As Paul explained to the Corinthians, the more the Spirit moves in power in our worship, the more we can expect aston-ished unbelievers to declare their worship of God with the exclamation, 'God is really among you!' (1 Corinthians 14:25).

---

[1] *The Worship of the Early Church*, p. 105.

Hymns and songs

The New Testament gives us few clues as to the content and forms of early Christian worship, but before leaving this theme we need to pause and consider the value and place of hymns and songs. Discussion of worship today degenerates all too readily into a slanging match, as if hymns and songs were two mutually exclusive options. Once battle lines are drawn, foolish and unwarranted generalisations are paraded. Far more useful is to identify what each kind of composition does best.

I believe in hymns. We can find hymns within the New Testament, most notably the celebrations of Christ in Philippians 2:6–11 and Colossians 1:15–20. On the basis of these examples, hymns may be said to be thoughtful compositions, carefully crafted, with clear doctrinal content. Hymns represent the worship of God with mind and voice. They involve not just enjoying the chance to sing, but the restatement of the great truths of our faith. Such hymns recognise that to think clearly and to express doctrine clearly is fundamental to loving God with our minds.

One good description of hymns is sung doctrine. Though we cannot prove it, it may well be that Philippians 2:6–11 was memorised by new believers. Such hymns remind and instruct us in the faith. Indeed, the didactic function of hymns should not be underestimated. Great hymns, often repeated, sink into the subconscious and inform daily faith more immediately than many a sermon. As one hymn-writer concluded, 'I don't mind who writes the theological books, so long as I can write the hymns.'

The finest hymns are essentially timeless. Wesley and Watts wrote devotional poetry, whereas most hymns are a more humble kind of verse, and there is a close connection between artistry and timelessness. The greatest hymns express ageless truths in deathless poetry, so they more readily keep up to date, for example 'And can it be' and 'When I survey'. They stay 'news' and an effective vehicle for contemporary worship. There is also great value in sometimes 'singing with the saints of old'. Present-day worshippers then experience the truth that we are not merely part of a single generation church. We should never deride or dismiss our forefathers in the faith, for the one Spirit has brought into being the church of Christ in every generation.

Although not all hymns have the same limitations, we may note certain common hazards. First, the risk of becoming over-cerebral. The right use of the mind in worship can spill over into an intellectual snobbery which begins to assume that only the mind matters. Such a tendency leads to hymns that are neither good poetry nor good communication. For example, one hymn begins with these thoroughly indigestible propositions: 'Consubstantial, co-eternal . . .' More like a can of condensed theological soup than a feast of praise!

Perhaps in reaction against this trend, many of the popular evangelical hymns of the Victorian era have a cloying senti-mentality, often with an overdose of 'sweetness' imagery. Others, with understandable but misguided zeal, oversell the emotional consequences of conversion – 'Now I'm happy all the day'. Well I don't know about you, but my wife, Claire, will readily confirm this is certainly not true of me! Such hymns tend no longer to be sung, or to be sung with a kind of nostalgic bravado.

More generally, many older hymns concentrate on speak-ing about God in the third person. Not that this is always unhelpful – the New Testament certainly speaks of the horizontal dimension of worship, addressing one another in psalms, hymns and spiritual songs (Ephesians 5:19). But a diet of worship made up largely of hymns *about* God makes worship begin to seem like a wedding without the bride. In late 19th-century and early 20th-century hymns there is a related tendency towards an almost wholly unrealised eschatology – God is sung about, but certainly not expected to put in a personal appearance during any worship this side of the second coming.

There is enormous value in hymns. Sunday services are greatly enriched by the inclusion of at least a couple of hymns, whether from the era of Wesley or Kendrick. None the less, hymns alone cannot provide a complete answer to our need for music in worship.

I believe in songs, which are also found in the worship of the early church. With the working definition of a simple, brief expression of praise, we may cite, for example, Revelation 4:8 and 5:12–13. Such worship is often repetitive in style. For example, in Psalm 150 we find thirteen uses of the phrases 'Praise the Lord' and 'Praise him' in just six verses. Extravagant repetition is certainly no modernistic innovation unknown to the worship of ancient Israel or the first Christians!

In the early Christian centuries, there are references to spontaneous compositions during worship, customarily giving testimony and expressing delight in God. Such extempore songs would no doubt tend to use simple words and simple tunes. The use of songs in worship enables us to worship with heart and voice. This points not merely to enjoying a chance to sing, but to singing of our personal love to God as Abba, our dear Father.

Our culture is no different from any other in recognising the value of love songs. Often such popular songs have the simplicity and repetitive qualities found also in worship songs. There is certainly real value in expressing intimate devotion to

God. There is also much to be gained from meditations on divine love, dwelling upon a single truth, allowing it time to come alive in God's presence. The 'Jesus prayer' is an ancient example which recognises the benefit of a disciplined and concentrated focus on a single aspect of God and our relationship with him:

> Lord Jesus Christ, Son of God,
> Have mercy on me, a sinner.

There is real value in simplicity and immediacy. We worship not only the God of eternity, but God with us. Not only Christ crucified and coming, but Christ present as King. Not only the rule of God to come, but the rule of God among us in power. In other words, our worship needs to express not only the transcendence and holiness of God, but also God's presence and overflowing love in our everyday life.

Up-to-date songs and musical styles can speak to believers and outsiders alike of the fact that worship is a living encounter and not a nostalgic memorial or museum piece. There has always been an evangelistic impact to contemporary worship. The outsider is no longer faced solely with the God of the 'religious' or the God of the past, which leads all too often to the retort, 'What's it to do with me?'

I first came across open-air worship in York, when David Watson encouraged teams to sing, dance and perform drama in the city squares, and we quickly discovered that its impact can be striking. On streets and in parks, in Britain and overseas, I have often heard the same question: 'What makes you people so joyful?' Many are deeply astonished to discover that our joy comes from Christ. They thought Christianity was all about gloom, doom and ancient, dreary dirges. Christianity has all too often assumed a cultural dress which is boring, stuffy, dull and dated. This is the terrible tragedy of Christian worship. We have taken the unsurpassable Lamb of God and dressed him up as mutton.

What then are the limitations of simple songs? First, they can be over-populist, uncritically dependent on the values of our society. For example, the rediscovery of a rich vein of songs describing our experience of God can risk becoming self-obsessed instead of Christ-centred. Secondly, there is a modern sentimentality, either 'matey' or gushy, as difficult to stomach as Victorian sentimentality. I am bound to say that I don't find it adds much to worship to be asked to sing repeatedly that Jesus is 'very nice'! Thirdly, many songs have a limited shelf-life and date very quickly. In every century most songs have not survived the generation of their composer, but the speed of turnover is now much faster. This is the very nature of modern culture, and songs are no exception. Such built-in cultural obsolescence is a plain fact of life, and needs to be accepted as quite unavoidable.

TRADITIONAL HYMNS	MODERN SONGS
Common strengths:	
scriptural	scriptural
with mind and voice	with heart and voice
sung doctrine	love songs
timelessness	immediacy
Common limitations:	
over-cerebral	over-populist
over-sentimental	over-sentimental
dated idiom of music/words	date very quickly

Hymns and songs are like shrubs and annuals. The garden looks best when both are present in due proportion. They are complementary, and it is thoroughly misguided to see them as competing, let alone mutually exclusive. In truth, they need each other, and quality worship needs them both.

21st-century worship

As we approach the 21st century we need to face the built-in obsolescence of many traditional hymns. Within a popular culture of ever accelerating change, there is an unavoidable problem with the dated idiom of both music and words.

In the pre-modern era, traditional songs were passed on from generation to generation. Last century the bourgeois family around the piano knew a common stock of songs. This is no longer true. Popular music is sectionalised according to generation, and, more importantly, is not on the whole expected to last. Songs typically express common sentiments in the idiom of the moment, and next year, or even next month, a new song will become the vehicle for such feelings and thoughts. To put it personally, I would be embarrassed to sing in the shower the songs my father sings from the forties and fifties. Even so, today's teenagers consider hopelessly dated the songs from my era in the late sixties and early seventies. Popular music hardly ever lasts today. That does not mean the music is inadequate, but rather it is operating within a cultural context where musical idiom is always on the move. Every generation has music for its own identity. And the same is true for every generation of Christian worshippers.

This cultural observation must be faced as a matter of indisputable fact. If music in existing churches is unchanging, new churches will continually need to spring up for new generations, and this will happen with an accelerating rapidity, as 'cultural generations' become shorter. The music in worship revolution of the last twenty years can never afford to stop. Last year's tunes will soon be relegated to the storeroom of the dated and unsung. One leader of a new church stream renowned for its worship songs told me of a complaint from some of his formerly radical 40-somethings: 'The young people aren't singing our kind of worship songs.' If a new church fails to accept the discipline of keeping up to date, it quickly becomes middle-aged and nostalgic.

We have to face the fact that many traditional hymn tunes are culturally non-viable. Some are timeless classics, but it must be recognised that most hymn tunes do not aspire to such musical stature and nor do they achieve it! Some are dated – some from the early 20th century employ the falling melodies of the music hall (though some Christians at the time would have been horrified to discover their connected-ness with their own culture!), which to a modern ear sound uncomfortably hackneyed and sentimental. Some are too far removed from contemporary rhythms and melodies, and sound plain dull to any not attuned from childhood to the conventions of Christian worship. Similarly, some of the 'new' songs of the seventies and eighties sound far too dated to be sung any more in contemporary worship. In short, some tunes will last unfailingly, some will gradually lose touch with con-temporary culture, and some have lost touch already and deserve a quiet burial without delay.

Both Calvin and *The Book of Common Prayer* spoke of the vital importance of worship in the common language of the people. What was true of Latin at the time of the Reformation is true of Elizabethan language today – it is frequently incomprehensible. Words and grammar are dynamic not fixed: words change their meaning. Thus, 'Before Jehovah's awful throne' speaks today of something horrible rather than something filled with awe; 'Lord the cistern's broken' suggests the need to call a plumber; and no one uses 'without a city wall' to mean 'outside it'.

We have now seen the death of thee/thou and -est/-eth language, and it won't come back. The end of the AV and the virtual end of the BCP mean that such archaisms, no longer in use in most school assemblies, are to be found solely in the hymns of Christian worship. They therefore feel increasingly archaic, anachronistic and incomprehensible, conveying the clear message to the outsider that the Christian church is old-fashioned and out of date, and that, if there is a God, he is trapped in the past. It increases the alien feel of religious language, unused in the rest of life, thus reinforcing the unhelpful dichotomy of the secular and the sacred: if you like that sort of thing, you can use the archaic language. We can give the impression that our God cannot be worshipped properly in the language of today – the language of 'real life'. No institution seriously committed to the present and the future can allow itself the indulgence of such self-defeating anachronism.

This issue is ever more pressing. Not only have certain forms passed from current idiom, there is also a need today to use, where appropriate, inclusive and non-sexist language. Above all, the English language is developing faster today than ever before. Shakespeare had an astonishingly rich and broad vocabulary, but so many words are now proliferating each and every year that he would actually be semi-literate faced with everyday language today. Our language will not keep still; so nor can the language of our worship.

Making it new

While we need a creative blend of hymns and songs, the repertoire of music in worship simply has to keep on changing. The 21st-century church cannot afford to ignore new songs. An unchanged diet of songs from the seventies or eighties will fail to bridge the gap just as much as an unchanged selection from the 19th century. Some of our best-loved hymns and songs may have a much shorter shelf-life than we would like to think.

In our church we had a problem with the evening service. The people wanted the meeting to move forward, and prayed with freedom and vigour during half nights of prayer. But when we met on Sunday evenings they seemed to dry up. Eventually we decided that the problem was a received tradition of how you ought to behave in a church service. Warm and relaxed people suddenly became stiff and formal, unable to loosen up until the closing prayer was complete. Our solution was simple: to destroy the destructive grip of such traditions we began meeting in a different room with a completely different and more intimate arrangement of chairs. What is more, we simply abandoned the tired remnants of the old service structure. We no longer called our meeting 'the evening service', but rather 'Open to God'.

Though the worship leader has some songs prepared, we now expect the Spirit to move freely during the worship and as a result of the preaching, so the leader is not someone who delivers a ready prepared meal to the congregation, but has to learn to become a facilitator, responding to the people and the Holy Spirit. We expect the leader to be a humble servant, always ready to adapt or even abandon the planned worship if God takes us in a new direction. There is no place for the kind of leader who doggedly ploughs through his pre-cooked package without flexibility – 'Here's one I prepared earlier, and I'm sticking to it whatever happens!'

There should never be any prohibition of traditional hymns, but nor need they be seen as compulsory at every Christian gathering. The hymns that enjoy an undimmed vitality always remain available, and can always be used if a worship leader or member of the congregation is prompted to include one. I am not suggesting for one moment that this free-form, flowing worship is the only model for the new century, but it is certainly one approach with a much greater life expectancy than the traditional hymn sandwich.

Missing priorities?

In recent years many churches have enjoyed a major redis-covery of worship. There was a time when worship in some churches seemed merely a prelude, a warming-up exercise before the sermon. It is now much more common to hear the priority of worship championed in live churches, and for our worship to be richly expressive both of our drawing near to God, and also of God drawing near to us. We expect to meet with God, to offer a vibrant and intimate sacrifice of praise, and to see God doing things among us in the context of worship, week by week. Of course there have been excesses and mistakes, but when I think back to the empty and lifeless routines which once went by the name of Christian worship, I thank God for the immense gains of the worship revolution.

Despite these great benefits, I am forced to the conclusion that much of the modern church has drifted from the prio-rities of the New Testament. I am no longer referring to the connections we have already explored between the calling of worship and the task of witness. In Acts 2, Luke identifies four priorities to which the Jerusalem church was devoted: the apostles' teaching, the fellowship, the breaking of bread and prayer. To be sure, one of the four priorities Luke lists is the breaking of bread, and he does add a couple of verses later that gladness and praising God marked their daily living. The Jerusalem church was therefore by no means devoid of the overflow of worship. How could they possibly be so soon after the unforgettable events of Pentecost! None the less, although it may come as a complete bombshell to some modern believers, Luke simply does not say that the first believers devoted themselves to worship.

We have come to expect modern Christians to stress the priority of worship, and this chapter has affirmed its vital importance as the first calling of all creation. My fear and concern is that far fewer today embrace the devotedness of the first Christians in two ways Luke specifically highlights – apostolic teaching and intercessory prayer. Where is the eagerness to receive teaching? Where are the prayer meetings as well attended as Sunday services? Preaching is too often derided or treated lightly. In some churches those devoted to prayer are an endangered species.

Some have lost confidence in preaching because it does not sit easily with the dominant communication techniques of the television age. Others have reacted against the dry intellectualism of a previous generation, where the principle of preaching was held to vigorously, but the content was often arid and more potent than the strongest sleeping pills. As a result, in many churches preaching has degenerated into idle theological speculation or into empty entertainment, a succession of anecdotes and tales of personal spiritual experiences. Some modern preachers have learned to tell good stories, and that is invaluable in the TV age, but their biblical exposition is unconvincing and less than competent.

Teaching is a wider ministry than preaching, and it is vital that we pursue teaching and training through small groups, practical workshops, videos, etc. None the less, preaching will always have a unique and essential part to play, for as the apostle Peter taught, it is not only in prophecy but also in preaching that we expect God to speak to his people: 'If anyone speaks, he should do it as one speaking the very words of God' (1 Peter 4:11).

Some appear to suggest that we have to make a choice between good preaching and good worship. There are churches where the worship is a rather cursory prelude to the main event of the sermon. In others, vibrant worship leaves little space for preaching. This is a false dichotomy that gravely diminishes spiritual health, for the best of contemporary worship and the best of contemporary preaching complement one another superbly. The same Spirit of God meets with us in worship and speaks to us through biblical preaching.

Despite the many demands of ministry in the modern world, today's church leaders urgently need to recover the apostolic dedication to the 'ministry of the word' (Acts 6:4). It takes a great deal of time and care every week to ensure that our preaching is grounded in the Bible, genuinely breaks open the Scriptures to feed the people, and builds in the people a growing confidence not merely in the preacher, but rather in the authority and relevance of the word of God. As Paul instructed Timothy, not only must we preach, we must 'preach the Word' (2 Timothy 4:2). The 21st-century church needs a recovery of nerve and a recovery of quality in demonstrating the centrality of preaching.

As to prayer, this was the only other task to which the apostles chose to be devoted (Acts 6:4). What is more, when the believers met together for earnest prayer, they expected God to meet them in power. Some churches today would run a mile from the suggestion that the Holy Spirit could fall on a prayer meeting the way he did upon the first Christians! 'After they prayed, the place where they were meeting was shaken. And they were all filled with the Holy Spirit . . .' (Acts 4:31).

I was most impressed in Brazil to see churches meeting on a regular basis for whole nights of prayer. The numbers who attended and the vigour of the praying was wonderful. Small wonder that the churches are growing! In contrast an English minister told me recently of his attempt to introduce a half night of prayer for the first time. Some of his congregation complained that it was excessive, inconvenient and smacked of over-intensity and extremism.

I have found a continuing struggle in seeking to mobilise for prayer. In my own life, in committees and in churches, prayer always seems the first thing at risk when time gets pressured. And yet the results are plain, for whenever churches get serious in prayer, not only do we see specific requests answered, we also enjoy a significant improvement in the spiritual climate. After a half night of prayer not only do individuals make real progress, but on the following Sunday both the worship and the responsiveness to preaching usually make a significant advance. The 21st-century church cannot expect significant progress without a recovery of passionate prayer.

Worship is indeed a priority, but not our sole priority. Should worship become the sum of our concerns, we will inevitably fall short of the spiritual vigour of the first Christians. Indeed, in some churches almost all the energy of every leader is put into the Sunday services, with a profound neglect of reaching out into the local community, whether in witness or in works of compassion and justice. If we do not adopt the apostolic priorities, in principle and in practice, not least their commitment to both teaching and prayer, it should come as no surprise when we do not enjoy similar impact, growth and joy. The 21st-century church cannot expect to be strong unless we are prepared to recover 1st-century priorities: 'They devoted themselves to the apostles' teaching and to the fellowship, to the breaking of bread and to prayer . . . And the Lord added to their number daily those who were being saved' (Acts 2:42, 47).

7

The High Performance Body

For the last twenty years, much thinking about the church has been dominated by the image of 'the body of Christ'. The very use of this term requires a certain daring. When the history of the church is littered with minor conflicts, major schisms, crusades and anti-Semitism, how can we call ourselves the body of Christ without shame and remorse? Nor was the first generation church so pristine that for them the phrase was a perfect fit. In both Acts and the Epistles we see a continuing undertow of the ever present sinful nature, made apparent in church tensions and conflicting priorities. When it comes to misunderstandings and stubbornness, party spirit and gossip, Christians are all too often just as angular and prone to difficult relationships as anyone else. Or sometimes even worse, especially those who get into the infallibility syndrome: 'The Lord told me, so how dare you even think of disagreeing!'

The church does not become the body of Christ in rare moments of greatness. Nor is it exclusively the exceptional individual, a Mother Teresa or a Jackie Pullinger, who can be spoken of as a member of the body of Christ. Rather, from the moment of conversion, every single believer enters the body (1 Corinthians 12:13). Belonging to the body is a given of the Christian life and a full-time calling for every believer. We are not the body of Christ solely on Sunday mornings, for Christ has entrusted his church at all times and in all places with the task and responsibility of being a visual aid to the gospel. Ours are the only hands and feet by which the life of Christ is revealed on earth.

Being the body speaks of responsibility and lifestyle. It also speaks of a new collective identity. The Christian does not lose personal responsibility or individual choice and freedom, but a larger dimension of life is entered. Though we need to come to faith personally, the fullness of God's purpose is more than individual; we are incorporated into a new community. This means that out of our commitment to Christ there needs to follow a commitment to a particular local church. How this is expressed varies from church to church, but the underlying principle is plain: our Christian calling, witness and obedience are fatally flawed if we merely attend a church, keeping other believers at arm's length.

In our church we invite those who want to get stuck in to make a threefold commitment: to the people, the life and the vision. To the people, because without loving relationships the church is just another club. To the life, because we expect people to be on active service, and not just takers. And to the vision, because the church of God is designed to be a people with a clear sense of purpose, in terms of both what we are seeking to do, and how we expect to achieve it.

The body of Christ was never intended to be an organisation you visit on Sunday mornings. It is a living body and a way of life. The Christian consumer, who attends a church but avoids close relationships and full participation, and the

Christian gypsy, who travels from church to church without ever buying into active involvement, are robbing themselves of their own calling as an integral part of the body of Christ.

Committed relationships among believers are only part of the picture. The New Testament makes it plain that the head of the body is Christ himself. For the individual believer, submission to the lordship of Christ is therefore incomplete without active local church participation. For the church, we must conclude that it is not possible to function effectively as the body of Christ without a clear recognition that the ultimate authority over the church resides not with tradition, nor with the minister, nor with the bishop or superintendent or other regional or national leaders, nor with the members, but with Christ himself.

I remember well a half night of prayer in which we sought to express this truth by divesting the minister, the elders and the members of any misplaced or excessive claim to authority. We knelt together, readily yielding our lives and our personal priorities to Christ. I know one Anglican church where they enacted the 'dethronement' of the vicar, and prayed together for a renewed enthronement of Christ as the active Lord of their church. It is Christ himself who is head of the body. Accept no substitutes!

Gifts and the body

Just as the various parts of the human body are essential for it to function properly, spiritual gifts are essential to the body of Christ, and we shall consider nine New Testament principles.

1. Gifts of grace

The spiritual gifts are not rewards, given according to how well we perform as Christians, or according to our relative worth as individuals. The New Testament term, *charismata*, literally means 'gifts of grace'. It is utterly inappropriate to look down on someone else for not having the same gifts as you. It is equally absurd to lay claim to a gift on the basis of active service, as if persuading God to provide an extra gift were like negotiating a performance related pay increase. Above all, a particular individual's gifts are absolutely not a reliable basis by which to measure God's approval or their own self-worth. God's gifts to believers are like our gifts to our children – not a bribe or reward for good behaviour, but an expression of devoted love.

2. *Each given at least one*

When soccer teams are picked in a school playground, it is all too easy to spot the kids who are brimming with sporting talent. If they are not the team captains, they are always the first to be picked. The eager beginning to team selection winds down towards the end, among the remaining motley crew of the overweight, the short-sighted, and those for whom foot/eye co-ordination has proved an abiding mystery. As a rule, the most skilful dominate children's soccer, which only in name can be said to be a team game. All too often, churches appear to function like these playground teams. The hyperactive few, comprising the super-gifted and the willing volunteers, rush around doing everything, while many others hang around at the edge of the game, unsure as to whether there is any real purpose in their presence other than as spectators.

The apostle Paul insisted that every believer has already been given at least one spiritual gift. To emphasise this vital principle he makes the same statement twice to the Corinthians:

'*to each one* the manifestation of the Spirit is given' (1 Corinthians 12:7);

[the Spirit] gives [spiritual gifts] *to each one*' (1 Corinthians 12:11).

All Christians need to learn to believe in themselves as those to whom God has already given at least one spiritual gift. We therefore have a responsibility to identify the gifts God has given – not only our own but one another's. Though some people have an immediately clear and accurate awareness of their own gifts, many are less sure, and I have found home groups to be ideal places for gift identification. When a group has been meeting for several months, and relationships have begun to deepen, participants can be invited to say what they appreciate most about each group member, and to identify their spiritual gifts. Quite often people discover they have been exercising gifts they didn't even know they had!

3. Entrusted for all

Just as the gifts are not rewards for merit, they are not trophies for display in a cabinet at home. Though individuals receive them, they remain gifts for the body, and not merely for the individual. Indeed, they are entrusted to the individual, with a responsibility to put them to use for the 'common good' (1 Corinthians 12:7). God's purpose in the distribution of gifts is to strengthen our relationships, and increase our sense of dependency on one another. If believers do not use the gifts God has given, they betray God's trust and weaken the life of the body. If the leaders prevent certain gifts from being exercised, or certain people from using their gifts, they obstruct the purposes of God.

4. All have something to give

If each has been given at least one gift, and the gifts are entrusted for the spiritual vitality of the whole church, everyone needs to find the confidence and the opportunity to use their gifts. If the body is to function properly, every gift must be exercised, and not merely the gifts of the assertive, the willing and the confident. This means we must establish an atmosphere of encouraging and supportive relationships, in which it is made as easy as possible for people to 'have a go'. In some churches the fear of failure, criticism or censure from the fellowship is so high that the members of the body have become paralysed, and dare not experiment with learning to exercise their spiritual gifts.

5. Natural and supernatural gifts

It is easy to recognise good hospitality. You've either got it or you haven't! It is deeply rooted in some people's character. A simple test is your reaction to the sound of the doorbell. If you immediately welcome the prospect of an unexpected visitor, you are naturally hospitable. If your first thought is to regret a possible disturbance of your privacy, hospitality is probably not your strongest quality. However, a spiritual gift is more than a natural disposition. The Holy Spirit must touch a character trait and enhance it with spiritual power.

We see this with preaching, for some preachers are born with natural fluency in public speaking while others are shy and stammering. Whatever the temperament, if God calls someone to preach, they must learn to be dependent on the Spirit – the naturally eloquent just as much as the tongue-tied. Without a humble dependence on the Spirit's empowering, human eloquence is gaseous and empty. A genuine spiritual gift always transcends our natural talents.

Other gifts have no such connection with our character and skills. Tongues, prophecy and healing require direct impartation from the Holy Spirit or they do not exist at all. None the less we should avoid sorting gifts into distinct categories marked 'natural' and 'supernatural'. If God empowers any gift within us, the results will always be remarkable. I think of one elderly lady who is naturally hospitable. She has provided meals and somewhere to stay for many young people who have moved to London, and she has seen many converted, filled with the Spirit, healed, and committed to active Christian service. This is more than natural hospitality; this is a gift of grace, empowered by the Holy Spirit. The key question is not, 'Are my gifts natural or supernatural?' Rather we should be asking, 'Am I allowing my gifts to be Spirit empowered?'

6. More gifts to be given

Because the Holy Spirit is Lord, he is always able to provide us with additional gifts. Sometimes this dynamic provision of gifts is directly related to an immediate or crisis situation. A believer is thrown in at the deep end and needs to pray for healing, or is given a prophetic word because the situation demands it. The Spirit is far too powerful for us to be able to opt out of difficult emergencies by saying that we just don't have the gifts to be of any help.

Emergency provision of spiritual gifts is not the main issue. Even as the Holy Spirit is continually at work within us seeking to reshape our character in the likeness of Christ, he is also at work providing new gifts. While we need to know what gifts the Spirit has already given, to suggest that these gifts are the sum of our potential is to pigeon-hole ourselves and to limit the God who always has more grace to give.

7. More gifts to seek

Not only does the Spirit reserve the right to give more gifts, but the apostle Paul calls upon believers to seek for gifts not yet given (1 Corinthians 14:1). We can naturally abuse this invitation. If we seek gifts for our own fame or influence, our motivation is fundamentally flawed, for these are gifts of service, not power. If we seek a gift obsessively, our priorities are distorted, for the divine Giver should always be more important to us than any of his gifts. We can become like a child captivated by a particular toy, who demands it relentlessly in the run up to Christmas. Such an obsession may certainly be keen, but hardly allows for a rounded relationship.

The only sensible way to seek a gift is to ask God, and so the New Testament positively encourages us to pray for gifts. Some say they wouldn't presume to ask God for specific gifts, but Paul's instruction allows us to be bold in our prayers, and to expect the Spirit to be generous. Indeed, Paul doesn't reluctantly allow occasional prayer for new gifts by those who feel particularly poorly endowed. On the contrary, he invites the whole church to seek spiritual gifts with real eagerness. Praying for spiritual gifts is not something to be done only in secret. It helps enormously to have others pray with you for a particular gift.

8. A hierarchy of gifts

We have already stressed that the spiritual gifts are not a measure by which we can compete with one another. There is no league table of Christians based on the gifts we have been given. On the contrary, Paul appealed to the Corinthians that those who appear to be the most insignificant among them should be treated with special honour and considered indispensable to the body. This is an instruction honoured more in the breach than in the remembrance, for it remains all too easy to neglect such people in the life of many local churches.

While the value of individual believers cannot be determined by their gifts, there is none the less a hierarchy among the gifts. Paul doesn't simply encourage the Corinthians to desire eagerly all the gifts, but stresses one in particular, namely prophecy (1 Corinthians 14:1). Similarly, while he would like them all to speak in tongues, he would much rather they all prophesied (1 Corinthians 14:5). Indeed, while in chapter 14 Paul invites them eagerly to desire the gifts, as well as following the way of love, at the end of chapter 12 he explicitly encourages eagerness for 'the *greater* gifts' (1 Corinthians 12:31).

There is no exhaustive list of spiritual gifts in the New Testament. In fact, none of the four lists of spiritual gifts is identical (Romans 12:6–8; 1 Corinthians 12:8–10, 28–30; Ephesians 4:11–12). It is therefore quite impossible to provide a definitive list of spiritual gifts which covers every gift the Spirit might give and records them in ascending order of importance. However, two of the lists do give us a clue, for they provide lists of leadership gifts: 'And in the church God has appointed first of all apostles, second prophets, third teachers, then workers of miracles . . .' (1 Corinthians 12:28); 'It was [Christ] who gave some to be apostles, some to be prophets, some to be evangelists, and some to be pastors and teachers' (Ephesians 4:11).

Similarly, the list in Romans 12 begins with prophecy. It therefore seems reasonable to deduce that, while there is no comprehensive biblical ordering of spiritual gifts, these foundational gifts are the higher gifts. Is there a gift of apostleship? I don't think so, for it is never referred to as such in the New Testament. It seems more reasonable to suggest that apostleship is a specific office, with apostles requiring a wide range of spiritual gifts, notably teaching and evangelism, prophecy and pastoral leadership.

We have already suggested that believers need to be encouraged to pray for spiritual gifts. I encourage people to pray for any spiritual gift to which they aspire, including tongues, that minor gift which was so commonly given to the first Christians. But we must emphasise the need to stir up eagerness for the higher gifts. In addition to the gift of prophecy which Paul highlighted specifically, we should surely encourage particular prayer for the foundational gifts of teaching, evangelism and pastoring.

9. *According to the measure of faith*

In Romans 12, Paul not only promotes the use of spiritual gifts, he also adds a qualifying phrase: 'Let him use it in proportion to his faith' (Romans 12:6). In part Paul is ruling out that false modesty which inhibits believers from serving with the gifts God has already given. The phrase also implies that our faith is not a fixed quantity, but can grow with good use or even diminish with neglect.

To receive a gift is one thing; to use it publicly is quite another. Speaking personally, I love to preach, for the public proclamation of the word of God is a high and privileged calling, and yet at the same time preaching remains always awesome and daunting. The novice preacher may leap to his feet, confident that he has all the answers and excited by the demands of the occasion. The seasoned preacher will learn to continue to declare his emptiness before God, his utter dependence, despite all his preparation, upon the Holy Spirit, so that somehow, through the all too inadequate human words, God might still reveal some jewels of divine truth (2 Corinthians 4:7).

Many with the gift of prophecy only have the first few words in mind before they speak out. At times, both in personal ministry and in public meetings, I would have much preferred not to declare a prophetic word, knowing the unavoidable risk of looking foolish or being misunderstood when we step out in faith. We need, like Timothy, to be reminded that we have not received a spirit of timidity (2 Timothy 1:7).

As to healing, we are called to pray in faith (James 5:15). On one occasion a couple in our church asked for prayer for the baby they were expecting. The mother's womb had been scanned, and the tiny life was seen to have two abnormalities. Together these symptoms suggested severe deformity, as a result of which the hospital indicated that an abortion would be advisable. Not surprisingly, the young parents asked some church leaders to pray. We began by thanking God for the miracle of the gift of life, and that this little baby was precious in God's sight. I then asked what we had real faith to pray for, since we didn't want to go through the motions of a faithless prayer. It became clear that we were all able to pray with faith that one of the symptoms would disappear completely. A further scan a couple of weeks later revealed that one symptom had disappeared and the other had reduced significantly. A few months later a completely healthy baby was born.

Using gifts according to our measure of faith is vital. There is all the difference in the world between a risk of faith and foolhardiness. If we pray for the sick simply according to our heart's desire, we will always pray for total healing, but our request, while full of compassion, may well be without living faith. It is far better to be honest about our measure of faith, and then our gifts will be exercised within the realistic limits provided by the New Testament. When spiritual gifts are used responsibly, our measure of faith will increase, and so, with wise use, our spiritual gifts will gradually strengthen and mature.

Equipping the body

The release of the full, biblical abundance of spiritual gifts has the potential to do away at long last with the nonsense of a one man band. The body life which God has planned for his church simply cannot be expressed if ministers are trying to do many tasks for which they are not gifted. If the people of God are not exercising the gifts the Spirit has given and seeking the additional gifts he longs to give, they are God's frozen assets – no good to anyone without a major spiritual thaw.

One bishop has suggested there are three distinct kinds of church life identifiable today:

1. The minister is the church, and does the ministry.
2. The minister delegates some ministry to the people, who help the minister be the church.
3. The people are the church, and the minister equips them for their ministries.

Each category is radically distinct. In the first, if anyone other than the minister preaches, leads worship or provides pastoral care, it can lead to annoyance: 'What do we pay him for!' In the second, many are willing to do their bit, but the underlying thought is that the congregation are helping the minister to fulfil his calling: 'It's really up to him, but because he's not gifted in a particular area, or because there is too much for one person to do, we'll lend a hand!' Only in the third way of looking at the church do we return to the church of the New Testament. Only here does the body of Christ break free from the chains of Christian tradition and history.

Only here do we enter the world of Ephesians 4:11–13, where various kinds of leader – apostles, prophets, evangelists, pastors and teachers – are appointed not to provide all ministry, but rather to 'prepare God's people for works of service'.

It would be absurd to suggest that the spiritual gifts do away with the need for leadership. In truth, when the gifts start to be freely released into the life of a church, the leaders' work has only just begun. I want to illustrate this by considering the development of pastoral care in Herne Hill, but the principles are applicable to every kind of ministry team.

Consultation and planning

The initial impetus was similar to Acts 6, namely that as numbers continued to grow, the staff were increasingly unable to keep up with the pastoral needs of the church. In addition, while many individuals were providing spontaneous pastoral care, because it wasn't co-ordinated properly, some were receiving a great deal of attention, while others were being neglected. Before providing any training or recruitment we prepared the ground. We held open consultations to identify key needs and possible responses. We also brought together a small planning team that had church or professional experience in different kinds of care provision.

Structuring the ministry team

We soon identified four strands of pastoral care. The home groups would provide primary pastoral care for their members. Area pastoral teams would be established to provide pastoral oversight, in particular covering the people who didn't attend home groups, cherishing the elderly, and providing personal support for those in particular need. A specialised counselling team was also required, and a prayer ministry team would make themselves available after services on Sundays.

Training and development

Training programmes have been implemented with a three-fold purpose: to equip people with the necessary skills; to build confidence in the gifts already received; and to begin to establish a sense of team identity. This training took a variety of forms, from one-off sessions to a structured course lasting a couple of months. In particular the counselling team developed a listening skills course, suitable for anyone, and a 'counselling part two' course for those with a particular aptitude. There has also been workshop based 'hands-on' training in prayer ministry, and several groups have used the outstanding CPAS video based training on bereavement support. We were also keen to draw on resources from outside our own church, and so a professional Christian counsellor was asked to present a series of training sessions. It is important to stress that the minister was definitely not the sole provider of training. On the contrary, my priority was to identify those in the fellowship who had the gifts and experience to deliver training of the greatest relevance and highest quality.

Providing real opportunities

It is no good making training an end in itself. I heard recently of a group of churches that provided excellent training in bereavement counselling. Several who took the course were suitable and available to become a bereavement support team. Only one problem remained: the ministers of the churches involved felt threatened by the idea of others entering this sensitive area of ministry, so no one was ever put to work. As a result, the training didn't release new ministries, it simply increased frustration. Training which does not lead to real ministry opportunities is always counter-productive and potentially disastrous. It conveys the impression that rather than fulfilling the biblical task of '[preparing] God's people for works of service' (Ephesians 4:12), professional ministers are operating a closed shop.

Recruitment and co-ordination

Attending a training course is never an automatic qualification for active ministry. Each of our pastoral teams developed its own recruitment policy, seeking to ensure that the right people with the right gifts are appointed at the right time. We inevitably made mistakes, and some have needed to drop out of a team where the demands are too high, or where their gifts or personalities don't really fit, despite first appearances. It is vital that the teams don't become exclusive cliques. They need to continue to recruit new people and everyone needs to be encouraged not to think of team membership as a ministry for life.

With regard to co-ordination, teams need to meet regularly for mutual support and prayer, and to ensure that the provision of care is as effective as possible. The teams are also linked to the elders, and we continue to present their ministries to the whole church through a photographic display, a brochure and regular mentions on Sundays.

Expecting the best

Someone recently asked me whether I feel threatened when so many gifted people are exercising ministry in our church. If the same question were asked in business, it would seem absurd. Just imagine a managing director who was so insecure that he made sure no one else in the company was able to do anything better than he could. Such an attitude would be a recipe for an ineffective company. It is equally a recipe for an ineffective church. It is surely part of the task of any full-time leader to equip others to excel to the very best of their abilities.

Leaders need to get beyond the foolish egoism of being threatened by the ministry of others. We need to believe in the believers, and convey the clear impression that we expect them not merely to help out the minister, but to excel. Where the gifts are released properly, there will be many people in the life of a local church exercising ministries far beyond the abilities of the minister. I once came across a dedicated and highly gifted elder who was incapable of praising the ministry of anyone in the church. He was hyper-critical, always and only seeing faults and failings. No one felt believed in or encouraged by his manner and words. Such an attitude is entirely inappropriate to authentic Christian leadership.

Helping to specialise

In a small church it is often a case of all hands to the deck, so specialisation is a luxury. In a larger church, specialisation is an absolute necessity. There are three kinds of specialisation we need to promote. First, we need to encourage busy people towards specialisation of ministry. It is far better to make a strategic contribution in one area of the life of the church than to parcel out fragments of time to several ministry teams.

Secondly, we need to encourage specialisation away from Sunday services. One grave distortion of every member ministry occurs when everyone who is keen to get involved wants a 'slice of the action' on Sundays. Genuine every member ministry is not about spreading Sunday slots ever more thinly among a growing number of gifted people. It is about becoming mobilised as the body of Christ throughout the week. Many vital areas of ministry take place most effectively far away from the public events of Sunday, including much evangelism and discipling, pastoring and training.

Thirdly, we need to encourage specialisation among leaders. The more teams that are released into the life of a church, the more complex church management becomes. If all the new teams report directly to the minister, he or she will soon become swamped, and there will be little time or incentive to encourage new teams into being.

When a church's ministry is concentrated upon Sundays only, most of the leaders can still afford to provide general oversight. The more a church multiplies and diversifies its ministries, the more essential it becomes for each team to know which church leader they relate to. Leadership teams have to come to terms with the fact that mobilisation and growth quickly make it no longer possible for every church leader to be fully up to date with every aspect of the life of the church. The point is managerial rather than theological. Just as a board of directors must sustain an overview, but as the business expands and becomes more complex they gradually move away from the minutiae of each company division, even so as a church expands and becomes more mobilised, a team of leaders must rely on one another to provide the necessary cover for their particular dimension of the life of the church.

We see a good example of leaders stepping away from the details in Acts 6. Having appointed the seven to get on with the task of serving the widows, the apostles handed over not only the activity, but also the responsibility. That is, it was up to the seven to perform the task, but also to decide how to do it and to make sure that it was done. The apostles gave away real responsibility. They didn't keep looking over the shoulders of the seven or undermine their authority by intervening and making decisions for them. Specialisation among leaders is twofold: trusting one another to provide leadership in particular areas, and also trusting other teams to whom real responsibility is handed over. Diversification of ministries within the body of Christ must lead to specialisation among leaders. The only alternative is overworked leaders and frustrated ministry teams.

Removing the barriers

Central to the New Testament is the liberation of men and women, rescued from captivity to Satan by the power of the cross of Christ. As a result of this divine liberation, human relationships can enjoy a threefold liberation from the old ways of hierarchy and domination: a racial liberation, in which any notions of ethnic superiority are excluded; an economic liberation, in which all come to Christ and belong in his church on an equal footing; and a sexual liberation, so that women are no longer to be despised or exploited: 'There is neither Jew nor Greek, slave nor free, male nor female, for you are all one in Christ Jesus' (Galatians 3:28).

It is a plain fact that churches can easily fly in the face of the New Testament and ignore this radical liberation. If the body of Christ is to function effectively, it is vital that a local church is pursuing in these three areas a radical and biblical repudiation of the prejudices and divisions ingrained by the culture of society and the traditions of the church. Such barriers are removed by clear biblical teaching, exploring the implications of new freedom in Christ. Study and discussion groups can tease out the practical implications. We want to develop a climate of awareness and sensitivity, but also a community where liberation is practical and genuine, evicting prejudice by encouraging a new way of living to flourish. Simple gestures can also help establish a climate of equality. For

example, those who organise our rotas for serving communion seek to provide teams that have a good balance by age,
gender, race, marital status and social background. We don't
want to be a white church which welcomes blacks, or a
professional church which welcomes blue collar workers.
Rather, we want to be a genuinely multiracial church, a
church for all nations and a church for all peoples.

The cross and racism

In 1991 we brought the racial dimension into the open. We
are based on the borders of an inner city, and in our morning
congregation are found over thirty nationalities and some
twenty-five denominational backgrounds. It would be foolish
to imagine that becoming multicultural has always been every
member's idea of heaven. Some twenty years ago a Nigerian
lady arrived one Sunday morning in a resplendent crimson
costume only to be told, 'We don't dress like that here, you
know.' Others from ethnic minorities kept coming to the
church through years of discrimination. While many related
to them warmly as brothers and sisters in Christ, some
ignored them during the week and avoided sitting next to
them on Sundays.

Having developed a strong sense of belonging together, we
wanted to declare a positive commitment to being a church
for all peoples, so we chose to spell out some essential
convictions:

1. All people are made in God's image, and there is
   absolutely no place in the Christian church for racist
   attitudes.
2. In society, there is not only overt and naked racism, but far
   more widely a problem of institutional racism. Non-whites
   are regularly the victims of personal prejudice, educational

and social disadvantage, higher unemployment and higher incidence of being stopped by the police. If we are complacent about the status quo, we allow such institutional racism to go unchecked.

3. Each of us is shaped by our upbringing to harbour all manner of prejudice. Therefore, not only do we take our stand against explicit racism, but we are also prepared to examine ourselves humbly, ready to discover and uproot the unconscious prejudice of many years. This is a vital part of growing into holiness.

A small group teaching and training programme was already under way, so we made a group available which would look at racial awareness. This group was led by people with race awareness responsibilities at work, in a hospital and a local education authority.

If we had simply offered the group, we could have appeared to be suggesting that race awareness was an appropriate Christian interest, but only for a minority. Therefore we also ran a sermon series for a month on issues of race. For some whites, a month of teaching on race issues seemed far too much, but with the history of slavery, apartheid and other forms of white racism it seemed to me that a full month was vital. Today, with the steady rise of racism in Western Europe, I would argue all the more strongly that a single sermon would be woefully inadequate. For some blacks, it was the first time they had heard clear teaching against racism in a multiracial church. We also gave an hour within a members' meeting to an introductory presentation on race awareness, in order that those who didn't join the small group could not avoid being exposed to these issues.

For our church, uprooting racial prejudice has been an

integral part of becoming an alternative community for all people, within a city where relationships are becoming ever more fragmented. But exploring issues of race is vital throughout the world. Sadly, we have all too often left such reflection to non-Christian groups. Shouldn't every church grasp this nettle and face up to exploring these issues? Let's have an end not only to overt racism, but also to the complacent harbouring of deeply unchristian prejudices. In Christ, the dividing wall has been broken down. Let's declare and demonstrate that liberation to our cosmopolitan multi-racial post-modern society!

Singles and ministry

A fourth dividing barrier which is particularly prevalent in our society must also be torn down. All too often there is a dividing wall between singles and marrieds. In many churches singles are very definitely second-class citizens. Some churches have decreed that all home groups will be led by married couples. Often it is tacitly assumed that all church leaders will be married. The disempowerment is twofold. First, in a reversal of the medieval Catholic pre-judice, there is an assumption that the married condition is universally the better or higher calling. In the light of Christ's own singleness, such a claim is palpably absurd. Secondly, single people are systematically excluded, whether deliberately or unconsciously, from many key areas of ministry.

In a society where an increasing number of adults are single, such a policy strips away from a large part of the body of Christ the opportunity to exercise their gifts freely. It is just as vital that we take a stand against this dividing prejudice as against the other three. In preaching, training groups and the continuing life of the church we need to proclaim and demonstrate the liberation and equality which have been won for all by Christ. Only when the church is liberated from the tyranny of these dividing barriers can the spiritual gifts begin to flourish freely. Only then will the body of Christ break free from the chains of cultural prejudice.

The next generation

Developing the next generation, bringing them forward and releasing them into leadership, doesn't always come easily. Many commercial organisations fail precisely at this point. Many political parties and voluntary organisations struggle to avoid becoming gerontocracies, dominated by an ageing peer group, who grow old on committees together.

For the church of Christ, raising up and releasing the next generation of leaders is not merely a matter of common sense and survival. It is a principle which is fundamental to truly biblical leadership, exemplified in Jethro and Moses, Moses and Joshua, Elijah and Elisha, Barnabas and Paul, Paul and John Mark, and Paul and Timothy.

1. The need to hand on skills and responsibility

Jethro knew how to pass on his insights into leadership in such a way as not to undermine Moses, but rather to make him an even better leader (Exodus 18). We need leaders ready to pass on their expertise with similar skill and graciousness.

2. The need to allow old moulds to be broken

Moses was accomplishing tasks beyond the dreams of Jethro. While the older man had invaluable insights to convey, he scrupulously avoided getting in the way of Moses' leadership. Despite the complaints of the people, Moses was a mould-breaking visionary. He would accomplish things never seen before in Israel, and as a result, the life of the people of Israel would never be the same again.

3. The need to allow younger leaders to excel

When Moses brought Joshua forward, he was establishing a younger leader who would accomplish a task beyond Moses himself: taking the people of Israel into the promised land (Deuteronomy 34:9). Likewise, when Barnabas recruited Paul to Antioch he was presumably the senior partner (Acts 11:25–26). Ultimately, Barnabas had to be big enough to recognise that Paul had the larger ministry, as an apostle to the Gentiles. We need leaders who are able to bring others forward and who are prepared to allow themselves to be eclipsed by a more gifted leader.

4. The need to affirm a calling and honestly recognise the cost

Elijah set his personal seal on Elisha's calling, affirming the younger man as his God-appointed successor. But Elijah also refused to romanticise the prophetic calling, helping Elisha to face up to the reality of the costs of ministry that Elijah had known and that he was to endure in turn (1 Kings 19:19–20). We need leaders who are ready to affirm others in ministry and who are not afraid to acknowledge that their own ministry has sometimes been no easy road.

5. The need to be resolute and undeterred in raising up the next generation

It didn't work out when Paul recruited Mark. In fact the immediate fallout must have seemed horrendous, when he lost not only Mark from his team, but also Barnabas (Acts

15:37–39). Paul avoided the easy generalisation that younger leaders were not ready to play a part in this kind of ministry. His letters to Timothy confirm his continuing resolve to get alongside and continue to develop younger leaders.

6. The need to give immature leaders a second chance

Nothing was further from Paul's mind during his argument with Barnabas than the thought that John Mark might mend his ways (Acts 15:38). In time the young man must have been given an opportunity to prove himself, for towards the end of Paul's life Mark became one of his closest colleagues (2 Timothy 4:11).

7. The need to teach and demonstrate that bringing forward the next generation is a continuing responsibility of Christian leadership

Paul didn't just develop Timothy, he also instructed Timothy to develop others. Those who aspire to the apostolic pattern of ministry must not only 'guard the good deposit that was entrusted to you' (2 Timothy 1:14). They must also make sure they pass the baton to the next generation, entrusting it to them in turn (2 Timothy 2:2).

To apply these principles to church life requires a new perspective on leadership development. I spoke recently with a young man who had been promoted to a senior management position at the tender age of 24. At his church, the greatest level of responsibility with which he could be trusted was to help on the bookstall once a month. We are squandering our human resources by failing to give young leaders a measure of real responsibility. As a result, they find much more fulfilment in the workplace than at church, where they feel neither believed in nor stretched.

It is in some of the new churches that I have seen these principles applied most consistently. In Ichthus, there are many leaders in their twenties and thirties who carry significant responsibility. Some find it difficult and need a great deal of support, but I am enormously impressed with the quantity and quality of leaders being developed. The Revelation Church in Chichester and Portsmouth has established a deliberate and systematic policy of apprenticeship. Not only are younger leaders considered an integral part of the leadership team, but every leadership or ministry role in the life of the church is 'shadowed' by a trainee leader, who is learning about ministry through hands-on experience. This policy is extended to all dimensions of the life of the church, including home groups and evangelism, congregational leadership and area oversight. Here are churches and leaders taking seriously the concept of the next generation. Leadership in the body of Christ should never be allowed to become a single generation group of leaders growing old together.

The gifted leader who has not learned the principle of developing the next generation may end his days with his church lamenting an irreplaceable loss. But the leader who has learned the apostolic principle of helping to raise up younger leaders can look forward to ending his days rejoicing to see how, in the service of Christ, the next generation excel.

The mobilised church

Recent medical research has consistently demonstrated that the British are getting more unfit. Exercise is being taken less, while we are consuming more fatty foods. For most car owners, if a journey is more than 200 metres, we choose to drive, which is not unrelated to the fact that the number of overweight men has doubled in recent years. Children are also taking less exercise. Because of heavy traffic and the growing fear of violence or abuse, almost all children are now taken to school and to friends' houses by car. As a result, children are not only less fit, but less resistant to illness, and there is even a possibility that their growth and adult health may be undermined. The private car is exacting a heavy price for its convenience. We are beginning to suffer from low performance bodies.

The body of Christ is designed to be a marvel of spiritual engineering – a high performance body in which the gifts of the Spirit enable us to accomplish far more for Christ together than we could on our own. However, when we fail to apply New Testament principles of body life, the church becomes decidedly low performance.

Restricted tasks or open opportunities

The low performance body identifies a fixed number of tasks that need to be filled in the life of a local church. Once the limited quota of Sunday school teachers, stewards and so on has been filled, any remaining attenders are surplus to the requirements of active service. Their sole task is to fill pews. Body life is reduced to a spectator sport.

The high performance body mobilises members into freedom. The range of ministries in the life of the church is limited only by the creativity of the members and the gifts of God. The functions of the body are no longer narrowly defined, but open-ended. If a team come together with a vision to explore a new dimension of ministry, no one stands in their way. Rather, they are given every support and encouragement in pursuit of their goal. We need, in

Tillapaugh's striking and attractive phrase, to unleash the church.

Ministry by office or gifts

The low performance body organises ministry according to office. In its narrowest form, only the minister leads worship, preaches, provides pastoral support, runs discipleship classes, etc. Still very common is the alternative form where only the appointed leaders of the church carry any kind of responsibility or engage in public ministry.

A friend of mine was a deacon in a church where they introduced personal prayer ministry at communion services. I am all in favour of this ministry through which I have seen countless people greatly helped, including myself on many occasions. Problems arose because prayer ministry in this particular church was going to be exercised exclusively by the deacons. It so happened that all the deacons were male, which dramatically reduced the opportunity for women to seek prayer for any personal needs. Still more fundamental was the fact that, good leaders as these men were, none of them had been appointed as deacons because they were gifted in personal prayer ministry. Some of them may have happened to be gifted in this way, but that was a fortunate coincidence. The ministry was imposed on office bearers without them being asked whether they were gifted for this task.

Similarly, in some churches every elder automatically takes their turn to preach. This flies in the face of the New Testament, which doesn't suggest that every elder preaches, and also in the face of common sense. If a church appoints someone who is not a good preacher to be an elder, it must surely have identified other key leadership gifts on which that elder needs to concentrate.

The high performance body encourages ministry according to gifts, not office. The leaders need to master discernment of gifts and humility of spirit. Their main concern cannot be to lay claim to tasks that come with their office. They need to concentrate on discovering to whom in the body the Spirit has given particular gifts and ministries.

Body in the image of Christ

Many churches develop in the image of the minister's gifts. Where his gifts are strong, the church is strong. Where he is less gifted, the church is weak. This is the hallmark of a low performance body.

The high performance body seeks to be shaped in the image of Christ rather than the image of the minister. I have never met a single minister gifted for every dimension of ministry. This seems to be a subtle strategy of the Holy Spirit to ensure that every leader needs the ministry of the whole body, restricting the gifts of leaders to keep them humble and to promote substantial opportunities for the ministry of others in the local church.

Only the Holy Spirit has the ability to provide gifts in the body for all round ministry. If a minister and leadership team are not gifted in a particular area, they need to identify the people the Spirit has provided, and release them into ministry. The church built solely or mainly around the gifts of its minister will always be a lopsided body, highly developed in some areas and barely functioning in others. The Christ-empowered church is a high performance body, in which the life of Christ is far more roundly expressed, with the gifts of every member being released to the full.

Initiative and responsibility

In the low performance body, initiative rests solely in the hands of leaders. In some churches the minister presides over everything, and is the only person in the church allowed to use any initiative. Elsewhere, there is a team of leaders who claim a monopoly of initiative and vision, and keep the rest of the church on a short rein.

In the high performance body, there is an enterprise initiative released among the people. The leaders deliberately and consistently encourage others to pioneer new dimensions of ministry. The leaders' tasks remain considerable, often stimulating initiative through training opportunities and supportive conversations. To give a couple of examples, I know of one church where a training course on AIDS awareness led to a regional initiative in support of ACET, the Christian AIDS charity. Elsewhere, an individual who was highly motivated about acute needs in the community was encouraged to put together a statistical report. This led to an action team which in time was able to initiate a church-based social work programme.

If a small group share a burden or a vision we need to encourage them to pray together, to share their dreams, conduct research and draw up a strategy for action. If every member's dreams are piled up onto the minister's desk, there is little chance of them ever being put into practice as he parcels out ever smaller fragments of time to each new idea. The same problem arises if such proposals are simply added to the agenda of a church leadership team. But if a group of believers share a dream, they can pour their energies into this specific opportunity, burning with zeal for their new ministry to be launched.

With initiative must go responsibility. There is nothing so

demotivating at work as to present a new project to your manager who promptly takes it over and squeezes you out. There is a vital distinction between proper accountability by which church leaders provide sufficient cover for a ministry, and over-centralisation, by which pioneers are robbed of their rightful responsibility. Over-centralisation is like a black hole, sucking new ideas into a central committee from which they never again emerge.

The high performance body avoids possessiveness among its leaders. They learn instead to create a climate of boldness, experiment and enterprise. A climate in which pioneering and creativity are encouraged, and where failure is not an unforgivable sin. Some churches are so frightened of a new initiative failing that they haven't tried anything new for years. The fatal error is not to try and fail; it is never to try at all. The high performance body releases initiative and responsibility into the hands of believers. It is time to call for a free market in new ministries and congregations.

The car in which I learned to drive was a VW Beetle. One word which summed up that car was reliable. One word that could never describe it was fast. I learned that turning from a side street into busy traffic took a great deal of patience. Our next car was a Ford Escort with an engine twice the size. It was a great pleasure to accelerate away on the open road, but after a few weeks I realised that my technique for turning onto a busy city street hadn't changed. I owned a high performance car, but I was driving it with low performance expectations.

We face similar dilemmas with churches. First, there are churches which are low performance bodies, because they have chosen to neglect the New Testament teaching on the body of Christ and the gifts of the Spirit. Secondly, there are churches that embrace the biblical teaching in principle, but they have failed to renew their structures and assumptions. We can have the potential of a high performance body while functioning with low performance expectations. Only when a church embraces biblical teaching, and as a result thoroughly reforms its structures and renews its expectations, can we begin to fulfil the intentions of Christ and the promises of the New Testament. Only then can we become a high performance body. Nothing less is needed if we are to be faithful to the New Testament and serious about reaching the 21st-century world.

8

The Abolition of Human Religion

If this chapter is too much for you to take, please don't throw out the baby with the bath water by writing off the entire book! For some readers my argument in this chapter will cover very familiar and uncontentious ground. For others, it may point the gun at some very sacred cows. Like it or loathe it, my invitation is that you give a fair hearing to the Scriptures on two vital issues that we cannot afford to neglect as the church enters the new millennium, namely buildings and leaders.

Buildings

The temple of God

The later books of the Old Testament reveal just how central the temple became in Jewish thought. When Ezekiel looked forward to the restoration of Jerusalem beyond the Babylonian exile, so dominant in his thinking was the new temple that he described its dimensions and layout in exhaustive detail (Ezekiel 40–43). Above all, he looked forward to the return of the glory of the Lord, filling the temple as of old.

Haggai demonstrated the same reverence for the temple, denouncing the materialism of the post-exilic Jews when he saw them pouring money and energy into their own 'panelled houses' while the temple was still in ruins (Haggai 1:3–11). Once the people heeded these warnings, not only would the Lord take pleasure in the temple, but his glory would return to fill the house. What is more, Haggai declared, the glory of the rebuilt temple would exceed the glory of the temple of Solomon (Haggai 2:7–9).

The centrality of the temple in later Jewish thought shows a considerable shift from God's instructions to Moses for the construction of the ark of the covenant and the tabernacle (Exodus 25–26). The tabernacle was a kind of tent, a portable shrine. Similarly, the ark of the covenant, the gold-covered container for the two stone tablets on which the Ten Commandments were carved, was designed to be carried from place to place. Wooden poles, overlaid with gold, were fitted through rings on its sides, with an express instruction that they should not be removed (Exodus 25:15). It had built-in portability.

The readily movable ark and tabernacle had several key implications. First, God's desire was not to appear to be remote, but to make his dwelling with the people (Exodus 25:8). Secondly, they would remind the people how God had led them out of captivity. Thirdly, they reminded them that their destiny was to be a people on the move. Fourthly, they restricted any tendency to attempt to tie down the living God to a single place. As a result, when David requested permission to build a temple, he met at first with divine resistance: 'I have not dwelt in a house from the day I brought the Israelites up out of Egypt to this day.

I have been moving from place to place with a tent as my dwelling' (2 Samuel 7:6).

Once God relented, Solomon constructed a building of great magnificence, using the finest artists of the Middle East (1 Kings 6–8). When the ark of the covenant was brought into the temple, God graced the building with his presence so powerfully that the planned worship had to be abandoned: 'And the priests could not perform their service because of the cloud, for the glory of the Lord filled his temple' (1 Kings 8:11).

In these dramatic spiritual experiences, the living God manifested his transcendent glory in such ways as to demonstrate not only his presence, but also his power. Although a permanent house had now been built for him, the sovereign Lord could not be controlled or tied down by his worshippers. The Old Testament makes a careful distinction between the temples of idols, which were seen quite literally to be their dwelling places, and the temple of God, which, strictly speaking, is the 'dwelling for his Name' (Deuteronomy 12:11). God was not to be thought of as restricted or contained within a single place, even though his presence and glory would be manifest there.

Despite God's presence and eventual approval of the temple, there remained an ambiguity in Solomon's building programme, just as in his other ambitions. The first book of Kings emphasises this ambiguity by comparing how long it took to build the temple with the time taken on its neighbouring building, the royal palace: 'He had spent seven years building [the temple]. It took Solomon thirteen years, however, to complete the construction of his palace' (1 Kings 6:38–7:1). The temple quickly became not only the centre for religious activities, but also a monument to national identity and a dynastic chapel for the royal family. Pride in national

identity and the power of the line of David were interwoven
with the worship of God.

These ambiguities were carried over into the most ostenta-
tious temple ever built in Jerusalem, the temple of Herod.
The Jews were always suspicious of Herod, despite his
attempt to curry favour by building the new temple. He
was an Edomite who had married into the Hasmonean
dynasty, the old Jewish royal family. Herod then wiped out
his in-laws, his wife included, to secure his own grip on the
throne, which he held for thirty-six years. Although a Jew by
religion, he had pagan temples erected, but his greatest building achievements were the modernisation of Jerusalem and
the rebuilding of the temple on an unprecedented scale.

If you are fortunate enough to stand on the Mount of
Olives, looking across the valley to the Temple Mount you
quickly understand how Herod's temple must have towered
above the city. He massively extended the mount itself,
creating a huge man-made plateau, looking down upon
the city and flanked by imposing walls. While previous
generations used rough-hewn stones for their fortifications,
Herod's stones were finely cut and dressed. The temple area
was enormous, taking up perhaps one sixth of the space
within the walled city, and the temple itself was extravagantly
beautiful, dominating the skyline. Despite the fact that Israel
had been conquered by Rome, these were proud days. As the
Babylonian Talmud stated of Herodian Jerusalem, 'Whoever
did not see Jerusalem in all her glory never saw a beautiful
city' (Succah 51, B).

Jesus and the temple

Jesus' disciples expressed the typical enthusiasm of tourists
when they were leaving the temple: 'Look, Teacher! What
massive stones! What magnificent buildings!' (Mark 13:1). It

is hardly surprising that they were caught up in the magnificence of a building which, like Solomon's temple, not only expressed the majesty of God, but was also a noble shrine affirming their national identity. Here was an eloquent demonstration in stone of the divine glory which promised the Jews' national identity and continuing survival.

The reaction of Jesus to the temple was complex, and was raised during his trial, when witnesses misrepresented his claims: 'This fellow said, "I am able to destroy the temple of God and rebuild it in three days"' (Matthew 26:61). Jesus did indeed prophesy the destruction of the temple in response to his disciples' enthusiasm, warning that every stone would be thrown down (Mark 13:2). But he also gave an entirely unexpected twist to temple language, when he spoke of his own body as the new temple of God: 'Destroy this temple, and I will raise it again in three days' (John 2:19).

The temple commanded qualified respect from Jesus. He not only attended and taught in the precincts, he even risked his own safety in driving out the money-changers to reclaim the building as a 'house of prayer' (Matthew 21:13). After his death the first Christians continued to meet in the temple courts, the natural public gathering place and the focus of city life. It was nothing less than devastating to the Jews when Jesus' prophecy was dramatically fulfilled in AD 70. Roman patience with the rebellious Jews had finally run out, and Jerusalem was not merely subdued but crushed, taken apart systematically, stone by stone. Herod's temple was razed to the ground, and a temple to Jupiter built on the site. There seems never to have been any suggestion in the Constantinian or Crusader eras that Christians might support any attempt to rebuild the Jewish temple. Not only had Jesus foretold its destruction, but he had rendered it obsolete by his death.

In the church, God had provided a quite different kind of temple in its place.

The new temple

The concept of a new temple was taken up and developed by the first Christians in two ways. First, there is an individual application, for every believer has become 'a temple of the Holy Spirit' (1 Corinthians 6:19). Whereas the temple in Jerusalem was the dwelling place for the name of God, Christians are more literally God's dwelling place, for God himself, in the person of the Holy Spirit, lives within them. Paul stressed that it is the human body which is the Spirit's temple. For those trained in Greek philosophy, the physical body was something to be despised in comparison with the mind and the spirit. Paul takes his stand against cultural values by insisting that the Spirit, far from avoiding contamination by our physicality, has chosen to live within us. The Holy Spirit therefore makes the human body not merely highly valued, but a holy place. All the sanctity and reverence attached to the temple as the house of God is now attached to the believer and his body. As a result, demands of holy living are laid upon believers, and so Paul urges the Corinthians to 'honour God with your body' (1 Corinthians 6:20).

As a building dedicated to God's use, the temple is sacred not only before men and women, but in God's eyes too. Therefore the Jews expected God to defend his temple and to bring judgement on those who sought to defile or destroy it. Even so, Paul argues that Christians, as God's new temple, are under the protection of God. Persecutors and spiritual deceivers destroy God's new temple at their own peril: 'If anyone destroys God's temple, God will destroy him; for God's temple is sacred, and you are that temple' (1 Corinthians 3:17).

The second application of 'new temple' thinking is corporate. Believers are not only individually temples of the Holy Spirit, but are also 'living stones'. Paul speaks of the church as a building, joined together in Christ and rising to become 'a holy temple in the Lord' (Ephesians 2:21). Peter describes believers as living stones, built into a spiritual house. In this corporate dimension the emphasis is not upon God indwelling his temple, but rather upon the function of the temple as a place of worship, for the task of these 'living stones' is to offer 'spiritual sacrifices acceptable to God'; that is to 'declare the praises of him who called you out of darkness' (1 Peter 2:4–5, 9).

The chief building responsibility of the church is therefore not to construct temples, cathedrals or chapels. Rather, we need to build quality relationships of love, centred on Christ and his lordship. The living stones must be built together in order for our worship to be pleasing to God. If a church constructed a glorious building and hired the best musicians that money could buy, but the people endlessly bickered and criticised one another, their worship would be less acceptable to God than the worship of a church too poor to fix the roof, but where the believers truly loved one another as brothers and sisters in Christ.

Where does Christ fit into this new building? Both Paul and Peter speak of Christ not as the entire temple but rather as the cornerstone. This was the crucial foundation stone in ancient buildings. Precisely hewn, the cornerstone was laid first, and determined the guidelines and layout for all the stones that followed. Quoting Old Testament scriptures, Peter explains that everything hangs on the individual's response to Christ. Those who reject Christ inevitably stumble and fall, but for those who believe, the cornerstone is precious and is able to set them in true with the other stones in the house of worship (1 Peter 2:7–8).

Old temple thinking

Jesus and the apostles completely revolutionised all temple talk. Almost without realising it, the church has often failed to sustain this revolution, preferring instead to return to the natural instincts of human religion. At the simplest level, the New Testament word 'church' is used always of believers, never of a building. We have given to buildings an honour the New Testament reserves for Christian people alone. The contrast with the New Testament is far more than a matter of terminology. If we are serious about recovering the convictions of the first Christians, we require nothing less than a fundamental shift of mindset. Old temple concepts have dominated much of our thinking about church buildings.

1. Many cultures are familiar with the concept of a religious building, so it seems only natural to refer to Christian buildings as 'the house of the Lord', or 'the sanctuary'. Biblically, however, the holy dwelling place of God is no longer a building, but rather the people of God. It is we who are the house of the Lord, for we have become the sanctuary of the Spirit.

2. Many Christians still assume that 'proper' worship depends on the availability of a suitable religious building, but in the New Testament, the physical location of worship is unimportant. The quality of worship is determined far more by our living faith and our relationships than the place where we happen to meet.

3. Many Christians consider their building to be sacred, but the truly sacred place is wherever the Spirit indwells. I recall a PCC member protecting his 'sacred' church building against the offence of Christian drama, by angrily condemning the youth group drama team. The truth is that this self-righteous man was the real offender against the temple of

God, by wounding those whom the Holy Spirit had made sacred. He had committed the cardinal error, which is seen all too often, of making a church building matter more than his relationship with other believers. Such attitudes, however sincere or well intended, are far from the ways of the Holy Spirit and the apostolic church.

4. Many Christians assume that the only place we can meet with God or begin to expect revelations of divine glory must surely be a church building. Yet because God continually indwells his people, and cannot be tied down to any one location, the presence of the Holy Spirit is available at all times and places. This is not to deny that we can indeed meet with God in our church buildings, but if we want to be biblical we must strenuously deny the idea that God's availability is restricted to such places. A group of committed believers in a derelict barn is likely to know far more of the presence of God than a civic gathering of non-Christians in the splendour of an ancient cathedral.

5. For many Christians, their church premises symbolise a sense of permanence and stability. In a world of constant change, their building represents something settled and immovable. The services next Sunday will be predictable in the time honoured manner, as it was in the beginning, is now and shall be for ever. In some churches, if a minister dares to move a table given in memory of a leader half a century ago, they practically walk in peril of their life!

The letter to the Hebrews teaches us as Christians to see ourselves as a pilgrim people, a people who are always on the move because God is always moving us on. When our buildings so easily strengthen attitudes of fixity and inflexibility, we do well to recall the mobility of the tabernacle. While we fasten our religious furniture in place, not just with screws and bolts but with the fixity of inflexible tradition, the ark of the covenant was not allowed to be seen without its carrying poles. As a pilgrim people, we need to rediscover a tabernacle mindset, always free to move forward with God.

6. Just like the temple in Jerusalem, the main church in the capital of many so-called 'Christian countries' has become the seat of national identity. In this building the monarch is crowned, political leaders are honoured, and prayers are uttered for victory in war. There is, of course, no such thing as a Christian country. While a country may have been influenced to some degree by Christian values – in culture, customs or laws – Jesus taught that the only way to enter the kingdom of heaven is to be 'born again'. This is neither something an entire country can do, nor an automatic birthright for the citizens of any nation.

Our objection is to more than the concept of a 'Christian country'. Even though Solomon and Herod both used the temple to their own political advantage, the Jews had a legitimate and unique claim to be God's people. No other nation can make that claim. In the Christian era, the fundamental basis of the church is that we are a united body of believers under the lordship of Christ, transcending all boundaries of race and nation. There can be few actions more blasphemous than the fact that, in the centuries of wars in Europe, Christian leaders in each of the warring countries prayed to the same God for national triumph. They were staking claim to the God of all as if he were a tribal or national deity.

It is inconceivable, on the basis of the New Testament, to argue for anything other than a strict separation of church and state. An established church is a fundamentally compromised church. A church that is not the official state church, but none the less allies its prayers uncritically with the nation's priorities, is a church that has abandoned the lordship of Christ. The church is an internationalist movement, in which our new identity in Christ takes decisive precedence over national identity and priorities.

7. All the world religions, including the Christian religion, tend to construct special religious buildings which declare the glory of their gods. These temples not only claim in some measure to be a divine dwelling place, they often compete with one another in extravagance, to the glory not only of the deity, but also of the builders or benefactors. Whether a chapel built in honour of the local industrialist, or a village church which bows and scrapes before the lord of the manor, religious buildings are often embodiments in stone and mortar of human power and pride. Denominations have poured money into their competitive and sectarian monuments, even as, in multifaith societies, steeples compete with minarets for prominence on the skyline.

Human ambition expressed in church buildings is a monument to folly. There is much to commend any building that is pleasing to the eye, but religious buildings which commemorate human pride can never be pleasing to God. God's priority concerns the living temple, where he looks for sustained growth in holy living and relationships of love.

Buildings that serve

Nothing that I have said denies the usefulness of buildings. Understood in terms of conventional human religion or the old temple, church buildings have a tendency to become tyrannical masters, distorting the message they were built to serve. Stripped of superfluous and specious religious significance, a good building remains an invaluable and effective servant of the gospel.

What kind of building best serves these biblical priorities? It should be welcoming, outside and inside. Even if some people habitually refer to it as a 'church', we should strenuously avoid giving any building the name reserved in the New Testament for believers. My preferred term is 'Christian Centre'. Every part of the premises should be multi-purpose – it is an appalling and profligate waste of resources to set aside our largest room for a single use on Sundays. Wherever possible, small rooms for training and counselling should be provided. It should be comfortable, but not over-luxurious, designed to make local people feel at ease, probably echoing in its decor something of the typical local style. The building should be designed and used to serve the local community and be made available as a resource for other churches in the area. Above all, the building should be conceived as a mission centre, not as a comfortable religious club. A place where believers are encouraged, inspired and resourced for worship and witness. A place where each believer is taught the faith so that they may know with confidence in daily living that they have truly been made a temple of the Holy Spirit.

The Christian revolution

We have seen that in the New Testament, Christ is the new cornerstone, and in him we are the dwelling place of the Spirit and the spiritual temple, filled with the worship of God. There can be no good reason for us to ape the attitudes or buildings of other religious systems. Their dependence on holy buildings has been rendered obsolete. Their extravagant temples, whether sublime or grandiose, are surplus to requirements. We no longer have any good reason or need to conform with conventional religious instincts, for the living God established a rupture with religious conformity in bringing salvation to us. In the death of Christ we are faced with nothing less than the abolition of human religion.

Leaders

The priests of God

Is there any place for priests in the apostolic church? The New Testament lists of spiritual gifts make no reference to priests. Paul identifies the key leadership roles to be apostles, prophets, evangelists, pastors and teachers, but he makes no mention of 'priests'. Peter describes all Christians as a 'royal priesthood' and invites them to become a 'holy priesthood' (1 Peter 2:5–9). In Revelation, all believers are made priests to God (Revelation 1:6; 5:10). No priests are called upon even once in the New Testament letters to deal with the eucharistic abuses or circumcision controversies of the early church. The only reasonable conclusion to be drawn from the total exclusion of any reference to a distinct caste of Christian priests is quite simply that they did not exist.

Hebrews explains their absence in detail, presenting Christ as the one true Priest who renders superfluous the mediation of any human priesthood. What priests accomplished provisionally in the regular sacrifices for the people, Christ accomplished once for all as the perfect sacrifice and the great High Priest. While the Jewish high priest was the only person allowed to enter the Holy of Holies, all believers now have direct access to the holy presence of God. There could be no greater departure from Jewish religious practice than this repudiation of any need for a distinctive, mediatorial human priesthood.

The sacrificial language normally connected with priestly functions is retained in the New Testament, but given an entirely different context: believers sacrifice themselves (Romans 12:1), they sacrifice their money (Hebrews 13:16), and they offer a sacrifice of praise (Hebrews 13:16).

Everyday life, not religious rites, is the arena for sacrifice and the setting for the new priesthood. There is no longer a barrier between priest and laity, religious and ordinary life, sacred and secular. The normal structures of human religion, both Jewish and Gentile, no longer apply.

Any suggestion that a distinct order of priesthood is necessary to Christianity is a blatant contradiction of the letter to the Hebrews. To say Christian priests represent the one true priesthood of Christ turns the letter's argument on its head. It introduces mediatorial priests where they are no longer required. For Hebrews, any return to a priesthood of the old kind involves an unnecessary return to shadows and imperfection. This would inevitably lead to a loss of the immediacy of encounter with God made possible by Christ.

The first Christians radically reshaped the language of 'priesthood' and 'sacrifice'. In one sense all are priests. Believers are their own priests, for all have immediacy of access to God's grace in Christ. What priests have performed for others before, believers can now do for themselves. In another sense, none can be appointed priests in the Christian church, for Christ has fulfilled the priestly role once for all, and continues to function as our all-sufficient, great High Priest.

Priests in early Catholicism

While the first Christians saw no need for the continuation of the priestly ministry, the subsequent era of early Catholicism saw a return to the old Jewish ways. For example, Hippolytus and Cyprian drew detailed parallels, comparing the Old Testament priests and sacrifices with the priests and Eucharist of the Catholic church. In the 4th century, Ambrosiaster acknowledged a fundamental change in church order away from what he considered the unseemly anarchy of the first generation, but he chose emphatically to assert the superiority of the later priesthood in contrast with the radical simplicity of the early church: '. . . all taught and all baptised . . . but when all do everything, that is irrational, vulgar and abhorrent.'

The biblical rejection of a Christian priesthood was still retained by Augustine in the 5th century. He declined to call bishops and presbyters 'priests' in the sense of mediators between Christ and congregation. By then, however, Augustine was unusually traditional in his New Testament emphasis. In the same century, Narsai, Bishop of Nisibe, represents the full flowering of the new version of Christian priesthood:

> The priest has received the power of the Spirit by the laying on of hands. Through him all the mysteries in the church are performed. The priest consecrates the font with the water for baptism, and the Spirit gives the baptised person adoptive childhood. Without a priest, no woman would be given to be married to a man; without a priest their marriage obligations are not completed. Without a priest the water would not be blessed and the house would remain impure. Those who do not possess the *ordines* cannot celebrate the eucharist, however pious they may be.

This traditional concept of the ordained priesthood evidently shaped the World Council of Churches' Lima statement, *Baptism, Eucharist and Ministry*, with its claim that 'the ministry of such persons, who since very early times have been ordained, is constitutive for the life and witness of the Church'.[1] No one looking to the New Testament for a

---

[1] *Baptism, Eucharist and Ministry*, A8.

doctrine of the church could possibly accept the word 'constitutive'. Leaders may equip, enable and direct the church, but a church does not depend on the presence of 'ordained clergy' in order to be constituted. On the contrary, priests in any natural sense of the word are surplus to New Testament requirements.

Clergy and laity or the people of God

Consistently in the New Testament, the *laos* are the inclusive people of God. Where there is a distinction between a congregation and its leaders, that is within the *laos*. There is no *laos/cleros*, people and priest divide. Our term 'clergy' is derived from the Greek *kleroi*, who were magistrates of a Greek city state. The concept of *kleroi* as a distinct caste within the church seems again rooted in the 3rd century, notably in Cyprian of Carthage's careful but contrived parallelism between the Christian presbyter and the Jewish priest, the Eucharist and Old Testament sacrifice. It seems that the political culture of the Roman Empire and the religious structures of ancient Israel came together in such a way as to dilute the radicalism of the New Testament.

Popular usage is clear – 'I'm a layman in this field' means 'I'm an amateur, or unqualified'. Once such terminology is applied to the church, it is inevitable that the 'clergy' will be identified with the church more fully than the 'laity', for example in the phrase, 'He's gone into the church.' This strips the vast majority of Christians of their full dignity as members of the body of Christ. It strips them of power, placing them at the bottom of a hierarchical structure, and it robs them of full opportunity to exercise their spiritual gifts and to live as full members of the priesthood of all believers.

Clericalism

While Paul lists apostles, prophets, teachers, preachers, healers, speakers in tongues, and so on, the churches have concentrated on developing a more or less fixed form of priesthood or ministry. As Donovan concludes, 'We have built a mighty institution out of a few references.'[1] Clericalism is the attitude that results. On the one hand, the professional and ordained clergy claim a monopoly of many ministries in the life of the church. This possessiveness inevitably robs the body of Christ of freedom to exercise the gifts God has given. On the other hand, the laity expect no one but the clergy to fulfil many tasks, whether in Sunday services or pastoral care. This attitude, as Peter Wagner has argued, denies the church effective leadership, constraining the minister to the narrow role of chaplain to the congregation, providing blessing and support to Christians while having only limited opportunity to establish direction or equip and mobilise the church.

Clericalism is undermined by an extensive list of omissions in the New Testament. There is no sole presidency at the sacraments by ministers, no unique representation of Christ by the church leader, no separate clergy, no ordination for life, no sole leader (not even assisted by an intermediate tier of so-called 'lay leaders'), no sole right to lead worship or preach.

Titles for leaders

Jesus must have recognised the insidious attractions of clericalism, because he gave explicit instructions about which titles were unacceptable among his followers (Matthew

---

[1] *Christianity Rediscovered*, p. 148.

23:5–12). What seems extraordinary is the readiness of the church to adopt and retain these outlawed titles, namely 'father', 'teacher' and 'master'. Such total disregard for Jesus' teaching reflects the power and pervasiveness of the clerical attitude which we need to combat.

The title 'reverend' surely falls under the spirit of Jesus' prohibitions. On the one hand, there is only one truly to be revered and that is Christ. To use such a title is to detract from his unique glory, which was guarded so carefully through the restrictions on titles that he established. On the other hand, in the priesthood of all believers, a single righteousness is conferred on all, and so all believers are made saints in Christ. For one group of Christians to reserve this title for itself is to detract not only from the glory of Christ but also from the true status and essential equality of all believers.

The centrality of teaching

The development of the Christian priesthood was based on the premise that the centre of gravity for Christian ministry is the breaking of bread. As early as Clement at the end of the 1st century, drawing on parallels with the Old Testament priesthood, a distinct group of believers were required to perform 'offerings and services' conferred by Christ, 'at the fixed times and seasons'.[1] However, the evidence of the New Testament contradicts such an assumption. The risen Christ's instruction to Peter spelled out the centrality of teaching: 'Feed my sheep' (John 21:17). The apostles developed a specialised role focused on the ministry of the word and prayer (Acts 6:4). Similarly, in the pastoral letters, teaching and preaching are the central, almost the sole designated

---

[1] 1 Clement 40, in Bettenson, *The Early Christian Fathers*, p. 32.

tasks of the full-time leader, there being no reference to presidency at the Eucharist. The conclusion is plain, as Schillebeecx observed: 'Ministry did not develop from and around the eucharist or the liturgy, but from the apostolic building up of the community through preaching, admonition and leadership.'[1]

The only form of apostolic succession found in the New Testament is not a succession based on episcopal ordination, supposedly passing on the anointing through the laying on of hands in an unbroken line that runs right back to the apostle Peter. On the contrary, the apostolic succession is in sound teaching, passing on to the next generation of leaders the responsibility to guard and proclaim the unchanging gospel (2 Timothy 2:2). Central to any biblical understanding of full-time Christian leadership is the task of Bible teaching.

Ordination

Closely linked with the *kleros/laos* divide is the practice of ordination, which was linked in the Roman world with the two classes of the *ordo* and the *plebs*. In Roman law, *ordo/ordinare* denoted the ruling status of a group quite distinct from the *plebs*; for example, *ordo clarissimus*, used of the Roman Senate. When Western Christians used the Latin term 'ordination' they imported a set of cultural assumptions about appointment to leadership into their understanding of the New Testament. That is, 'ordination' points to the rite of entry to the clergy (*kleros/ordo*), over against the laity (*laos/plebs*). Those who are not so ordained are by definition removed from the ruling group, from power and from presiding at any of the religious rites. The influence of Platonism

---

[1] *The Church with a Human Face*, p. 119.

strengthened this dualism, so that by the Middle Ages it was customary to speak of two orders, the religious and the secular, and two ways of life, the spiritual and carnal. Naturally those ordained to the religious orders, with their spiritual way of life, ruled over the secular.

This network of concepts – 'priest', 'clergy', 'laity', 'ordination to the priesthood' – is a seamless robe. Such terminology and thinking preserves the exclusive claims of a religious élite. What is more, they find their natural home not with the radicalism of the New Testament, but rather with the conventional patterns of human religion.

Commissioned for ministry

The first Christians certainly commissioned leaders to new ministries, and we can draw several principles from Paul and Barnabas at Antioch (Acts 13:1–3; 14:26–28; 15:36–41).

- Paul and Barnabas were already in leadership at Antioch. None the less, hands were laid on them, with prayer, before they set out on their first missionary journey.
- This particular laying on of hands was a specific commissioning to a short-term missionary journey. When Paul later suggested a further journey, he plainly could not take for granted that their first commissioning guaranteed a lifetime's missionary service from his colleagues.
- The ordinary church members at Antioch seem to have played a full part in this commissioning and laying on of hands. It wasn't left to the leaders. There is certainly no suggestion that only those who had been 'ordained' in the apostolic succession could commission others to ministry.
- The missionary leaders were 'set apart' both by God and the church. On the one hand the Spirit commanded them to be set apart through a prophecy. On the other, the

church prayed for them publicly. They recognised their calling, released them from leadership at Antioch and identified with them in their future ministry.

In short, this laying on of hands seems to have been a repeatable action, a commissioning to a specific task, done to those who were already leaders by the whole church, and not merely or exclusively by a group of 'clergy'. It is a commissioning, an appointment, a 'commending to God's grace'. Obligations are also laid upon the church that recognises God's call to ministry and accepts the authority of those so appointed. Can we describe such an event as an 'ordination'? Only if we remove from the term 'ordination' the historic implications of lifelong entry to a separate priesthood. And only if we are prepared to 'ordain' to their particular ministries not only vicars or pastors, but also elders, missionaries and other leaders.

New Testament leaders

The fact that there is no biblical job description for elders should alert us against any rigidly defined approach to church leadership. The rarity of references to elders in the New Testament suggests that establishing a standardised leadership was by no means the apostles' main concern. (Still less can we define the New Testament role of 'deacons', since we are told nothing at all about what the early deacons did!)

The Greek term *presbuteros*, usually translated as elder, was used in the New Testament with several strikingly varied layers of meaning.

- It can retain the general meaning of *older*, thus pointing to the older believers taking a leading role in the church as a result of their seniority.
- It can also be suggested that Paul tended to look for some leaders from among his early converts to take responsibility

for the church, which takes us to the meaning *older in the faith*.

- When Timothy is told not to be too reticent because of his youthfulness, he is presumably coming to terms with his appointment as a teaching and presiding elder. Here *presbuteros* is a title linked neither to age nor to years in the faith, but to *spiritual maturity, linked to a specific gift and calling to church leadership*.

- When the qualities to be looked for in a prospective elder are listed in the later Pauline epistles, the emphasis is upon right living rather than charisma, which may point to a pattern of leadership which is becoming less functional – the recognition of a charisma – and *more of an office*.

- In John's letters, the term is used not simply of an office in the church, but as a definition of *the identity and status of a particular leader*; that is, '*the* elder' (2 John 1; 3 John 1).

- Beyond the pages of the New Testament, we see the full flowering of *the ordained office of presbyter/priest*.

The first churches demonstrated clear enthusiasm for leadership teams as well as every member ministry. They also retained a high degree of freedom in working out the detail of their own pattern of local leadership. In short, the New Testament shows neither uniformity, nor a clear, linear evolution, but rather a wide number of variations on a theme. Our task is surely to retain that fluidity, while ruthlessly removing any of our traditions that run contrary to the essential convictions and spirit of the first Christians.

Anti-clericalism

It is vital that we don't swing from clericalism to anti-clericalism. Strictly speaking, anti-clericalism is not possible where there are no clergy, but I use the term to express a disregard or disrespect for Christian leadership and full-time ministry. There is clear evidence in some churches of this equally unhelpful trend. The following factors are vitally important:

1. Respect is due to leaders. The New Testament never makes the mistake of suggesting that leaders are surplus to requirements. On the contrary, believers are encouraged to pray for, obey and submit to their leaders (Hebrews 13:7, 17). A minister is not the doormat of a church. He is appointed to be the servant leader of the church, leading with a serving spirit.

2. Leaders need teams and teams need a leader. Throughout the New Testament, leaders function in teams, not in splendid isolation. In recent years, many churches have embraced this principle, and moved away from quasi-priestly authoritarianism. However, we need to recognise a fundamental distinction between a creative leadership team and a bureaucratic leadership committee. A bureaucratic committee assumes that everyone has to have a say about everything, and nothing can ever be done without the entire committee being fully informed first. A creative leadership team allows for specialisation, so that individuals can take responsibility for particular areas of ministry, which they then get on with, reporting back to the team only as necessary.

A bureaucratic team will resist any emphasis upon a team leader, wanting everything to be controlled by the committee. A creative leadership team supports and strengthens the authority of the team leader. For example, although Paul travelled as part of a team, there was no mistaking the fact that Paul was the team leader.

3. Initiative and accountability must be combined. When Peter was confronted with Cornelius and others speaking in tongues and professing faith he made a decision to baptise them. This produced an uproar back in Jerusalem, where Peter had to justify his actions (Acts 10–11). We see here two complementary principles of Christian leadership: initiative and accountability. Both necessarily apply in any church where a full-time minister is in partnership with a team of leaders whose paid work is beyond the church.

On the one hand, the team leader reserves the right to use his initiative in order to exercise proper leadership in response to the promptings of the Holy Spirit. It would have been totally inappropriate for Peter to leave Cornelius kicking his heels while the apostle rushed back to Jerusalem to establish with the other leaders a policy on baptising Gentiles. In the same way, Paul took the initiative in mission to the Gentiles without securing an agreed policy from Jerusalem first. At times any team leader worth their salt will need to take the initiative without delay.

On the other hand, the team leader must remain accountable. They should not be mortified or take offence if their colleagues require an explanation for an unexpected initiative. Wise leaders accept the fact that they may have been wrong in their initial decision and so it is right and proper to be held accountable. The wise team accept the fact that the team leader may well be prompted by the Spirit without prior notice. They provide proper accountability, but they won't quench the Spirit by preventing the proper use of initiative by the team leader.

4. *The teaching office.* We have argued that the teaching ministry is central to New Testament leadership, but we have also noted that the New Testament does not suggest that every elder should preach, regardless of gifting. From Paul's instructions to Timothy, we can reasonably suggest a teaching office in the life of a church, so that where a church has a full-time minister, teaching and visionary leadership

can be identified as his central tasks. Not that he is the only teacher or leader, but these are the tasks for which a church depends upon their full-time minister the most. If someone is not gifted to preach, they should be asked to lead a local church only in exceptional circumstances.

Towards a second reformation

As with temples, much in the concept of a priesthood is common not merely to Judaism and traditional Christianity, but to human religion. Human religions generally accept the need for a caste of intermediaries between God and ordinary men and women, and their priests normally perform religious rites and sacrifices from which everyone else is excluded. The first Christians therefore violated the canons of normal human religion – 'an oddity indeed – religious groups without priest or sacrifice'.[1] The debate about the office and function of Christian leadership is part of a wider debate about Christianity as a subversive religion. As Ellul has argued: 'For the Romans nascent Christianity was not at all a new religion. It was "anti-religion". This view was well founded. What the first Christian generations were putting on trial was not just the imperial religion, as is often said, but every religion in the known world.'[2]

The development of the church is the disturbing, even tragic history of the subversion of Christianity from within, compromised by culture and conventional human religion. What we need is not a modest adaptation, but a radical overhaul of the traditional doctrine of the church. As Kierkegaard frequently insisted, the conventional church and the Christian religion stand in urgent need of subversion

---

[1] J. G. Dunn and J. Mackey, *New Testament Theology in Dialogue*, p. 123.
[2] J. Ellul, *The Subversion of Christianity*, p. 55.

by Christ. Authentic Christianity declares the abolition not only of human religion, but also of human priesthood.

There is an unmistakable vibrancy about the churches of the New Testament. They face many problems and uncertainties. They make mistakes. They are infiltrated by the nominal and the carnal. And yet . . . there is an attractiveness and reality among them which forces us to conclude that those first Christians had indeed discovered a new way of living; Christ-centred, mission-orientated and Spirit-empowered. To recapture that vibrancy involves not only recovering their dynamism, it also involves a process of unlearning the assumptions of conventional thinking about the church, unexamined or considered 'only natural', among Protestants and Catholics alike. In Snyder's words: 'The clergy–laity dichotomy . . . is one of the principal obstacles to the Church effectively being God's agent of the Kingdom . . . it creates the false idea that only "holy men", namely, ordained ministers, are really qualified and responsible for leadership and significant ministry.'[1]

As he did so often, Luther rediscovered a biblical radicalism concerning Christian ministry before his instinctive traditionalism and a reaction against the chaos of extremists made him draw back into a more conservative institutionalism. He argued that a priest has a particular function or office which makes him worthy of respect. However, once he leaves that task he is no different from anyone else. This is square against the 'once a minister/priest always a minister/priest' dictum which is taken for granted by many Christians – Protestant as well as Catholic. The sacrament of ordination he wholly repudiated as a Roman invention, and he asserted rather

---

[1] Howard Snyder, *The Community of the King* (InterVarsity Press [USA]), p. 95.

that all are priests, inasmuch as all have been baptised into Christ. He considered baptism our ordination into the universal Christian priesthood.

It would be more accurate to the New Testament to suggest that every believer's appointment to ministry comes with the indwelling of the Holy Spirit. It is the cross which makes Christ the great High Priest, and confers a universal priesthood of believers. And it is the Spirit, given by Christ, who baptises us into the body of Christ, conferring membership and equipping us for our various ministries. The Holy Spirit makes actual and effectual the new community that has been made possible by the cross.

There is a twofold revolution in the New Testament. First, the cross of Christ sets believers free from the need for an intermediary priesthood and all that follows from it. Secondly, the coming of the Spirit actualises the new way of being: it is in the power of the Spirit that the missionary church erupted upon the unsuspecting 1st-century Empire, as the spiritual gifts were bestowed and the believers were energised with holy power.

Tragically, as we have seen, the normal pattern of human religion has proved a more attractive and comfortable model for most Christian churches. What is more, as Paul prophesied, the history of the church has included many who hold fondly and reverently to the outward form of religion while denying its inner and experiential power (2 Timothy 3:5). There is no possibility of being a radical and apostolic church without a clear and thorough understanding of the impact of the cross and the Spirit. To put it technically, a biblical ecclesiology is built upon the foundations of a biblical soteriology and pneumatology.

According to the New Testament, the cross of Christ precludes much of the traditional office, practice and terminology of the 'clergy', Protestant as well as Catholic. The coming of the Spirit brings about revolutionary possibilities which traditional understandings of the church struggle to accommodate. Some fundamental choices are required when our traditions; under the influence of natural religious instincts, are found in conflict with the church life of the New Testament. Despite the natural instincts of human religion, we have neither holy buildings nor an élite priesthood, for all believers have been appointed the dwelling place of the Spirit and members of the holy priesthood. So despite the familiar use of such language, we do not strictly speaking 'go to church' on Sundays, nor do we 'go into the church' if we enter full-time ministry. At all times and in all places, whether or not we are in full-time ministry, all Christians don't merely attend, but actually *are* the church of God. In Christ is found the abolition of human religion, whether pagan, Jewish or even Christian, with its holy buildings and exclusive, élitist priesthoods: 'What agreement is there between the temple of God and idols? For we are the temple of the living God' (2 Corinthians 6:16).

We end this provocative chapter with a searching question:

*Will the 21st-century church dare to recover the
Christ-centred radicalism of the first Christian generation?*

9

Multiplying Churches

The event that put church planting back on the map in the UK more than anything else was surely the Challenge 2000 national DAWN congress early in 1992. Representatives from almost every Protestant grouping, both historic denominations and new church streams, met together and set goals which amounted to 20,000 new churches by the year 2000, aiming for 20 per cent of the population attending church regularly. The acid test of any goal is action that produces results, and significant new developments have arisen at two levels. On a national basis, many denominations are holding training events in church planting for the first time ever. At a local level, many churches are rising to the task. Churches that have never before considered church planting are taking the challenge seriously and establishing local goals. Even though, with hindsight, the DAWN goals were naive and inflated, the impetus given to church planting by this initiative still deserves to be recognised.

What is happening in Britain is paralleled around the world. For example, Heiner Rust, former senior minister of Hanover

Baptist Church, secretary of Home Mission for the German Baptists and a leader of renewal in Germany, has come to recognise the need for many new churches in order to reach the German people with the gospel. I visited a new congregation the Hanover church had planted recently, and heard about their vision for an accelerating programme of church planting in the coming years, each church plant tailored to reach the people of a specific district around Hanover. At one time they considered providing a training centre for church planters, but suddenly there are many such centres appearing, and Heiner Rust has concluded that the greater immediate need is not further courses, but churches that are ready and able to seize hold of today's planting opportunities.

The need is urgent for a fresh evangelistic advance into Europe – a continent that is in moral and spiritual darkness as a result of turning away from the gospel for several generations. Germany and Britain were two key nations in the missionary advance into the non-Western world, but in this century they have shed one another's blood twice in world wars. In a continent that is showing signs of a rising tide of militant nationalism and racism, it would represent a profound demonstration of new unity and hope in Christ if German and British Christians began to support a new millennium initiative throughout Europe in evangelism and church planting.

I recently spent some time in Brazil to learn at first hand from their tremendous church-planting advances. I asked Reginaldo Kruklis, a key leader in Sao Paulo, about Brazilian church-planting methodology. 'There is no organised method,' he explained. 'We preach that every believer is called to be a witness and that church planting plays a key part in evangelism.' The rate of church planting is staggering. At Reginaldo's previous church, three new churches were planted in three years, while the congregation of the sending church doubled. As for the Pentecostals, many are planting at several times this rate. One retired Brazilian Baptist pastor suggested to me that a decisive factor in the rate of church planting is the level of bureaucracy. While the Pentecostals and new churches are strong on mission and make decisions quickly, older churches can suffer from bureaucratic overload which severely inhibits church-planting advances.

In Brazil, church leaders seem not to need to stir up reluctant troops or organise every new initiative in evangelism. Enthusiastic teams approach their pastor to share their vision for a church plant in a particular area, eagerly seeking permission to get started. The people own the vision for church planting and church growth and have willingly taken responsibility for mission. Leadership of church plants is often given to someone with a day job, who then attends evening classes in ministry and mission. From what I saw, these leaders are equipped to do a magnificent job. We have much to learn from what God is doing with great power throughout the developing world.

Seven key reasons for church planting in the West today

1. The vast numbers who are unreached

Some 90 per cent of the English population have no church involvement. The twenties are the least reached generation, among whom this figure rises to 94 per cent. In London alone this means that over 6 million need to be reached with the gospel. In Europe, Canada and Australia the situation is just as serious. The Western world is an immense mission field today. There needs to be a huge response to a huge task, and part of that response is to plant new churches.

2. *The inadequate number of existing churches*

In 1851 there was one church building for every 500 people in England, and 40 per cent of the population were regular attenders. In 1981 there was one church for every 1,200. This means that if every church service were full today, only 16 per cent of the population would be able to attend. In London it is worse: in 1989 there was one church for every 1,900 people. Many urban areas and housing estates are not served by any kind of church at all. Meanwhile, a significant number of old churches have closed or are facing closure due to terminal decline. There are simply not enough existing live churches to serve and reach the nation.

3. *Live churches with full buildings*

While many churches show every indication of dying in slow motion, a good number of evangelical and charismatic churches have enjoyed considerable growth in recent years. It is no longer a rarity to hear of projects to expand the seating capacity of church buildings. Such growth is thrilling, but the capacity of a building is a self-limiting factor. When land is expensive, few churches have the option of moving to a new site to allow for continued growth. Studies have revealed that when a service is 80 per cent full on a regular basis, it has reached its working capacity. Latecomers are no longer guaranteed to be able to sit together, so inconvenience starts to deter some from attending at all. Others look around at a sea of faces, with little evidence of empty seats, and they begin to lose the incentive to invite new people.

During my last year in publishing I invited David Watson to our sales conference beside Lake Windermere, to speak about his latest book. It was an unforgettable morning, as the Hodder sales force, accustomed to visits from best-selling authors like Jeffrey Archer and John le Carré, listened intently to David speaking of the reality of faith in Christ when he was dying of cancer. I had known David as a student in York, where I attended his church, met with him as President of the Christian Union, and knelt before him when he prayed for me to be filled with the Holy Spirit. Now I was his editor, and later that year I would ask him to pray for me again when I left publishing to train for full-time Christian ministry.

As we drank coffee together, I asked David to look back to his time in York. The enormous growth of the church had tailed off once St Michael's was full. While conversions continued among students and non-Christians brought to guest services by Christians from out of town, it seemed that the regular congregation were showing a diminishing zeal to witness. David told me that had he stayed in York, he would have begun to wonder whether St Michael's should seek to obtain another redundant church building, moving across part of the congregation in order to provide a real opportunity to reinvigorate urgency in witness and renew strong conversion growth. What David was beginning to explore, many of us have pursued in more recent years. A live church that has grown until the building is full is a joy to see. But the fact that many of our live churches are nearly full is a very good reason to establish many new churches and congregations, whether on-site or in new locations.

4. The micro-communities of modern living

The urban environment is not like an overgrown town with a single shopping and commercial centre. A city is made up of many small communities. Some are defined geographically, around a particular shopping parade or some other focal point. Others are defined ethnically: those from the same country or island, who share the same language or come from the same tribe, often spend much time together, even if their homes are far apart. Other micro-communities are cultural, so that those with a particular interest in common mix together socially. The city is therefore a complex web of relationships, in which we can play a part in several different overlapping micro-communities, some of which bear no relation to where we actually live.

If we are to plant churches in this context, we need to identify and reach distinct micro-communities. Visibility is a key principle. In order to take the gospel into unreached estates and areas, a church needs to be established in each micro-community. In this way the gospel is indigenised rather than asking the people to leave their micro-community in order to go to church. If we were able to plant a live church for every thousand people, then everyone who washes their car, buys a newspaper or walks the dog on a Sunday morning would stand a very good chance of seeing a live church gathering for worship and witness in their neighbourhood.

As to the non-geographical micro-communities, a Chinese or Arabic speaking church is much more likely to be heard of and visited by members of that ethnic group. Similarly, some African-led churches in Western cities specifically target a particular tribe and worship at least partly in their tribal language. In London, Kensington Temple has demonstrated the evangelistic effectiveness of starting new congregations for distinct ethnic minorities. If we really want to see the gospel penetrate into the micro-communities of the modern city, we need to establish many new culturally specific congregations.

5. Reaching the poor

In many cities in Britain, the United States and around the developed world, many ageing and decaying housing projects for the poor have no live church in the neighbourhood. It is vital that the gospel is taken to the poor inner-city communities of the older cities. In the developing countries, the rate of urbanisation is extremely high and as millions flock to the cities in hope of work and wealth, new shanty towns spring up every month. In these new cities, which will be the mega-cities of the new century, the task is even greater: vast millions will need to be reached who will be new city dwellers, mainly young, and living in extreme poverty.

Traditional churches have usually failed in this task. Often the strong churches are in middle-class areas. Some ignore the poor, whether in Chicago or Sydney, Manchester or Rio. Others have tried bussing the urban poor to a live church. I have seen bussing used both in England and Brazil with the same problems arising: the poor usually feel uncomfortable and out of place in a middle-class environment; styles of clothing and topics of conversation are often markedly different. In some areas, adults with literacy problems are thrown into an environment of highly abstract discourse, where they cannot relate on equal terms. The evangelistic impact of bussing initiatives is generally slight.

Sao Paulo is a mega-city of enormous size, with a staggering rate of population growth. Up to 2 million people live in terrible poverty and squalor. I visited a recent church plant there in Jardim Olinda, a favela of some 5,000, of whom 30 per cent are children under 7. Here was a church of the favela, a genuine community church, not only proclaiming the gospel but demonstrating the gospel through practical programmes to help with adult literacy, preparing young children for school, guitar classes and teaching health care to pregnant women. This particular favela had been thrown up on the slopes of a small stream, which had inevitably become an open sewer. The church was recruiting volunteers to fit piping around the stream, reducing at least some of the major health risks of the community. During my visit I was thrilled to see the baptisms of several new believers from the favela. Stuart and Georgie Christine, who have pioneered this project, are now launching further favela church plants. Their vision is to see a whole network of favela churches across the city and beyond. In the 21st-century church, throughout the cities of the world, ancient and modern alike, only if we take major church-planting initiatives can the good news be taken effectively to the poor.

6. Reaching the 21st-century world

As we saw in the first section of this book, not only are the vast majority of the population unreached, but most of them wouldn't dream of going to a traditional church. This underlines the fundamental error of the argument that there are enough churches already. As we have already noted, the statistics indicate a severe shortage of churches, even if every church were live and packed full. More than that, not only are many church buildings in the wrong place or in bad disrepair, most existing churches are so culturally remote as to be irrelevant to the task of reaching the post-modern world.

The only way to reach the vast majority is to multiply culturally engaged churches and congregations. This means that many new churches will be needed if the 21st-century church is going to be serious about mission in today's world. Many existing churches show no sign of being prepared to face the cost of bridging the cultural gap. It is not their priority. Others are cautiously open to change, but show little evidence of being prepared to change radically enough to bridge the chasm that has opened. We have already suggested that some churches need to consider adding an additional congregation that is dedicated to an experiment in cultural engagement, with no strings attached by traditionalist Christians.

I was very impressed in Rio de Janeiro to meet people from two recent church plants which have broken through to a new contemporary style in the power of the Holy Spirit. It should come as no surprise that they are reaching significant numbers of younger people. Just as impressive is the fact that the sending church has given them absolute freedom to incarnate the unchanging gospel in fresh and creative ways. May thousands of new churches bloom for the sake of taking the gospel to this generation!

7. *The call of God*

I am instinctively wary of the latest church fashion, so I was very cautious when everyone began talking about church planting. I needed to be convinced about church planting in three ways. First, that this policy has a strong biblical basis. Secondly, that it makes good strategic sense in our cultural context. Thirdly, that it represents part of the Holy Spirit's purposes for today's church. I can now say without hesitation that I fully endorse church planting and the multiplication of congregations on all three counts. Church planting is not cheap, in terms of both personnel and money, nor is it the fastest way to win individual converts. But it is the best way to establish the gospel in unreached communities.

Getting started

In early 1993 a delegate at a national conference for British church leaders suggested that church planting is a modern fad about which the book of Acts has nothing to say. This was a sad and astonishing indictment not of church planting, but of our massive neglect of the study of church planting in the

New Testament. To be sure, there are no church buildings in Acts, so their church planting couldn't be building-centred. Nor did they have denominations, so there could be no denominational strategies, funding or planning. Nor indeed were the first Christians organised in parishes, so the problem of planting across parish boundaries which impedes and frustrates some Christians today was entirely absent.

I have not the slightest hesitation in stating that church planting was fundamental to the apostolic strategy for reaching the world with the gospel. We will consider the church plant at Philippi as a model of apostolic best practice (Acts 16:12–40), identifying key principles and offering practical application for today. Within the book of Acts there are many contexts for evangelism, including healings, preaching and public debate. The missionary teams didn't work to a blueprint, doing the same thing in every town. Likewise, we need to know our local setting, to identify where God wants us to be and the best ways to witness there.

Before anything could happen, *the sending church at Antioch needed to embrace the church-planting vision*. It not only gave continuing support and encouragement to the team, it also needed to give them freedom to plant according to context, for no two New Testament church plants are identical. In the same way we need sending churches to be right behind church-planting initiatives.

Planting is expensive, and not merely in terms of the financial investment to launch the new project. A church will need to be ready to give up some of its best people for the plant. Some good friends will no longer worship together in the same congregation. The price is worth paying for the sake of the gospel, but too much reluctance to accept the cost will undermine the motivation of the planting team. Continuing prayer is also vital, together with the personal support and encouragement of the church leadership team.

The church-planting team then needed to be selected and trained. Luke doesn't tell us Paul's methods, but team preparation is vital. A great variety of methods have been used to provide such training, but the necessity is beyond dispute. Team members need a good grounding in personal discipleship. They need to know how to lead someone to Christ. If we want to follow the New Testament pattern, they also need to know with confidence that they have been empowered by the Holy Spirit for mission (Luke 24:49).

Church-planting teams are no place for superficial eagerness. Some may be invited personally to join the team and others may be encouraged to apply for consideration, but in my view a pioneering team is no place for unselected volunteers. We don't want anyone to be overextended, nor do we want the planting team to have to divert attention from evangelism to pick up the pieces for someone who shouldn't have been on the team in the first place.

Not that everyone stays on a team long term. A distinction can be drawn between the pioneers, who help to get a plant off the ground, and the settlers, who remain part of the new congregation for the foreseeable future. Where someone is struggling to stay on board, they need to be referred back to the sending church as soon as possible. The primary task of the initial team is evangelism, not the care of Christians.

Once they arrived in a new location, *Paul's team conducted preliminary research to identify and visit the natural meeting places of the city* (v.13). No church evaluation or evangelistic strategy is complete without a clear sense of the character of the local population. Whether for a church plant or in the continuing life of the church, such information is essential. How else can we begin to identify the appropriate means of communication by which to take the gospel to the people of our area?

In our own community analysis, we use two main sources of information: first, the national census and local health authority statistics, available through the local library, and secondly, a door-to-door community survey. The survey is compiled and analysed, with the help of a computer, by a medical statistician from our church, who ensures that the community profile we develop is as accurate as possible. The key factors we assess include age distribution, the incidence of single parenthood, the main ethnic groups, the frequency of abortion and drug abuse compared with the national average, the number of people living on their own, major concerns about local living conditions.

The community survey brings several results in addition to helping us understand the local area. It is a positive exercise in public relations, demonstrating that the church is really inter-ested in local people. It has introduced us on the doorsteps to some Christians with no church involvement, and to others who are ready for the first time to hear and respond to the gospel. Finally, the survey helps instil in a church-planting team a strong local focus for their mission. We have seen those involved in community surveys readily agreeing to 'adopt a street' for continued prayer, leafleting and visiting.

When the team sought out those gathering for prayer on the Sabbath, *they were targeting a group more likely to be open to the gospel*, rather than trying to reach everyone in Philippi at the same time and with the same methods (v.13). The apostolic approach is subtle and precisely targeted. While the ultimate intention was to reach everyone, they began by seeking to reach the most responsive, and chose their method accordingly. Only later would they turn their attention to the more resistant.

All too often churches aim to reach everyone in their vicinity simultaneously, with a single technique. Just as TV programmes and advertising are tailor-made for different kinds of people, we need a fresh understanding of specific target groups for our diverse evangelistic events. We also need to identify those who are most reachable, for while they are by no means our only target group, we need to make a particular effort to reach those we are most likely to win.

Contact was initiated at the level of friendly conversation, the informal witnessing in which every Christian has a valuable part to play (v.13). We can never stress enough the importance of friendly conversation and what Festo Kivengere used to call 'gossiping the gospel'. Friendship evangelism is often assisted by missions and special events, but nothing can replace the timely word of witness in relaxed conversation with a friend.

None the less, we simply cannot afford to rely solely on witness to close friends, colleagues and neighbours. In any urban setting the sheer density of population means that many thousands will never make friendly contact with a Christian unless we make a deliberate effort to meet them. Paul's mission team didn't set up home in Philippi and concentrate on establishing a few close friendships before embarking on witness. Rather, they went where the locals gathered and got into conversation there.

This indispensable strategy has its roots in the ministry of Jesus. He could have devoted his wonderful preaching skills to a career touring the synagogues as an itinerant preacher, but instead he chose to take the good news out on the streets, to the people who rarely attended a synagogue and to the poor who were looked down on by many 'churchgoers'. What is more, he didn't stay in one place, establishing himself as a preacher within a single town, but kept on the move, always giving new people an opportunity to hear the good news. Friendship evangelism is about more than witnessing to friends. An apostolic strategy for church planting and evangelism requires that we give a friendly witness where others in the community meet together, whether in the city squares and shopping malls, the pubs or parks. Some of our church planters have formed a pub quiz team. Mixing in the pub, socialising with men who wouldn't be seen dead in a church, they are taking the gospel to the people, not waiting for the people to come to church.

In due course, *Paul seized an opportunity to speak evangelistically*, and some came to faith (v.14). We don't know whether Paul preached or spoke in a more intimate way, but every evangelist needs to make room for proclamation. Sadly, some of our best evangelists become so overworked with other local church responsibilities that their evangelistic appetite begins to wilt through neglect.

It is vital that the gospel is proclaimed, but we also need to call for a decision. Our preaching should not merely inform; we need to preach for a verdict. Church leaders need the expertise and confidence to press home the gospel and seek conversions. At many colleges, little or no training is given in how to invite decisions at the end of a message. In some there is little or no training in personal witnessing. Indeed, some college lecturers have probably never led anyone to Christ. Quite simply, if a college claims to train for ministry it must be far more than an academic institution. How much we need professors who are scholarly soul-winners rather than detached academics. There is an urgent need today for increased provision for training in evangelism, church growth and church planting.

Establishing a church

The first believers in Philippi had no pews or organ, no vicar or constitution, no microphones or overhead projector. But they were a church, a local gathering of believers committed to the service of Christ together. How were they established as a new church?

First of all, the team set *the seal of believers' baptism upon the new converts* (Acts 16:15). The first Philippian Christians were baptised without undue delay, just as the Ethiopian eunuch was baptised within minutes of conversion. While discipling is a continuing task, once someone is certain in their faith they are ready for baptism. When we baptise, we not only set a public seal upon believers' inward faith, we also declare their incorporation into the church of Christ. The first baptisms of a new church plant are always an event of great excitement and rejoicing, when God places the affirmation of first fruits upon our endeavours.

After accepting Lydia's offer of hospitality, they realised that this businesswoman's house was *an ideal place for the church to meet* (v.15). The right meeting place can be a make or break decision for a church plant, requiring much prayer. There are practical issues concerning the suitability of lighting, heating and seating, as well as reliable availability. There are also spiritual issues, requiring an awareness of what else the building is used for. At one time we used another church's hall that was then hired out to Hindus to celebrate Diwali. Before we met there again, a small team spent an hour praying in the room to ensure spiritual liberty.

Lydia can be described as God's '*breakthrough person*', the right believer at the right time with the right resources – in her case a large house and a gift of hospitality – to help establish the church plant (v.40). We had just such a breakthrough couple for our first church plant, Effra Community Church. Their sense of calling, vision and commitment to their area was rock solid. Before anyone else caught the vision, they stayed in the area when they needed to move house. When a home group began to meet in their new flat they started to see what it might lead to eventually. At the moment we have a team meeting regularly for prayer about another area. Some members of that prayer team have 'lit up' since they began to meet, and once again I suspect we have been provided with God's strategic 'breakthrough people'.

Paul's team must have worked hard *to integrate the converts as a new church*, and Luke hints at their success in establishing the church as a community of faith when he refers to meeting 'the brothers' at Lydia's house (v.40). Such language was not used lightly in the early church. They not only believed that God had adopted them into a new family, they made every effort to strengthen good relationships. Paul's frequent appeals to Christians to build relationships of love indicate the importance of this task. It is wonderful to see the depth of committed relationships in a church plant that is prospering. Fellowship thrives on a common task and vision, and some of the strongest bonds of love that I have ever encountered have been in church plants.

A church is built on new relationships of love, but also requires *a foundation of teaching and prayer*, which Paul and his team could be relied upon to provide. However, the team had to do themselves out of a job, so it was vital to establish a self-sustaining preaching ministry within the new church. In the same way, we need to be sure today that a church-planting team has sufficient teaching and preaching gifts. But we need to be flexible, expecting new gifts to be given and new ministries to emerge. If we believe in the believers, and provide the right support and training, we can enjoy the privilege of seeing new leaders rise to the challenge, growing into ministries they may never have discovered in the sending church.

It is a universal truth that *where the church advances, opposition intensifies*. At Philippi Paul had to deal with a period of intense spiritual opposition when he delivered the slave girl whose shouting was a continual distraction (vv.16–18). The fact that this girl spoke the truth about Paul and his team didn't make the spirit within her any less of an opponent to the gospel. As Shakespeare observed:

> And oftentimes to win us to our harm,
> The instruments of darkness tell us truths.
> *Macbeth,* Act 1 scene 3

Effective evangelism and church planting are impossible without taking account of spiritual warfare. In half nights of prayer, prayer walking and prayer meetings in homes, we need to recognise and pray that we will overcome the forces that despise the gospel of light. I am reluctant to encourage believers to address directly the principalities and powers for the simple reason that this does not seem to be how the early church prayed. But I passionately believe that when we church plant with prayer, we must pray for protection as well as advance, and for the frustration of the evil one and all his deceptive tricks.

Spiritual opposition was only half the story, and Paul and his team were also *prepared to take the heat of human opposition to the infant church* (vv.19–24). Sadly, in the history of mission and revival, the most strident opposition to evangelism, growth and significant advance of the gospel has often been voiced by the leaders of existing churches. If church planting accelerates in this generation, growing opposition from some churches appears inevitable. We must expect and not be dismayed or distracted by any misrepresentation, whether in the press or in ecclesiastical gossip.

In jail, Paul and Silas *demonstrated determination and resolve*, even before the miraculous earthquake that set them free, when they continued to pray and sing praises (v.25). Persistence is not a quality with which many are accustomed within a society based on instant gratification. But persistence and determination are the staple diet of church planting once the initial novelty wears off. In effective church planting, persistence must be modelled by leaders and learned by the team. As Tom Marshall has observed, when things are going smoothly the leader may seem almost unnecessary, but when things get tough, leaders who know persistence will come into their own. If some are losing heart and the initial momentum is weakening, the team leader has a special responsibility to show stickability.

Finally, before their departure from the city, Paul and his team met again with the believers in the home where the church now gathered regularly. Having established the church, taught them the faith and shown them how to respond to opposition, they had one final gift for the new church; *the vital resource of encouragement* (v.40). The New Testament calls for an overwhelming extravagance in mutual encouragement, which is light years away from conventional British understatement and reserve: 'Encourage one another daily, as long as it is called Today, so that none of you may be hardened by sin's deceitfulness' (Hebrews 3:13).

Mrs Thatcher used to speak about terrorists yearning for the 'oxygen of publicity'. If the army of God is to sustain high morale for the advance of the kingdom, we need the oxygen of encouragement. In all too many churches, leaders and people alike are starved of encouragement and so grow weary, defensive or withdrawn. Some people feel embarrassed about saying an encouraging word in case it sounds foolish or does no more than state the obvious. How much better did Paul understand that an encouraging word is never wasted, above all for a young church plant: 'They met with the brothers and encouraged them' (Acts 16:40). Without encouragement, we stunt one another's spiritual growth.

Churches that reproduce

The speed with which Paul moved on from Philippi may cause some surprise. No sooner was he out of jail than he prepared to leave. His strategy was not to build the church around himself, but rather to do himself out of a job. Having established the church, he expected the believers to stand on their own feet, and not to be dependent upon the apostolic team for ever. The reason for Paul's relative haste is, of course, that his vision for Philippi was part of a much larger strategy. Luke explains that Paul was eager to plant a church in Philippi because it was 'the leading city of that district of Macedonia' (Acts 16:12). Once the church plant had taken root, Paul knew it was time to move on. Carrying a responsibility to take the gospel throughout the Gentile world, Paul evidently intended to plant a vibrant church in each regional centre.

Planting a church in Philippi was only the first step in the apostolic mission strategy for the region. When Paul moved on he didn't expect the young church to turn in on itself and concentrate solely on looking after the believers. Nor did he expect them simply to continue the task of witness in Philippi. There is not a hint of paternalism in Paul's attitude to the churches he planted. He is never patronising, never encourages an unhealthy dependency, never conveys the impression that they may not be able to cope without him.

Rather, he speaks of them warmly as his partners in the gospel (Philippians 1:5). Throughout the area for which Philippi was the leading city, the apostle handed over to the Philippian believers a regional mission responsibility.

This same policy is apparent in Paul's first letter to the Thessalonians, whose seaport city was a major trade centre, the capital of its province and the largest city in Macedonia. Paul commends them because they have taken the 'Lord's message' through Macedonia, Achaia and beyond (1 Thessalonians 1:8). This regional responsibility couldn't possibly stop short at 'hit and run' proclamation. We must surely conclude that Paul expected every church he established in a strategic city to embark on a church-planting programme throughout the surrounding region.

Planting, not cloning

The gospel has an unchanging content, but the duty of an evangelist is to find new forms of presentation to make the gospel clear in each new setting and generation. The church of Christ cherishes an unchanging gospel, but the task of church leaders is to implement church structures and activities which promote strength and health in the church of today. That means the forms are the servants not the masters of the gospel – existing structures must always be expendable.

The structures of any church can easily become our master if we are not careful. Secondary practices, preferences and customs gradually become considered essential and intrinsic to the gospel. Creative experiment hardens into a rigid and fixed way of being church: 'Ours is the only way that is right!' When we plant churches we need to give freedom to the new church to develop a life and style of its own, which cannot be altogether predictable and must not be controlled by the sending church. There is often an unspoken pressure for us to reproduce the secondary characteristics of an existing church. That is not church planting; it is church cloning. We are not called to open a church franchise, but to establish communities of love.

The apostle Paul didn't travel with a blueprint of church structures. Despite the hostility of some Jewish Christians, he was committed to the liberty of the churches he planted. They wanted every church to be a Jewish church, but even at Corinth, where the church nearly collapsed into the immoral behaviour rampant in that city, Paul was prepared to take the risks of establishing an indigenous church. Rather than being organised just like the church in Jerusalem or Antioch, each new church was given responsibility to incarnate the gospel in its own particular context. Real church planting has no place for clones or carbon copies.

It is absolutely vital to recognise that apostolic church planting is more a process than an event. Because we are used to new church buildings being opened with a day of celebrations, we are conditioned to think of an institution with a launch date or opening ceremony. For the first Christians, church planting was all about relationships – with God, with one another, and with the surrounding community. Relationships aren't opened like buildings; they grow with love, patience and time. A church is never planted in a day. You take adventurous steps of faith one at a time, waiting for the new plant to take root in the soil of the local community.

The multi-congregational church

A few years ago, all church planting seemed to lead to a new, independent church. The rapid growth of Ichthus and Kensington Temple in London has established the viability of an alternative model: the multi-congregational church. Since we have repeatedly emphasised the liberty of the local church in the New Testament to explore its own development, it would be quite absurd to suggest that this is the only model, but it certainly has some major advantages.

The power of celebrations

Many are now familiar with the church growth analysis that identifies three sizes of meeting: the cell, for personal support; the congregation, for teaching and participation; and the celebration, for motivation and envisioning. In a multi-congregational church, the members of a small, pioneering congregation are able to meet as part of a larger church on a regular basis. In our church, the planters join the central celebration on Sunday evenings. This can help sustain momentum and morale when the going gets tough.

The homogeneous unit principle

When church growth teaching was first popularised, this was the principle that many of us couldn't stomach. In practice, many growing churches tend to attract a certain kind of person who naturally feels at home within a congregation made up largely of their peers. It is easy to see why this happens, since in all human activities the same principle applies – like attracts like. Few Christian leaders have been prepared to make this a pre-emptive strategy, deliberately targeting a particular kind of person. We want to reject the concept of a socially exclusive church, yet we have to face the reality that the kind of congregation which grows fastest is usually made up of people who have a lot in common. For the church that decides to become multi-congregational, the principle of an inclusive church and the homogeneous unit principle can, for the first time, be embraced simultaneously. Culturally specific congregations can readily be multiplied within the spectrum of an inclusive church.

Some churches resist strongly the concept of separate congregations for micro-communities. I remember Peter Wagner describing a new church in California for Vietnamese refugees. At first they were a small handful, renting the premises of a Baptist church. As the Vietnamese congregation became established, the conviction gradually grew that it was not the Lord's best plan for them to remain isolated. They explained this conviction to the Baptists, and suggested they might join together as one church. The Baptist leaders readily welcomed this proposal with one condition: if they were to become one church they would have to worship together, as a single congregation.

I can sympathise with this opinion, because at one time I would have voiced it myself. However, the Vietnamese had a problem: if they were absorbed into an English speaking church, some of their members would instantly feel out of place and marginalised. Worse still, their evangelistic impetus would be undermined, because at present they were easily accessible to other Vietnamese, who would be much more wary about visiting an American Baptist church. No compromise could be found and the churches remained separate.

The vision of the Vietnamese believers was later fulfilled, when they became part of another church in the area. This time it was agreed that although there would sometimes be whole church celebrations, they would continue Sunday by Sunday to meet as a separate congregation. The American church that welcomed them into their fellowship had the wisdom to understand that to function as one church was the best way to express new unity in Christ, but to continue as distinct congregations was the best way to maximise future conversion growth.

Expertise and resources

In the multi-congregational church, the new congregation continues to have full access to all the resources of the whole church. This not only applies to finance or office equipment, it can also mean, for example, that people with acute needs can be referred to the central pastoral or counselling team. In practice, the benefits are quickly mutual. On the one hand, the sending church has a great deal to give because of its size and resources. At the same time, the church-planting team are out on the front line, and will rapidly be able to teach most sending churches a great deal about practical evangelism and urgent prayer. Since we planted out, those involved have nearly all turned up at whole church half nights of prayer. When you are in the front line, you know you cannot get by without earnest prayer!

A Sainsbury's strategy

In Britain Sainsbury's have pioneered the move from city centre supermarkets to out of town mega-stores. Senior directors have recently acknowledged that there must inevitably be limits to the concentration of shopping into hypermarkets. It has been suggested that the year 2000 may see the development of a new strategy, developing smaller outlets which complement the hypermarkets by providing specialised products for niche markets. In this way, Sainsbury's intend to maximise their volume of customers and give the consumer every opportunity to use one of their outlets.

The multi-congregational church is able to develop a 'Sainsbury's strategy'. On the one hand, the new congregations can be like a chain of specialised shops, each given the liberty to target a particular group and develop its own style. On the other hand, the central church can be seen as a mission centre providing a range of ministries, rather like the wide choices of the hypermarket. Of course, such a strategy is only workable if the individual congregations are given a high degree of room for manoeuvre in order to specialise for their target community. Only when the congregations are given the respect and liberty to find their own style of cultural engagement can the 'Sainsbury's strategy' really begin to succeed.

Believing in the believers

The pioneering Anglican missiologist, Roland Allen, wrestled with the enormous contrast between Paul's missionary methods and the approach of Western missionaries in the modern era. Allen exposed and rejected the typically paternalistic and patronising attitudes that were producing converts who remained dependent for life upon the missionaries' leadership. Allen concluded that what he called the 'spontaneous expansion of the church' was directly related to Paul's confidence in the resourcefulness of the new believers. Paul didn't simply discover the power of positive thinking; he believed passionately in the power of the Holy Spirit in his converts. As a result, he not only entrusted them with making their local church work, but he gave them regional evangelism and church-planting responsibilities. What is more, Paul knew how to help others believe in themselves, inspiring them with confidence that the same Spirit of God they had seen at work in Paul and his team was now empowering them. 'If we have no faith in the power of the Holy Spirit in them, they will not learn to have faith in the power of the Holy Spirit in themselves. We cannot trust them, and they cannot be worthy of trust; and trust, the trust which begets trustworthiness, is the one essential for any success in the Pauline method.'[1]

If a church is to be truly indigenous and culturally engaged, a great deal of freedom is required. Freedom to discover what it means to serve Christ in a local community. Freedom to pioneer new ways of being church in a particular cultural context. Freedom to become different from the sending church or from the conventional churches of that denomination or stream. And freedom to believe in and experience the equipping power of the Holy Spirit.

The minister or leadership team that tries to control every initiative has missed the point. If we want church planting to multiply, we need to encourage free-range initiative and vision. I long to hear more often of home groups or those living in a particular area discovering a sense of burden, beginning to pray together and offering to conduct preliminary research. In this way we may begin to enjoy in the West the wonderful momentum of church planting seen in the developing world – church planting by the people and for the people. I spoke to one leader in Brazil who told me that one Sunday a group of believers asked if they could borrow the church minibus. On asking what they had in mind they explained, 'We've been praying for some time for our part of town, so we thought we'd do an open air to prepare the way for a new congregation!' This, in Roland Allen's glorious phrase, represents something deeply unconventional to the organised Christianity of the Western world – *the spontaneous expansion of the church.*

I have met newly married couples and also those in middle age who have suddenly discovered an unplanned pregnancy.

---

[1] *Missionary Methods – St Paul's or Ours?*

In the same way, if we embrace the radical implications of every member mission, a church may have the pleasant surprise of discovering that a new church plant is on the way, without having deliberately planned it! We will never find in the New Testament a ready-made structure to impose upon our evangelism or church life. But if we are serious about the need for a massive advance in church planting today, we need to return to our roots, and learn afresh from the methods, convictions and enthusiasm of the greatest church planter – the apostle Paul.

PART THREE

TIME TO ADVANCE

10
The Church Meets Post-Modernity

The emerging tomorrow

The Independent newspaper came up with a memorable explanation of post-modernism which went something like this:
'No one knows what it really means. Therefore if you want to
impress people it is advisable to refer to post-modernism as
often as possible!' The term 'post-modernism' has the characteristic, over-considered clumsiness of modern academic
terminology. In a literal sense it is impossible to be post-
modern, since the natural meaning of 'modern' is simply
that which pertains to life, values and thought in the present
day. However, what the term seeks to recognise is that there is
an unmistakable and seismic cultural shift under way at the
end of the 20th century, which is increasingly impacting the
whole of life. Strictly speaking there are two distinct components. *Post-modernism* is an established school of academic
thought, increasingly influential in many disciplines of the
arts and social sciences. *The post-modern condition* is the connected, but not identical, perspective on life that is becoming

increasingly influential among ordinary people at the dawn of the 21st century.

In order to understand some of the major ingredients of the post-modern worldview, we need first to recognise the characteristics of the era we are leaving behind, which has come to be known as modernity. A worldview is different from a well thought out philosophy. A worldview is a way of seeing; a set of commonly held assumptions about the nature and purpose of human existence. Modernism as a worldview grew in the fertile interaction of post-enlightenment rationalism and the Western experience of the age of empires and the industrial revolution. Rationalism held several confident assumptions: the power of reason to make sense of a reasonable world; the possibility and availability of objective, even absolute truth; the universal reliability of propositional, abstract truth statements; a settled sense of self. The explosion of new technologies through the 19th century created a social history that seemed to demonstrate conclusively the triumph of reason: science and technology could harness natural resources for the unhindered and accelerating advance of civilisation. The scientific theory of evolution was extrapolated to become the pseudo-scientific myth of evolutionism – the confident and assured ascent of man towards a future that was guaranteed to be unreservedly utopian. There was an instinctive trust and respect for authority figures and an underlying, confident expectation that human existence is meant to be purposeful.

Post-modernism rattles the blithe confidence of this optimistic myth of unfettered advance. Heisenberg's uncertainty principle made scientific objectivity more complex, even as Einstein's theory of relativity unsettled the previously inviolate assumptions of Newtonian physics. Beyond the narrow confines of the scientific laboratory there has been a loss of confidence in the availability or even the possibility of universal, absolute and objective truth. People prefer no longer to say, 'Is it true?', but tend instead to ask the narrower, personal question, 'Is it true for me?' Subjectivism has overturned the assumptions of objective reality. Just as there are now splinters of personal truths rather than any absolute and universal framework of truth, the sense of self has splintered. With every season, the fashion gurus invite the young, beautiful and rich to yet another makeover. Madonna is the icon of self in a post-modern age, reinventing herself with every new album and concert tour. Self is no longer a matter of depth, substance and character, but rather of image and first impressions: what matters most is not maturity and wise judgement, but how politicians and entertainers come across in their thirty-second sound-bite on the evening news.

The downside of modern technology has smashed the naive idol of an assured, utopian destiny. We see the world's non-renewable resources being rapidly exhausted, as the West continues with an extravagant lifestyle to which the developing nations can never realistically aspire. There are simply not enough natural resources for them ever to catch up, even if the shackles of debt enslavement to the Western banks are ever broken. We have all become familiar with the consequences of toxic waste, destruction of the rain forest, and many species of wildlife facing imminent extinction. For those privileged to be living at the dawn of the 21st century, astonishing technological and medical advances have brought immeasurable advantages to human existence, but electricity and running water, antibiotics and organ transplants can do nothing to reverse the disquieting trends of family and community breakdown. Even in the medical sphere, the gains have become ambivalent, for the prospects of genetic manipulation and cloning raise at least as many spectres as hopes for the generations of the new millennium. Future expectations are increasingly dystopian. Many are beginning to express a deepening anxiety about the brave new world our children's children are likely to inherit. The Peter Pan generation of twenty- and thirty-somethings are deferring the responsibilities of parenthood as they seek to prolong the carefree indulgences of late adolescence, living for the now in self-indulgence and escapism, with very little expectation of purpose in life. We can also identify an underlying suspicion, even cynicism, towards almost all authority figures.

Here we must note a huge discrepancy between theoretical post-modernism and real post-modern people. The theoreticians have long argued that a further inevitable factor in the new world order is the collapse of moral absolutes. The new consensus, they claim, is not immoral but rather amoral – a refusal to accept that there is any longer a universal framework of moral absolutes to which everyone must adhere. The post-modern condition in the real world is rather more complex. In private morality, the right to do your own thing is widely championed. But the campaign against apartheid, the protests against live animal exports, the anti-road demonstrators, and the parents who campaign against child abusers moving to their neighbourhood all share the same conviction: certain kinds of behaviour are, quite simply, wrong, and must be resisted strenuously. The moral consensus has changed, so that certain patterns of behaviour that were illegal or met with general disapproval fifty years ago are generally accepted today. But ordinary people show no sign of turning their back on the assumption that we need to recognise and preserve a framework of clear and universal moral standards in order to continue to function as a reasonably civilised society.

We can sum up aspects of this seismic shift in expectations diagrammatically:

Modernist	Post-Modernist
objective reality	subjective reality
universal, absolute truth	pluralistic, personal truths
propositional statements	story and perspective
objective reality	subjective reality
triumph of progress	raped planet, broken lives
live with a purpose	live for NOW's experience
trust in authority figures	cynical towards authority figures
settled sense of self	fragmented sense of self
certainty and confidence	uncertainty and pessimism

The landmarks of loss of confidence can be traced in the headlines of post-war history. Confidence in political leadership has been repeatedly sapped by the hysteria of McCarthyism, Nixon's cynical machinations and Clinton's tawdry assignations. Too many of the great leaders who gave hope for a new kind of society fell victim to assassins, above all John F. Kennedy, Martin Luther King and Mahatma Gandhi. The immediacy of media in the age of television exploded the myths of heroism in warfare, when the carnage of Vietnam filled American news programmes. Oil slicks and declining fish stocks, rain forests on fire and the prospect of a silent spring as the population of British songbirds plummets with no insects left to eat from insecticide soaked fields, escalating levels of asthma among children and urban highways gridlocked with the sheer volume of cars; in so many ways the downside of the technological revolution has become inescapable, its damaging consequences long term or even irreversible.

The influence of television has undoubtedly intensified many of these trends, and has doubtless become the single most influential factor for ordinary people in shaping the post-modern way of looking at life. As TV stations proliferate in the satellite, cable and digital age, the percentage of the population likely to have watched any particular programme is diminishing. A shared life experience that can be discussed the next day over coffee, is transforming into a private world of entertainment; an individualised construct, tailor-made to personal preferences. The remote control has added incalcul-ably to this experience – it reinforces our sense of being in control and speeds our channel surfing. Those who would have left the TV passively on a single channel in the days when you still had to walk over to it and press a button to change channels, can now 'multi-task' in front of the TV. If nothing is sufficiently absorbing to capture our interest in full, we begin to watch several programmes simultaneously, bringing workaholic intensity even to the life of a couch potato.

Television is full of stories, personal viewpoints, makeovers of faces, clothes and homes in which the guest's image is reconstructed. Current affairs programmes have lost almost any sense of respect for senior politicians, who are grilled rigorously. The most appreciated interviewers often cultivate a sardonic, or even cynical, superiority towards the political high flyers they are questioning. It has also become almost obligatory for any issue to turn into a gladiatorial combat between two opposing points of view. There is rarely any quest for resolution or consensus. What matters for the ratings is that no ground is given, with the contributors – or is it contestants? – scoring knockabout debating points. We become collaborators in the fiction of serious television. Allowing ourselves to be entertained by a pantomime of earn-est debate, we as viewers are provided with a superior view-point above the clamour of contradictory convictions. TV's worldview is profoundly pluralistic and relativistic.

The ironic detachment of the post-modern condition is particularly apparent in advertising. The post-modern advert is all too knowing in its attitudes. Many ads tacitly acknowledge that they are expected to make a hard sell, and yet, however oblique and ironic their approach, the attempt to persuade or cajole us into the purchase is unremitting. We are hounded by the clamour of a thousand siren voices with another product to sell, another point of view to promulgate. Every time we turn on the TV, there are more perspectives, more stories, more reinvented selves. Our sense of identity is profoundly dependent upon the cathode ray. TV tells us what to like, what to wear and provides isolated post-moderns with a virtual community in the familiar faces of their favourite soap operas. We may no longer know our real neighbours' names, but we know the secret life stories of everyone who lives on Coronation Street or Ramsay Street. The nightly TV schedule has become for most people their fullest induction into the experience of the post-modern condition.

Stuck in yesterday

I rushed down the steps and onto the platform, only to see the train already leaving the station. The doors were closed, the train was moving and I was left behind. Anyone who travels by public transport will sooner or later have that kind of experience. You feel frustrated, but also powerless, as the train relentlessly draws away from the station. The same kind of experience now faces churches that refuse to adapt. The train of post-modernity is leaving the station, and forms of Christianity that are wedded to the dying culture of modernity will eventually die with it.

Evangelicals are therefore faced with a crucial question: Can evangelical convictions be separated from the modernistic culture which has been their breeding ground in the West for so long? That is not to say that modernism is automatically pro-evangelical. The modernistic quest for certainty and the triumph of reason resulted in the liberalism that rejected the possibility of supernatural interventions, such as miracles or the resurrection of Christ. It also produced the dogmatic secular rationalism of those who assert that 'science has disproved religion' – a generalisation as sweeping and meaningless as to suggest that 'history has disproved poetry'. When an atheistic scientist presents his scientific analysis, he is endeavouring to be a good scientist, but when he attempts to draw theological conclusions from his scientific data, he has crossed the boundary between two distinct intellectual disciplines. The fact that he is an excellent scientist is no guarantee as to the quality of his theological reasoning, and his scientific credentials are neither here nor there in an unrelated field of academic enquiry.

The cultural spawning ground for theological liberalism also generated the equal and opposite dogmatism of the fundamentalists. In response to secular rationalism, the fundamentalists produced a rationalistic account of Christian faith in which everything would be proved in the court of reason. They believed in every biblical miracle, but endeavoured to explain their authenticity by non-miraculous means. They wanted a watertight Bible, in which everything could be reduced to an abstract proposition within a rigorously detailed systematic theology. Some would have preferred the New Testament to contain Calvin's Institutes rather than Jesus' parables. After all, Jesus' stories are so open-ended, leaving us with more questions than answers. Others struggle to take account of the extraordinarily diverse genres of biblical texts and the subtle interplay between different perspectives and theological emphases within the Bible, particularly when differing emphases are held in tension within the strands and layers of a particular book.

Fundamentalists are theological flatlanders, obliterating the richly diverse terrain of the landscape of biblical theology, reducing everything to a codified, one-dimensional series of abstract propositions. In their pursuit of rationalistic certainty, they typically become sectarian, negative and suspicious, intellectually arrogant towards any who disagree with them on any minutiae of biblical interpretation. It certainly is the case that the Christian faith is reasonable – we can give a reasoned defence of our convictions – but there is too much of the supernatural in orthodox Christianity for it ever to become narrowly rationalistic. That is, the Christian gospel simply cannot be circumscribed and hemmed in by the limits of the human mind.

Rationalistic fundamentalists not only exhibit an intellectual arrogance towards those who have drawn different conclusions from the data, they also tend to be deeply suspicious of almost all spiritual experience. Their instinctive first reaction to hearing of a healing, a dream or a vision is to be wary and negative. They may allow for spiritual encounters in principle, at least in biblical times, but their governing assumption is that such happenings in today's world, if not altogether invalid, are best treated with extreme scepticism. Ironically, because fundamentalism and liberalism share the same cultural assumptions, they are equally indisposed to the possibility of contemporary divine self-revelation and miraculous intervention. Rationalistic religion in all its forms dogmatically excludes from contemporary life and spirituality any surprising eruptions of the divine presence.

It is extremely difficult for any of us to be self-critical of our own cultural context. The worldview which we inhabit seems instinctively and inevitably to be both natural and right. This universal human tendency produces particular risks for Evangelicals. The earnest desire to defend the unchanging gospel so easily spills over into an instinctive defence of the package deal of our particular cultural expression of evangelical convictions. The badge of honour among some Evangelicals is an emphatic adjective – *conservative* Evangelicals. If this meant a zeal to conserve the unchanging gospel, it would be an adjective of unambiguous honour for every orthodox Christian. But for some it has come to mean an instinctively reactionary posture towards anything new in both society and the church.

In academic theology, this attitude of intellectual arrogance was summed up in the words of Charles Hodge, who is said to have asserted that there was nothing new to teach in conservative theology. The denial of any possibility of new insights, new approaches to the analysis of the biblical data, new reflections on theology in the light of present-day knowledge, new applications of theology to the issues of a new cultural setting whether in the arts, science and technology, social policy, the welfare of the planet or countless other avenues of human enquiry, such narrow-mindedness can only mean one thing: here is a dead-end theology, too arrogant and closed to be willing to learn or develop in any way. Bible colleges still suffer from the uninformed zeal of fundamentalistic students, who are sweepingly confident that they have all the answers before they have even discovered what today's pressing questions really are.

More widely influential and no less disturbing is the power of the prevailing culture upon culturally captive Evangelicals. Even though the old culture is breaking down, we still face the residual impact of an evangelical Pharisaism that was deeply legalistic. At one time, Evangelicals were defined by a zealous conformity to their secondary distinctives. Evangelicals didn't drink or smoke, avoided dances and the cinema, minimised make-up, maximised dress length and generally preferred old-fashioned clothing and cautious leisure pursuits. However, an Evangelical from the world of fifty years ago would be astonished at the clothing and hairstyles, the relaxed attitude to alcohol and the new informality in worship that characterise most Christian events at the end of the 20th century. Some evangelical leaders took the initiative in repudiating the old sub-culture, recovering the Pauline emphasis upon the profound liberty of every individual in Christ. But the most decisive factor in the death of the old-style evangelical conformity was probably the in-built defiance to yesterday's rules that prevails almost instinctively among the post-war generations. Perhaps we have ceased to be the slaves of yesterday's evangelical conventionality, only to join the rest of our society as slaves of the new and young, the hip and trendy.

Yesterday's gone

One cultural captivity is easily exchanged for another. As the cultural tide began to recede for the closed universe of secular rationalism, the growing influence of existentialism was paralleled by the rise of charismatic renewal. Positively, charismatic renewal sought to recover the biblical doctrine of the present availability of the Holy Spirit and his gifts. Negatively, charismatic renewal resulted in some becoming tongues-centred and others 'my blessing'-centred. There was a trivialising addiction to novelty, to this year's fashionable emphasis, and to a cult of personality centred upon 'anointed leaders'. There were illusions of ultimacy, as if tongues or inner healing or prophecy or power evangelism or spiritual warfare or regularly falling to the carpet could instantaneously and permanently transform the life of the devout individual, the renewed church or even a whole nation.

In recovering the biblical emphasis upon present-day experience of the Spirit, many first and second generation charismatic leaders failed to emphasise that one of the key ways in which we encounter God is through his unchanging Word. As a result, some expressions of charismatic renewal show signs of degenerating into a kind of 'evangelical lite' – full of today's experience of God, but cultivating an underlying, increasing and ultimately enervating tendency to biblical illiteracy.

What of the new churches? In global terms, their impact remains minuscule, but in Britain the house churches of the seventies have become the new church streams of the nineties. Careful examination suggests that they have become part of the problem as well as part of the solution. In their beginnings, relatively young leaders emerged with fresh new approaches to church life. There was a genuine and vigorous attempt to re-engage the local church with the work of the Spirit and the task of mission. Ichthus is probably best understood as an evangelistic movement in south east London that seeks to give expression to its mission in the form of local congregations.

A generation after their inception, some of the new churches are best understood as a late flowering of modernism. This applies in particular to those groupings that seek to find in the New Testament a definitive and inflexible blueprint for church structures. The general consensus of New Testament scholarship is that we find an experimental diversity in the life and leadership of the first churches. Their early development of leadership teams and their patterns of interrelationship between churches seem unusually pragmatic and delightfully spontaneous. Modernistic thinking craves order and fixed systems and therefore looks to the New Testament to provide an absolutist blueprint for church structures in every culture and generation. Modernistic new churches are almost unavoidably separatist. They may deny that they are a denomination, but they are also inclined to affirm that they alone are planting 'New Testament-type churches'.

The logic is impeccable. They see themselves ultimately not as *a denomination* but rather as *the church*. The more extreme strand of Restorationist teaching reinforces this exclusivity. Many Christians willingly speak about the importance of restoring New Testamental values and priorities to the church – surely an attractive and vital task for the church in every generation. Restorationists describe their particular brand of church as the equivalent of the restoration of post-exilic Israel in the Old Testament. No longer content with New Testament parallelism, where the universal church is seen at least to some degree to be the new Israel alongside God's continuing purposes for the Jews, these Restorationists lay exclusive claim to Israel typology. If their churches are the true Israel of the Restoration, all other churches are either outside God's promises altogether, or at best represent those Jews who were content to remain in exile. According to hyper-Restorationism, their churches really are the only true – or truly faithful – churches, fully implementing New Testament structures, and fully in line with the purposes of God. If you cannot buy their theology of the church, the sectarianism leaves a sour taste.

According to Restorationism, once the original church order has been implemented, the blueprint more or less guarantees rapid advance. Such networks of churches are therefore particularly prone to triumphalism, talking up their advance to the full while discreetly playing down their share of the inevitable struggles and failures of church life. They readily convey the impression that, without exception, all their churches are vibrant, large and growing rapidly. If triumph has not already arrived, then it tends to be promised just around the next corner – perhaps during their next major conference or immediately following implementation of the latest refinement to their church structures. There is a fine line which indiscriminate enthusiasm finds easy to cross, between envisioning and hype, between faith-building confidence in the truth of the gospel and spin-doctoring salesmanship, recruiting for a new denomination.

The most obvious parallel in recent church history is with the Exclusive Brethren: an earnest desire to be thoroughly biblical in church order, a dogmatic insistence that theirs is the fullest, finest or even the only legitimate expression of church life, and a tendency to be suspicious or even arrogantly dismissive of other kinds of church, especially the historic denominations. Modernistic evangelicalism has been plagued throughout its history with a tendency to fragment. Almost every new denomination has emerged as a result of Evangelicals becoming over-confident that they have at last cracked the code and discovered in the New Testament the definitive pattern of church life and order. The new churches in Britain have surely been around long enough for this kind of naive and extravagant claim to have lost all credibility. If the primary concern of New Testament ecclesiology was establishing the right structures, twenty-five years of new church experiment ought to have been long enough for the resultant success to be unambiguous and conclusive. Some Evangelicals have craved more certainty and finality about church structures than the New Testament churches can ever provide. For *several hundred years* modernistic Evangelicals with separatist tendencies have been making similar claims for *several thousand denominations*, many of which, in their infancy, have been presented as the full and final expression of the New

Testament teaching on the church. History teaches us that this kind of new church is really rather old-fashioned. We have seen separatist claims of ultimacy many times before.

The last child of dogmatic modernism, those new churches that are exclusive, separatist and triumphalist, are best understood as a kind of Pentecostal Brethren, combining pentecostal enthusiasm for the gifts of the Spirit with the Exclusive Brethren's tendency to sectarianism. This edge of pre-ecumenical exclusivity is likely to prove increasingly unpalatable to ordinary Christians in a post-denominational age. With the hardening of the arteries among early leaders, second and third generation leadership will almost inevitably lead to an increasing institutionalisation. Like the new farmers at the end of *Animal Farm*, the new denominations may soon become indistinguishable from those they once expected to replace. Milton once caustically observed that presbyter was but priest writ large. In similar vein we note that modernistic new churches began by claiming to have restored apostles, but what they have ended up with are, in all but name, the bishops of a new denomination. That is not to say that individual churches are not doing a good job. But denominational maturity requires a frank repudiation of all inflated claims about the ultimacy of any particular pattern of church structures and government. Only then can new churches play their full part in ecumenical partnership with the historic denominations.

Searching for tomorrow

At the opposite end of the church spectrum are found those few churches dedicated to a thoroughgoing and radical exploration of what it means to function as church in the post-modern context. Here is the advance guard of post-modern Christianity, unafraid to sacrifice the sacred cows of conventional churchmanship, enthusiastic in their zealous dedication to experiment with the new. We may trace three major hazards at this end of the spectrum. First, just as modernism feeds rationalism and fundamentalism, post-modern assumptions are likely to feed a suspicion of intellectual rigour and hard reasoning that can lead to anti-intellectualism or even irrationality and also to biblical illiteracy. Why make an effort when you can effortlessly enjoy the experience? Secondly, being a maverick on the margins can become self-authenticating, tempting self-styled radicals to assume that whenever their latest experiment in worship or church life is criticised by other Christians, the very fact of such opposition must prove that their experiment is right. Thirdly, post-modernism promotes a new quest for an authentic spirituality, rooted in the wisdom of the past and contemporary in its expression. Positively, this can free Christians from the generational arrogance that assumes that the latest is always the best and re-opens the spiritual disciplines of 2,000 years of living faith. Negatively, a distinctively post-modern reconstruction of the past can result in a kind of ahistorical, arbitrary confection.

The strengths and weaknesses of the post-modern exploration and recovery of the past are exemplified in the current high standing of 'Celtic Christianity'. One music publisher told me that such is the present vogue for all things Celtic that the very appearance of the word 'Celtic' on a CD cover is enough to increase the sales significantly. Positively, some in the more remote and rugged parts of Britain are rediscovering their own ethnic and spiritual roots in an ancient expression of the faith that combines liturgy and spontaneity in worship, a community of disciples under a common covenant of love and spiritual discipline, a devotion to worship and mission, and a willingness to develop a rich creation theology alongside a theology of the cross. In all these ways, many have found the rediscovery of Celtic Christianity profoundly enriching. It makes a refreshing change from what C.S. Lewis called the 'chronological snobbery' of modernism, where the prejudice is that if anything is new it must be better, if anything is ancient it is probably boring and second rate.

At the same time, there is a curious parallel between the pre-Raphaelite movement at the end of the 19th century and today's Celtism. The pre-Raphaelites invented a pseudo-historical era of mythical purity and simplicity, just as some of today's self-styled new Celts seem singularly indifferent to historical precision as they search for a pre-Reformation nirvana in the history of the western European church. We may be able to trace three strands of disillusionment that have quickened this quest. First, a disillusion with the historical Protestant denominations, sometimes still rehearsing the disputes and conflicts of the Reformation, often culturally ineffective in the post-modern setting, and traditionally inhospitable to contemporary use of the full biblical range of the gifts of the Spirit. Secondly, a disillusion with the late modernistic pretensions of the kind of new church that claims to provide the definitive restoration of the New Testament's infallible blueprint for church order. Thirdly, a recognition that something more than conventional charismatic renewal is required to bridge the cultural gap to the post-Christian generations of the third millennium.

Not all that claims the name 'Celtic' has the same origins. Some is self-critical and historically precise. Some looks more like an arbitrary amalgam, a romanticised, wish-fulfilment fantasy typical of the new world of faction (a curious mixture of fact and fiction that has become fashionable in TV docu-drama), where objective reality and historical objectivity are lost in a soup of subjectivity. Authentic Celtism is reconstructing an ancient spirituality in a new cultural setting, whereas pseudo-Celtism is likely to prove a passing fancy – a fad that will fall from fashion as quickly as it arose. In short, if the sectarian kind of new churches are the last flowering of fundamentalistic modernism, at the opposite extreme, pseudo-Celtism – as opposed to authentic neo-Celtism – may be the first instance of a post-modern cultural captivity at the margins of contemporary evangelicalism.

Despite the risks of going overboard and of disproportionality and eccentricity in their emphases, the wider church has great need of the creativity of these pioneering post-modern radicals. Some of the risks they take will inevitably lead to failures, but when the church is not best known for its burgeoning creativity, these radicals are likely to lead the way for others. We have no need to follow them into experiments that fail, but whenever they get it right, countless others in the historical denominations are sure to benefit eventually. We must be grateful to those not afraid to take risks on the cutting edge of cultural engagement in the laboratory of experiment where post-modern expressions of church are beginning to take shape.

A post-modern evangelicalism

What then are some of the key ingredients for an evangelicalism reconfigured for the post-modern world?

- We need to recover a biblical *humility*. Our vision and theology are incomplete, for we see through a glass darkly. The apostle Paul is a great hero of evangelical exposition, and we need to recover his emphasis upon the *mystery* of the gospel. Anyone who thinks they have sewn up every last detail of Christian doctrine understands very much less than they suppose.

- We need to learn better how to be *generous and gracious*, both to one another and particularly to non-Evangelicals, recognising our common faith even where there is much disagreement among us on secondary issues. We also need to affirm that evangelicalism finds its place within orthodox Christianity, but is by no means the sum of orthodox expressions of the faith.

- We need to create a climate of *openness*, learning once again to be creative, willing to experiment and eager to explore, both in theology and church life. The Word does not change, but we need to be open to new insights and applications derived from the eternal truths of biblical revelation.

- We need to concentrate upon *guarding the essential gospel* rather than our particular package deal. While not dispensing with gospel essentials, we must be careful not to major on minors, over-emphasising our secondary concerns.

- We need to discover more about *the creative exploration and application of the gospel in a new cultural setting*. We should never change the heart of the gospel, but its expression always needs to be made new.

- We need to demonstrate a fresh willingness *to separate out the timeless gospel* from the cultural clothes of modernistic evangelicalism. The Bible is surely designed always to confront the subtle compromises of our ways of being church and pursuing the life of discipleship, and never should be so misread as merely to reinforce our instinctive theological and cultural prejudices.

- We need a style of preaching *that makes no claim to have all the answers*. We don't need preachers who impose upon us with overbearing authoritarianism, promoting specious standardisation for every Christian's prayer life, marriage, successful career and so on, often developing a compilation of mythical stereotypes of narrow saintly conformity. We are fellow sinners, understanding only partially the implications of the gospel and giving no more than a fragmentary expression to the gospel in our daily lives, so we need to beckon one another onward. The idea is not that others should meet us where we have already arrived, but that they should join us in a voyage of spiritual discovery, exploring and discovering a fuller, deeper conformity to the ways of Christ. We are fellow pilgrims, working out together what it means to live as 21st-century disciples.

- We need to be more concerned with *conforming to the character and values of Jesus Christ* than with the conventions of traditional evangelicalism. The disciples of Christ need to look a lot more like him if we are to make any significant headway and bridge our credibility gap to the generations of the 21st century.

11

Learning from Alpha

The success of Alpha has been phenomenal. In 1993 there were 200 courses running, which by September 1998 had escalated to 10,000 Alpha courses registered worldwide, with Christians in seventy-five countries now involved. In Britain there are more than fifty student courses, over 1,000 youth courses and even prisoners can join Alpha groups in nearly 100 prisons. The total number who have attended Alpha now exceeds more than 1.5 million, with many different kinds of church now eager to take part.

The impact of Alpha was demonstrated in November 1998 by an article featuring Nicky Gumbel in *Newsweek*. Significantly, the profile was not placed in the section devoted to religion, but was a back page interview. This is the prestigious slot which *Newsweek* reserves for the high profile opinion formers who are changing the face of our society. In his replies to the *Newsweek* journalist, Gumbel was typically self-effacing, dismissing the suggestion that Alpha's success had been helped by his own immensely appealing style of communication, both verbally and in print. He chose to emphasise two key factors: first that the unchanging message of the gospel is deeply attractive to a generation searching for spiritual reality; secondly that the latest marketing and advertising methods make sense as a way of making the Christian message as widely accessible as possible. *Newsweek* dubbed him 'Adman for Christianity' and highlighted his emphasis upon up-to-date promotion and marketing: 'All we're trying to do is take a message that's been around for 2,000 years and put it in [fresh] packaging.'

If we examine Alpha carefully we can identify ten key ways in which it has successfully bridged the gap to today's generations.

1. The fear· of an unfamiliar, religious environment is defused by Alpha beginning each session with a meal. In an unchurched society, this is very seeker friendly, putting people at their ease by meeting in a familiar social environment.

2. Post-modern people, particularly in the urban context where most of us live, experience increasingly unrooted lives. By meeting in groups, Alpha provides an opportunity to develop a sense of belonging, making friendship integral to the beginnings of a Christian lifestyle.

3. The opportunity to relax over a meal and interact in a group gives time for the enquirer to evaluate the Christians as real people. Rather than passive pew fodder, the believers can be tested out to see whether they really are religious dipsticks from another planet. Of course, if we are, that rather weakens the suitability of Alpha for our church . . .

4. The weekly talk is designed to be accessible, practical, jargon-free and shot through with humour and illustrations. The fact that Nicky Gumbel is a great story-teller

and the collector of an encyclopaedic supply of quotations, anecdotes and witticisms means that Alpha has been able to build in a quality control for the speakers at local Alphas. As Gumbel himself has observed, 'They are giving pretty well the same talk.' In some churches this is taken a step further by announcing a definite time limit for the Alpha talks. 'Alpha consumers' therefore know exactly what to expect and can be confident that the preaching will not ramble on all evening.

5. There is no pressure to convert quickly, recognising that coming to faith is usually a process rather than a crisis without preparation. People are given the space to make up their own mind in their own time. While there is opportunity for response, Alpha is expressly designed to exclude anything that is forced or manipulative. This respects people's integrity as free individuals, and recognises their need for space as they discover and explore the often unfamiliar terrain of the Christian faith.

6. In a society where the Bible has become a thoroughly unfamiliar book, the weekly exposure to passages gradually unlocks the Scriptures to the uninformed enquirer.

7. There is an interactive learning experience in the discussion groups. This connects with modern styles of teaching both at school and in workplace training, so is familiar to the unchurched. This is far removed from the traditional passive learning experience of preaching without feedback, in which someone six feet above contradiction tells you exactly what to think. Passivity in the pews leads to inactivity in the faith.

8. The discussion groups affirm the autonomy of the individual, which is a profoundly important value for postmodern generations. We want to know that we are free to express our own opinions and free to ask any questions

we like. This affirmation of individual freedom allows the enquirer to make a journey towards settled convictions and personal, living faith in their own time and way.

9. There is a reasoned defence of the gospel, but also an opportunity to encounter God in personal experience, particularly during the Holy Spirit weekend. The course seeks to provide an opportunity for us to engage in a search for God with our whole being – neither switching off our mind nor engaging in an exclusively theoretical enquiry.

10. The whole experience is fun and friendly, down to earth and enjoyable. There is not a whiff of Pharisaical legalism or super-spiritual piety in the entire course. This is Christianity for real people rather than religious air heads.

Among the most common criticisms of Alpha are the following: reflecting its origins in early charismatic renewal, it places a disproportionate emphasis on tongues; the first invitation to make a commitment, while not at all pressured, comes rather early in the course, long before some are anywhere near coming to faith; many great doctrines of the faith are under-represented (hardly surprising in a fifteen-session course). Perhaps surprisingly, Alpha's apologetic for the faith is still thoroughly modernistic, even though the experiential component would have felt quite alien in most churches earlier this century. In short, Alpha is not perfect, nor has it ever claimed to be. Whatever its limitations – and Alpha must surely still be seen as a work in progress rather than a finished product that should now be set in stone – an enormous number of churches and new converts have great reason to be thankful to God for this remarkably popular and well-received evangelistic course.

The post-Alpha church

We have identified many factors that give Alpha its unusual cultural accessibility. Almost all of them are entirely transferable, and could readily be adapted for other evangelistic enterprises, and even for our continuing discipleship programmes. Indeed they need to be implemented more widely, and with considerable urgency, since Alpha makes many more connections with the post-modern world than the Sunday services of most churches. This has resulted in two common problems for which Alpha itself cannot take the blame. There are Alpha converts who don't want to become churchgoers, but prefer to repeat Alpha *ad infinitum* because it is so much more lively and real than church. There are also organisers of Alpha courses who find themselves reluctant to press church attendance upon the new converts because they secretly and reluctantly recognise that their own church really is both boring and irrelevant.

Alpha suggests that church needs *more meals and fewer meetings*. Just as the army used to say that if something doesn't move, you should paint it white, churches sometimes behave as if no hour is complete without a church activity. Christians are so busy propping up the unwieldy programmes of their church that they have almost no social life. We don't have non-Christian friends because we have become immersed in the cradle to grave sub-culture of church activities. Jesus enjoyed many meals with both friends and strangers. A theologian coined the decidedly ponderous phrase 'table fellowship', but the reality is much more warm and friendly. Jesus enjoyed relaxing and spending time with people over a meal. The meals are so important in Alpha, bonding people together and putting them at their ease. Christians need to eat more – with fellow believers and with non-Christian friends, neighbours and colleagues. Coffee after a service and a church lunch aren't superfluous to the spiritual life of a church. They help us to express an often overlooked priority of the first Christians – 'they devoted themselves . . . to the fellowship' (Acts 2:42).

Alpha suggests that *more quality control and commitment to excellence is required for effective preaching.* When I published John Stott's superb book, *I Believe in Preaching*, I could not help but point out to the great man that all his quotations that enthused about preaching were from preachers, not from those who have to listen to us once or twice a week. The Alpha outlines and books make good connections with the world of today. They provide a rich supply of contemporary illustrations, statistics, and practical application, combined with good use of story and humour. On their own, these techniques would add up to no more than superficial preaching, lacking good biblical content. But just as we need preachers immersed in the word and urgent in prayer for their noble and daunting task, we also need preachers willing to maximise the impact of their words by careful consideration of contemporary communication skills. Sermon preparation is not complete with a clear outline of a well-honed series of points and a single statement that sums up the heart of the message. We need to learn how to use stories and humour to seize the imagination, aid the memory and help people to re-engage with the message if their mind has wandered. A good story part way through the sermon is like an advertising break in a serious TV programme: it can renew people's interest for what is to follow.

Alpha suggests that we need to *make more space for interactive learning.* Particularly in smaller churches, there could be an occasional session of 'grill the preacher' after the service. The learning experience is incomplete until we have had time to chew over what has been taught. Some churches have experimented with home groups exploring further the theme from last Sunday's sermon. Where buildings permit, some churches have even moved the congregation into smaller groups on a Sunday, so that there can be immediate feedback and discussion, clarification and further exploration of the preacher's theme, while the message and passage are still fresh in everyone's mind.

Alpha demonstrates the need for a *thorough integration of mind and heart* in our exploration of living faith. Just as there needs to be thoughtful substance in our preaching, there also needs to be opportunity for responsive openness to God. Some churches are like wild west saloons, but instead of hanging up your gun on the way in you might as well hang up your brain – loving God with the little grey cells is not seen as a spiritual virtue. Other churches are like shelves of books in an unused library: full of information, but lacking all evidence of life. We need to reject the false dichotomy that has produced some churches that are deeply suspicious of the mind and others that would prefer to amputate the heart. The Holy Spirit is not being kept so busy on Alpha weekends that he is unable to put in a personal appearance in local churches week by week! Those who have enjoyed an Alpha weekend will begin to struggle if the Holy Spirit seems conspicuous by his absence from our regular worship services.

Finally, Alpha has proved *the value of multimedia communication*. In a typical Alpha setting, at least three media are used: the written course book, the verbal presentation and the discussion group. Some churches use the Alpha videos, and there is growing and hardly surprising evidence that home groups find it much easier to follow a video than listen to a preacher on audio cassette. Other churches have added Powerpoint presentations and video clips from well-known movies, and have made good use of the performing arts.

Alpha seems to have come at just the right time to unleash a great surge of creativity, often from Christians who have been unable to find space for such contributions in Sunday services. It is time that Sundays caught up – not just with Alpha, but with the multimedia world of the digital age.

Alpha, in short, is not merely an exceptionally popular evangelistic course. It provides us with many signposts towards new ways of being church and communicating the gospel in the world of the 21st century.

12
Making It Happen

There can be no room for complacency as the church prepares for the 21st century. The issues we have explored in this book count for nothing unless a generation of leaders is raised up with the gifts, skills and determination to make it happen. What then are the qualities to be looked for in leaders who aspire to rebuild the church in the Western world? Our response to this vital question is illuminated by the example of one of the finest leaders of the Old Testament: Nehemiah. Just as Nehemiah became convinced that the time had come to rebuild Jerusalem, the time has surely come to rebuild the church.

Facing the captivity of the church

When Nehemiah heard reports of the devastation of Jerusalem he faced up to the harsh reality (Nehemiah 1:2–4). Empty optimism was no substitute for recognising the enormity and urgency of the task. Leaders today must begin with similar hard-nosed realism. Luther once wrote of what he called the Babylonian captivity of the church, enchained by the doctrinal confusion and moral corruption of the late medieval period. Today we must face up to the Western captivity of the church before it is too late.

We are captive to consumerism when church becomes another place where we are takers but never givers. Consumerism is deeply self-centred, with all energy focused on the question, 'What's in it for me?' Consumer Christians look for spiritual stimuli without moral requirements or active involvement – religion served up according to their personal preferences on Sundays and freedom to do their own thing all week. Such couch potato Christianity is stubbornly deaf to the demands of the gospel and the lordship of Christ.

We are captive to existentialism when the church gets wrapped up in seeking novel spiritual experiences. Extremists end up despising sound teaching, looking only for the latest sensation. A variant form of this captivity among leaders is *pragmatism without principle*, asking whether an approach will work, without asking more fundamental questions about whether it is biblically appropriate.

We are captive to anti-supernaturalism when our fears of excess or the fact that God's power is beyond our control leave us spiritually paralysed, not daring to be open to God. In one large evangelical church a missionary speaker was illustrating his message with some thrilling miracle stories. A mood of indifference was beginning to gather around him, so he observed, 'Many of you don't believe healings happen today, do you?' Several heads nodded in agreement. They claimed to believe in Christ and his resurrection, but in practice they were as sceptical, cynical and narrow-minded as any other materialists.

We are captive to the hobby mentality when church is treated as a way to kill an hour or two on Sundays, providing an 'interest outside the home'. The Christian gospel is not designed to furnish us with a religious club, but rather to call us to an alternative way of living. If the 21st-century church is to be effective in reaching the world, the army of God needs to be mobilised for mission, taking the gospel more seriously than anything else in life.

We are captive to low expectations or even survivalism when our highest ambition and hope is just to keep things going. A century of decline for most churches in Europe has instilled a defeatist attitude, even as many outsiders expect Christianity to limp towards extinction. The history of the church in recent generations and the expectations of our society mesh together to form a prison of unbelief. Many churches and church leaders are trapped by a poisonous, God-limiting whisper within: 'Revival could never happen here!'

Above all, we have in this book examined *the disastrous captivity of the church within a nostalgic sub-culture*, out of touch with the contemporary world. We have also put the spotlight on the *religious captivity of the church*, conforming all too often to the instinctive ways of human religion. Only when we face up to our acute captivity can we begin to make plans for the liberation of the church. Only as we begin to achieve this liberation, by recovering the convictions and priorities of the apostolic church, including its commitment to creative cultural engagement, can we talk seriously about effective mission in the modern world.

Humbling before God

In prayer Nehemiah humbled himself before God, confessing on behalf of the Jewish people and requesting success in his bold attempt to recover lost ground (1:4–11). The vital importance of staying humble before God can be lost in the valuable modern emphasis on good self-image. It is glorious to know that we are loved deeply and personally by the living God, and that we each have unique qualities that God is able to use to build his church and extend his kingdom. But God still delights to use those who are humble of heart (Isaiah 66:2).

We need to humble ourselves before God in utter dependence. Jesus taught that we can do nothing apart from him, and that we cannot bear fruit unless we remain in him (John 15:4–5) We need to give more than mental assent to this teaching. It needs to be prayed into the depths of our being, so that it informs and shapes the very core of how we see ourselves and how we relate to God.

We need to humble ourselves before God in repentance. Not only do we need to be ready to repent of our own sin, we need to repent on behalf of the church, which all too often has become spiritually weak, evangelistically ineffectual and morally compromised. When I have uncovered significant problems in the history of a local church, I have invited the church members to take time for repentance in prayer together.

We also need to confess the sins of our nation and ask God for mercy, even though we cannot actually repent on behalf of our fellow citizens. At first the collapse of communism in Eastern Europe seemed to signify the triumph of capitalism. With the passing years we see more clearly that while communism was an evil sham, with self-serving politicians proclaiming equality while enjoying the pampered lives of a privileged élite, the Western world is also morally decadent, with corruption in high places, violence on the streets, and broken relationships in countless homes. If the future of the capitalist world is anticipated upon the streets of our major cities, we may be perilously close to hell on earth. We urgently need to humble ourselves before God and seek mercy for our nations.

We also need to learn to lead with a humble attitude. The leader or preacher who longs to be used by God needs to learn transparency, so that Christ is always the focus of our proclamation and leadership. Even as the apostle Paul was prepared to declare his own weaknesses in order to bring the greater glory to Christ, we need to ensure that our style is Christ-centred, not self-elevating (2 Corinthians 4:7). If a preacher leaves his audience with no higher thought than that he's a wonderful man, he has not fed the flock with the word of life. He has inflicted instead the junk food of vanity. Anyone who leads without a humble spirit and a servant heart has not yet understood the rudiments of Christian leadership: no matter how gifted as leaders they may be, they risk having more in common with a political wheeler-dealer than with Jesus Christ.

We must also humble ourselves before others. The least of the brethren must always be worthy of the leader's attention. We must humble ourselves before our fellow leaders within a local church for correction and improvement, as well as encouragement. And we must humble ourselves before the leaders of other churches, slaying the lions of pride and independence that prevent us learning from one another. I well remember Gavin Reid observing that in the States, church leaders more often understand the wise humility of getting behind those with a national ministry, knowing their own lives will be enriched by supporting these key leaders and evangelists. Sadly, in Britain and Australia we are more prone to the tall poppy syndrome, knocking the successful or indulging in cheap cynicism to 'cut them down to size', rather than humbling ourselves and supporting those leaders of leaders whom God raises up in every generation. Only with the measure that we learn to humble ourselves before God and before others can we expect God to use us in mighty ways. For, as Peter and Paul both knew in their own experience, it is those whom

God is able to humble that he will raise up in due season (1 Peter 5:6).

Handling conflict

Nehemiah was not derailed by conflict. Despite or even because of his excellence in leadership, conflict and criticism dogged Nehemiah's path. He faced verbal opposition from those who ridiculed his vision as impossible and his achievements as pathetic (4:1–3), and also from those who impugned his motives, claiming that his vision was self-promoting (6:6) and the rebuilding of the walls was a mere cover for armed rebellion (2:19; 6:6–7). He faced physical intimidation (4:11; 6:1–4), and he faced conflict among his own men when they began to lose heart and have second thoughts about the rebuilding programme. First they became overwhelmed by the immensity of the task, and complained they could never complete it. Then they focused on physical danger, and as many as ten times over they repeated their appeal for the project to be abandoned (4:10, 12). None the less Nehemiah remained undeterred, and rallied his followers to the vision with the confident assurance that God would fight for them and secure victory (4:14, 20).

In any local church the minister tends to become a lightning conductor for conflict. If things are going well, praise God. If there are difficulties, blame the minister! The problem is that many ministers take responsibility for conflict in such a way as to internalise the pressures. I have met leaders struggling with high stress and self-doubt, with withdrawal, cynicism or burn-out, because they are facing the high seas of conflict and they feel it must be all their fault. Some question whether full-time ministry is really worth the hassle. Others wonder whether it is really worth the cost to bring growth and renewal to a church like theirs. You only have to read the life of Moses, Jesus or Paul to realise that conflict comes with the territory of leadership. It is quite inevitable. What is more, while Satan loves to fan the flames of conflict at every opportunity and we must never forget the reality of spiritual warfare (Ephesians 6:12), the various patterns of conflict promoted by the principalities and powers usually have distinctly human characteristics – gossip and backbiting, party spirit and malicious talk. The key issue is not how to avoid all conflict, but how to interpret its various forms and respond with as much wisdom and grace as we can obtain in Christ.

Leaders can face impossible expectations. The demands of ministry may be set so high that no one could fulfil them. They may be too diverse, so that while the expectations could be met individually, they pull a leader in too many directions at once. Or there may be simply too many demands, so that there are just not enough hours in a week for them all to be met. These expectations may come from the leader himself or from people in the church. Usually they arise from both directions. I have seen leaders ruining their health or damaging their family life to meet expectations that are a mountain no one could ever reasonably be expected to climb. Like many other professions, local church ministry is a bottomless pit, for there is always more good work that could be done, both within the church and within the local community.

Leadership teams need to agree not only key priorities, but also which expectations cannot be met. Leaders need to develop a thick skin, so that when misplaced demands are expressed they don't cut to the quick but become more like water off a duck's back. We need to return regularly to the principle of Jesus: what matters most is fulfilling the realistic and tailor-made expectations of the Father in heaven (John 6:38). I used to belong to a small support group for several couples in full-time ministry where a simple prophetic word was given which distilled a vital truth: 'Remember the one who called you, and remember the ministry to which you were called.'

Leaders can face the pressures of ownership. Earlier we argued that a vision needs to be owned, but we are now addressing a different kind of ownership, which amounts to possessiveness: 'This church belongs to me.' Group ownership often arises following a momentous event in the life of a local church. They may be the founding generation, or the generation that implemented and paid for a major building project. If the church has been through a couple of decades where numbers have been static, with few newcomers joining the church, the group claiming ownership may be the 'happy family' who have been together through unchanging years. In other churches, after you have attended for a few months you begin to discover that many of the key leaders are related to one another and that a single family has taken over the church, running it as a cross between a dynastic succession, a family business and the Mafia! I have had a very positive experience of several members of one family serving in leadership together, but others have told me horror stories of churches where a large family's overriding motivation has been not to serve but to control.

A sense of identity and belonging is a great plus in the life of a church. A welcoming church that draws newcomers into the church family has great growth potential. But the best of virtues can turn sour. Where belonging turns into possessiveness, newcomers are mistrusted and seen as a potential threat. A clique that lays claim to ownership of a church needs to surrender it back to the lordship of Christ. If a church is bedevilled by such ownership, you may have been part of the church for several years, but you still feel you are an outsider, needing to be careful not to intrude upon the hallowed inner circle.

Personal church ownership comes in two forms that are both highly toxic. First, the minister may become too possessive, feeling that he alone has the right to take any initiative. With this attitude he runs the characteristic risks of authoritarianism, imposing decisions no one else wants and preventing anyone else from using their initiative. I came across one church where the minister's wife was designated a prophet and no one else was ever allowed to prophesy. If that's not misguided ownership, I don't know what is! We ministers need to be ready to hear from our fellow elders or other leaders whenever we are tempted to become too domineering.

The second form of personal ownership is found where a dominant individual becomes over the years a power broker, who almost always gets his way. Although it is quite possible for someone to slip into this role for love of power, they usually have the best interests of the church at heart. At first they make an invaluable contribution to the life of the church, serving tirelessly for many years. However, the role shifts imperceptibly, until the servant of the church becomes its master. Without realising it, and still with the best interests of the church at heart, the power broker comes to assume that he is indispensable or that the church owes it to him to follow his lead. It is not for nothing that the New Testament cautions about the kind of leader who has a finger in every pie, and in all things 'loves to be first' (3 John 9). We also neglect at our peril Paul's warning about the unsuitability for leadership of anyone who is overbearing, bullishly pressing his views until others surrender to his domineering assertiveness (Titus 1:7).

A friend of mine received a phone call from a senior denominational leader after several months at a new church, which gave a timely warning: 'I've met a man in your church who wants to try to take you over.' I have spoken to many leaders who have had the painful task of dealing with a power broker. There is no dodging this demanding and often acutely stressful duty of leadership. If a power broker's grip is not broken, in time he will break the church.

Leaders may also face conflict as a result of numerical growth. In theory almost everyone is in favour of growth, assuming that the status quo of church life will never change, and so the minister is praised for attracting some new faces. As growth continues, it begins to feel destabilising, for it becomes apparent that the newcomers don't take for granted the old priorities or style of the church. The minister is warned about forcing the pace of change. In time, the growth produces a new consensus, a critical mass is achieved for new priorities to shape the vision of the church. Those who have chosen to be immovable may now choose to accuse the minister or the newcomers of hi-jacking the church! Many churches go through a contradictory period when many are joining 'because the church is so loving', and others are leaving 'because there is no love here any more'! This is a desperately exacting period for any church leader who wants the best for all. Growth forces some painful choices. If mission is our first priority, we have to be prepared to let some members go. If keeping the present members happy comes first, we have to cut back on mission.

I recently met with the leaders of a new church which had grown out of a church where two divergent visions had emerged. One group had the vision to become a large and rapidly growing fellowship, big enough to have an evangelistic impact over a wide area. The other group's vision was to be a smaller community, a happy family open to growth but with a very local sense of mission. These groups could have fought each other for years. Instead they had the wisdom to become two churches with distinct visions and contrasting expectations of growth. As two churches there was harmony and mutual respect. If they had stayed together they could have faced years of sterile disagreement and heartache.

In any church where the members play an active part in the decision-making process, the impact of growth also needs to be understood in terms of the balance of power. If growth is sustained, two periods of turbulence are guaranteed. The first comes when the newcomers added to those who want to move forward begin to outnumber the traditionalists. Around this time there may be a 'last stand' on a relatively minor issue, or a wave of complaints that this group feel neglected or unwanted. The second comes when the newcomers begin to outnumber all of those present before growth accelerated, and the centre of gravity is about to shift irrevocably. At this stage the leadership team usually needs new recruits, so that the newcomers receive adequate representation. Some leaders who have played their part in bringing about the momentum of growth will need to hand over the reins, to ensure that new blood is drawn into the team.

Leaders will face conflict wherever there is an attempt to restore biblical priorities. In the Old Testament there is an endless cycle within the history of Israel, moving between periods of moral and spiritual compromise and periods of renewed obedience and fervour. In the same way it seems to be a principle of church life that over the years we can go off the boil or drift back into the patterns of natural human religion. The lives of the Old Testament prophets bear stark witness to the fact that wherever there is a call to repentance, resistance and conflict cannot be far behind. Wherever there is a recovery of apostolic priorities, some will prefer to resist or to leave rather than embrace the demanding radicalism of biblical reformation.

The work of the Spirit will also stir up strife. I wish this were not the case, but the witness of history is plain. One of the reasons John Wesley took to preaching in the open air was that a number of Anglican vicars barred him from their pulpits when he preached the need for personal salvation. When Jonathan Edwards saw revival come to New England, the most vigorous opposition came from some churchmen who considered all these sudden conversions and public exclamations of repentance to be altogether unseemly. When the modern pentecostal movement began, the first reaction of some other Christians was to write them off as another heretical sect. This was done in deeply regrettable and inflammatory terms which revealed far more about the judgementalists than the Pentecostals they rejected so vituperatively.

In all these cases there was not only active opposition from some within the churches, but also the passive opposition of indifference from those who were orthodox in belief but didn't want their ordered religion unsettled by a new movement of God's Spirit. The Holy Spirit is not divisive himself, but wherever he begins to move in power, some will feel threatened and their reaction can become hostile or even accusatory. I have not met a single leader who has sought to bring renewal to an existing church without facing some measure of real and painful opposition, nor without some members deciding, whether or not with good grace, to leave. One Anglican bishop suggested to me that the Holy Spirit invariably confronts a natural priority of Western religion: control. If we are serious about openness to the Holy Spirit, we can no longer hold faith and worship in the iron grip of human control.

Above all, the clash of cultures will produce conflict. As new converts come into churches today, a familiar tension becomes apparent. Those comfortable within the old sub-culture cannot understand why their enculturation of the gospel, their old and familiar ways of being church, cannot simply be adopted as a package deal. Meanwhile, those becoming Christians from within today's world have no desire to buy into an old-fashioned sub-culture, and cannot see why they should.

What we are faced with is a potentially traumatic clash of cultures. Cultural assumptions are by their very nature usually unexamined and taken as self-evidently correct. As we saw earlier, the familiar ways seem natural, and the local church may easily assume, 'Our ways are the best and necessary expression of the gospel.' For example, on one occasion in Brazil I was due to preach at a church which had struggled to grow for over twenty years. Before I spoke, their new minister sought to build faith by stressing that they had all the resources necessary to be a growing church: 'We have an organ. We even have pews!' I was careful to suppress a smile, for in our church only after we got rid of the organ and the pews did growth really begin to accelerate. In the church culture of that minister, church furniture had become confused with the gospel. Optional extras had come to be deemed essential for the effectiveness of the church. When such assumptions are brought into question, the first reaction is likely to be deep seated and emotional – hostile, threatened, bemused or even explosive. Out of this clash of cultures the future mission and character of a local church will be determined. In many cases, the old wineskins simply cannot cope with the new wine. We must either create new wineskins or fail to play a significant part in the church of the 21st century.

This clash of cultures represents a determinative crisis for the historic denominations. Before them is the prospect of an inability to implement radical cultural adaptation. It is all too easy to resist innovation and dismiss contemporary approaches as 'not in our tradition'. All too often the pre-eminent virtues are inflexibility and conservatism. Creative pioneers are not considered to be a source of present hope and future renewal, but are rather considered threats to the system – mavericks who are inadequately grounded in denominational identity. In many denominational colleges and seminaries little or no account is taken of the principles and urgency of cultural engagement. Contemporary and charismatic worship finds no place on the syllabus, perhaps with the forlorn hope that if they are ignored for long enough perhaps they will go away. As a result, some historic denominations face the danger of continued decline and gradual replacement by new expressions of Christianity. The shelf-life of intransigent traditionalism has grown perilously short. What the historic denominations urgently need is the boldness to endorse at every level a sea change in church life, breaking out from an archaic and institutionalised sub-culture whose viability is increasingly tenuous. There are encouraging signs emerging that such a rebirth could well be under way in several, if not all, historic denominations.

The clash of cultures is the inevitable and uncomfortable price required by full-blooded recovery of cultural engagement. The same price will need to be exacted from new churches if they are to remain in touch with new generations. In the accelerating ferment of change of the 21st century we will all need continually to face new cultural contexts if we really intend to be a missionary church for the modern world.

Releasing vision

Nehemiah released vision and achieved goals. He researched and planned each stage of advance. He remained adaptable as circumstances changed, while never losing sight of his ultimate goal (4:13, 16). He motivated others with his words of encouragement and example of fortitude (4:19–20, 23). And he frequently reaffirmed the God-centredness of his vision (4:14, 20).

Some churches continue from year to year without ever asking the question, 'What's the church for?' In this way, our priorities are determined by the existing activities of the church. This is the most narrow and limiting way possible to determine vision. We have sought in this book to explore the priorities of the first Christians, for it is from the churches in the New Testament that we need to draw the essential guidelines to renew our vision. Therefore, *the first stage of vision building needs to be clear and practical biblical teaching.*

Within a rounded teaching programme, we need to demonstrate that church growth takes place in at least seven interconnected dimensions, all of which are relevant to every church, no matter how large or small. First, there is discipleship growth – growing in holiness and knowledge of the Scriptures. Secondly, there is spiritual growth – growing in prayer and worship. Thirdly, there is fellowship growth – growing together in loving relationships. Fourthly, there is mobilisation growth – growing in gifts and ministries and in an underlying attitude of generosity and kindness. Fifthly, there is growth into the local community that we seek to serve. Sixthly, there is conversion growth. And seventhly, there is numerical growth. The church that only wants to grow in one dimension cannot hope to stay healthy for long. Vision building needs to take account of all seven dimensions of growth if we want to be a church that grows in quality as well as quantity.

Good teaching cannot be the whole story, for in the light of the general purpose of all churches a more specific question must follow: 'What is this particular church for?' No church can do effectively all the things that churches could do. Some churches inflict on themselves an impossible treadmill by having a vision that is too broad, trying to reach every kind of person and meet every kind of need. Others try to replicate the vision of a well-known and successful church, without having the necessary resources for the vision to be carried through. Of course, there are also churches with no vision to accomplish anything at all, except survival and the continuing comfort of Christians, but that is a different kind of problem altogether!

Just as a company can suffer from over-expansion, a church can stretch resources too thinly by trying to achieve too much. In order to maximise our impact we need to learn to specialise. Far rather achieve excellence in one ministry than mediocrity in six. There were countless things that Jesus could have done in three years' public ministry. He could have spent those years many times over among the poor, bringing them healing, hope and the teaching of the kingdom of God. He could have given time to leaders, intellectuals and people of influence, seeking to win support among the powerful. Instead he had a specific and narrow focus from which he did not drift: 'I have come down from heaven not to do my will but to do the will of him who sent me' (John 6:38).

The second stage of vision building is therefore earnest prayer, not only by the leaders of the church, but by all the people. Only through prayer can we discover the Father's specific purposes, as individuals and as a church. In my experience, half nights of prayer, setting aside four hours, from eight till midnight, are particularly effective for vision building. When we take prayer seriously, God takes seriously our seeking after wisdom, and we make real progress in discovering Christ's specific calling and purposes for us.

Teaching and prayer are both vital, but they need to be

informed by hard information. Just as a company considering a new product needs to invest in market research, *the third stage of vision building is to gather and analyse statistical information about both the church and the local community.* We research the church, in order to have a clearer idea of the available gifts, resources and concerns. We research the community, in order to identify the character of the local population, the age distribution, ethnic and social mix, local priority needs, etc. When the age distributions of church and community are compared, and the church resources are lined up against local needs, we can begin to make judgements about which opportunities we can realistically expect to deliver. It is quite wrong to imply to local people that we will meet their every need. No church could possibly do that. But it is surely quite absurd to attempt to build vision without a clear and informed awareness of the kind of people and needs in the local community we seek to reach.

The fourth stage of vision building is sharing hopes and dreams. Any minister and leadership team will have a number of aspirations and ideas to declare, but such dreams are not the exclusive preserve of leaders. A dream is not a decision; it is an intuition. Some dreams are merely human aspirations. Some would soon turn into nightmares if we tried to implement them. But some of our vague hopes for the future have been planted within us by the Spirit of God. Many people are frightened of saying something foolish, so every effort must be made to help them overcome natural reticence. An open and encouraging climate needs to be developed, so that everyone in the church feels able to share their dreams.

Our church developed a year-long programme of vision building through the sharing of hopes and dreams. Each home group was invited to spend an evening filling a huge piece of paper with ideas by completing the sentence: 'In five

years' time I would like our church to . . .' We wanted everyone to pray before attending and everyone to feel free to
contribute. We would rather have had several impractical
ideas written down than miss an insight God had given to
someone who was shy and reluctant to speak out. I attended
each of these 'dream evenings', seeking to facilitate the participation of as many as possible. The dreams made a heady
cocktail: ways of being and things to do, improvements to our
present activities and completely new initiatives – all were
mixed together in abundance. Once every home group had
completed this task, the large sheets of dreams were pinned
up on public display, and we invited everyone to consider
them prayerfully. Then we met to pray together in order to
identify the key themes which were emerging. Gradually the
themes came into focus, until we could produce a draft vision
statement.

Some leaders prefer to do all the vision building personally. I remember reading the autobiography of one
American pastor who even sought to dispense with an
architect for an ambitious building project because he had
seen the new premises in a dream. Each leader has to
develop their own approach to vision building, for there
is no single method suitable to all personality types and
churches. The important thing is to build vision, not to use
a particular method.

As for me, I encourage wide participation for three reasons.
First, in our educational context, modern methods encourage
individuals to take part in problem solving and discovery
learning rather than leave everything to a single leader. Secondly, in the business context, at one time the standard
management procedure was 'top-down', but today there is
a growing trend to involve staff much more widely in the
strategic development of the company. This doesn't remove

from managers the responsibility to take executive decisions, but the top-down procedures are complemented and enriched by a 'bottom-up' flow of information and ideas. My third reason is biblical: the prophecy of Joel, which Peter quoted on the Day of Pentecost, explicitly states that everyone who receives the Holy Spirit, young and old, male and female, will receive godly dreams and visions: 'I will pour out my Spirit on all people. Your sons and daughters will prophesy, your young men will see visions, your old men will dream dreams' (Acts 2:17). As a leader I expect to receive fresh dreams and visions from the Holy Spirit. But I also have every confidence that the Spirit wants to give a measure of vision to all believers.

Once the dreams have been sifted to discern those that count, and then sorted into some kind of intelligible order, *the fifth stage is to present the vision publicly*. We did this by compiling a small booklet. This is the beginning, not the end, of vision building, for the vision needs to be adopted by the church, whether formally or informally. Dreams do not become real vision unless they are owned by the church. Otherwise, they are someone else's responsibility, and everyone passes the buck.

Owning the vision is therefore the sixth stage. The whole church needs a broad sense of ownership, so that particular projects receive prayer, encouragement and the necessary financial support. Individuals need to own a particular aspect of the vision, so that they take responsibility to deliver the goods. Nothing much will ever happen if everyone dumps their bright ideas on the minister with the memorable words, 'The church really ought to be doing something about this!' Nor will much advance be made if every new idea is tacked onto the end of the leadership team's agenda. Only if individuals are ready to use their initiative and risk their own efforts can the ministries and impact of a local church begin to multiply fast.

Once the vision is owned, the cycle of vision building needs to begin again. Vision is not something achieved once and delivered from on high by the church leader or the leadership team. Vision building is an iterative process, for the vision needs continually to be made new. Individuals and communities are always developing, and churches can change quite dramatically during a period of significant growth and renewal. The church that relies on a five-year-old vision has chosen a diet of stale bread.

Achieving goals

A vision that is never delivered is worth no more than a day dream. While a vision expresses the broad direction in which we are heading, it needs to be broken down into key stages of progress. We cannot deliver everything at once, but if we analyse our overall aims we can begin to identify the steps by which we can achieve the vision over several years. For this reason, if a church is to make real progress in implementing its vision, it makes sense to declare annual goals.

Goals need to be measurable and achievable steps. In this way we can see whether the goal has been achieved at the end of the year. If it has, we can move on to the next stage. If it hasn't, it may have been an unrealistic goal. Or maybe the goal is good and we have made real progress, but it will take longer to deliver than a single year. Or maybe the goal was both good and realistic, but we have gone about it in an unhelpful way, or lacked the motivation to make it happen.

To attempt to measure by the same criteria the progress of an inner-city church and a wealthy suburban church would be absurd. Because some large middle-class churches have found goal setting successful, it is tempting for an inner-city church to consider the goals set in suburbia, recognise them to be irrelevant to the inner city, and then dismiss the entire approach as useless. This represents a fatal confusion of method and content. The principle of goal setting is equally relevant in every context, but the onus is on local leaders to identify the specific goals that are relevant to their locality, mobilising the people for the gospel's advance. To borrow goals from another church is to invite disappointment. To be useful, goals must be relevant to the particular setting and resources of a local church. We need to answer a practical question: 'Of all that we would like to do for God, what in particular can we achieve this year, with the Spirit's help?'

Useful goals not only need to be relevant and specific, they must also demand real faith. If our most adventurous goal is to meet for worship every Sunday next year, we may have little sense of achievement in twelve months' time! Faith in turn requires a measure of risk. It is just the same in business. The company that never takes any kind of risk will eventually fail just as surely as the company that takes unnecessary and inappropriate risks.

Churches can easily develop a play-safe attitude, a pathological allergy to any kind of risk. There were huge risks attached to the very existence of the first church in Jerusalem. There were huge risks attached to Paul's missionary journeys, and to the endeavours of the pioneering European missionaries. If we are serious about the gospel and serious about reaching a desperately lost world, then we need to be ready to take the right kinds of risk. The task of church leaders is to set the risk level just right. Not so high as to seem crazy, resulting in believers panicking or losing heart. But too high for creeping complacency, so that the church gets hold of real urgency in prayer. As John Wimber used to say, faith is spelled R-I-S-K!

Keeping going

Nehemiah sustained advance, encouraging jubilant celebration when the initial rebuilding was complete (Nehemiah 12), but then turning to a new stage of reform, promoting inner purification and the moral rebuilding of Israel (Nehemiah 13). It is quite impossible to sustain growth in the medium term without being prepared to modify local church management. A leadership structure that has assisted growth at one stage will soon begin to impede growth unless leaders continue to identify and implement the necessary changes.

The larger a church grows, the more urgently adjustments are required to management methods. In a church of up to around 100 believers, everything can be fairly informal, for everyone can know everyone else. Up to 200, leadership can be centred upon the minister, who can still know every individual, but around this size he will become a severe bottleneck if he tries to give a direct lead in all areas. Up to 300, a central leadership team can provide sufficient overall leadership, with the minister functioning as a kind of managing director, but communication across the church will need to become increasingly well organised and managed. Beyond this point, a decentralised management structure needs to be developed. If everything is still channelled through the central leadership team they will eventually become a bottleneck. Meanwhile the minister will need to take on an increasingly specialised role, hands off from many of the ministry teams as the chief executive, the central leader and teacher.

The life of a church is both cyclical and linear. There is both a weekly and an annual cycle of events, and it is all too easy for these cycles to dominate our attention and use all our energy and resources. However, the church not only has a responsibility to provide Sunday meetings and special seasonal events, we also have a task of mission to complete, which is our linear task. Once a church has enjoyed a period of growth and the building is nearly full, it is all too easy for our concentration on mission to lapse. Similarly, once some key goals have been reached, it is all too easy to slip back into the familiar cycle of events. It is absolutely vital that we provide breathing space, so that the church doesn't become a breathless treadmill for leaders or members. But it is also vital that leaders work hard to avoid an all-too-familiar trap: churches that make good progress for a few years, then go off the boil for a decade. I recently came across a church that had enjoyed steady growth over the years, but now there was no staff member heading up evangelism and half a dozen working in administration. Every effort was being put into back-up, with no one in the front line. It looked suspiciously like a well-oiled machine – very well maintained but busy going nowhere.

Three key disciplines help sustain growth. First, we need to give thanks to God for what has been achieved. In this way we avoid slipping into pride or complacency by constantly reminding one another that all we have achieved has only been possible with God's help. Secondly, we must renew the vision, which regularly needs to be modified and sharpened in the light of experience and progress. In this way the fellowship's ownership of the vision is renewed for a fresh phase of advance. Thirdly, we have to understand that leaders need to be on fire, not burned out. As a church grows, the demands on leaders become ever more complex and consuming. Suddenly you realise you are running on empty, too busy with the demands of the church to spend time with God, whether alone or in leaders' meetings. Even as a river will not run higher than its source, a church will not burn brightly with vision if the leaders don't make time to pray. If the church is to sustain growth, here is an essential duty for all who aspire to any kind of Christian leadership: we need to keep on fire, our spiritual resources continually renewed by the Spirit of God.

13
Future Church

The enormous impact of charismatic renewal upon the church in the last thirty years is unmistakable. So where is renewal going? It is an irresistible question, which must have several answers. Just as the whole church has a range of future possibilities, even so there are a number of futures for renewal. What gives the edge to this question is the fact that first generation renewal is drawing to a close. Several early leaders have died, others have retired or are drawing near to retirement, so need to begin to hand over the reins. At the same time, the fresh sparkle of novelty has been increasingly replaced by familiarity. So where next?

Petering out?

Church history is littered with one generation movements of reform. The first flush of enthusiasm has often waned fast. Even as St Francis of Assisi was dying, his devoted followers planned a building in his honour which would violate his guiding principle of poverty. Spiritual inertia is a mighty force which drags people back from radicalism to religious conformity.

Recognition and approval can prove even more stultifying than inertia. When the Anglo-Catholics were at the height of their influence in the Church of England, some were appointed to the bishop's bench. Others began to wonder when their turn might come and began to play down their distinctive catholic convictions. Recognition and promotion, far from strengthening the hand of radicals, can make them soft as putty. There are signs in some quarters that renewal is being tamed – a new domestication of the Spirit could be under way.

Perhaps the worst trap of all is cynicism. The cynic is often a disappointed idealist, who began with hopes that were too naive, too inflated or too short term. Some thought renewal meant jam today and jam tomorrow, with none of the inner fight of Romans 7, which remains inescapably at the heart of authentic Christian living. Renewal is a form of revivalism, and every revivalist movement runs the risk of promising glorious triumph just around the next corner – or during the next conference. Change in local churches and in denominations is apparent for everyone to see in Britain today, but these things do not happen tidily, or overnight, or without a backlash.

Marginalised?

All reform movements run the same risk. In pursuing reform of existing churches the reformers can end by dividing from one another. Some are bound to find it necessary for reasons of doctrine, strategy or personality to separate from existing groupings, and they will probably see others separate from them in due course. The secessionist future seems an inevitable trajectory. History suggests that those who suffer in secession sometimes include the seceders themselves, for their message is likely to be marginalised should they be unable to avoid the indulgence of judgemental and sectarian outbursts.

I am not suggesting that everyone should join one of the historic denominations. As a matter of fact I suspect the gospel will be best served in the coming years by the emergence of countless new church plants and several new networks of churches, both within and beyond the historic denominations. What we need to ensure is that we don't write one another off by claiming that our grouping is the only true church. In recent years several new church streams, although sadly not all, have demonstrated a positive and inclusive spirit, remaining true to their own convictions while avoiding the continual castigation of other churches. With this approach, centred on Christ and creed rather than denominations and power, we can look forward to diversity without division and recrimination; multiplication of churches and streams without marginalisation.

The other route to the margins where movements for reform become increasingly irrelevant is the quest for the exotic. At its best, renewal represents a rediscovered openness to the immanent availability of God among his people. It is a decisive corrective to all expressions of Christianity, including the 'stiff upper lip' school of evangelicalism, which are tempted to hold to the form of the gospel while neglecting, if not actually denying, its power. But a quest for the exotic distorts this rightful recovery of emphasis on the presence of God. Time and again in Christian history this has led to the twin errors of illuminism and sensationalism.

In illuminism, the Spirit is said to offer a short cut to a 'spiritual' knowledge which avoids the disciplines of Bible study and the use of the mind. In sensationalism, particular signs of the presence of the Spirit move to centre stage, and the enthusiasts of the movement devote themselves whole-heartedly to their special emphasis, gift or phenomenon. Over the years I have heard various gifts or experiences presented as the latest be-all and end-all of Christian living. Real life is more complicated than that. Sadly, those locked into the quest for the exotic will move on to the next illusion of ultimacy – the one gift or experience which is, at least for the present, the supposed answer to every need. The quest for the exotic is particularly strong in our culture. Existentialism has made us gluttonous for new experiences. Television has accustomed us to constant newness and instant gratification. So we often bring to our faith the desire for novel experiences which deliver instant results. Instant spirituality is like an instant meal in a plastic pot to which you only need to add boiling water – it can only be an insipid imitation of the real thing, momentarily enticing but ultimately unsatisfying.

Event- or truth-centred?

It has been said that classical orthodoxy is truth-centred (the glorious and saving truths of the gospel are celebrated and proclaimed), while classical gnosticism is event-centred (spiritual experiences are sought after eagerly, without any biblical and doctrinal framework). This reflects two routes into renewal among Evangelicals. For some, the coming of the Spirit swept over them out of the blue, bringing a separation from their previous convictions. For others, openness to the Spirit grew out of fresh study of the New Testament. In this second group, renewal was not over against evangelical convictions, but rather a growth into a full-bodied, more fully biblical evangelicalism. Those whose commitment to renewal is drawn from biblical convictions will be truth-centred in their Christian living. The events of the coming of the Spirit are then measured by the resultant conformity to Christ, not by tingles down the spine.

Renewal is becoming the inheritor of the evangelical consensus in Britain today, but the jury is still out on whether it is a worthy inheritor. Renewal must prove that the baby has not been thrown out with the bath water. We urgently need to see a recovery of biblical preaching. We urgently need to see fuller expression of the Spirit's biblical passion for both evangelism and social justice on a national and a global scale. We also need to see a recovery of the classical evangelical inheritance: the truth on fire of Wesley and Whitefield, Edwards and Spurgeon. Not, of course, exhumed as a dead orthodoxy, but creatively made new in the 21st century.

What is the future for renewal? There are many futures, and more than one will come to pass. But if the finest future of renewal involves taking up the reins of evangelicalism, then that future entails a recovery of evangelical identity and priorities. To be a vibrant and radical movement for reform, renewal must come to see itself not merely as a 20th-century novelty, but as a movement with a great and glorious past. We need to go back to the future – classical evangelicalism on fire. For this to happen we need to reaffirm in practice the authority of the Bible and the centrality of the cross, and we need to make sure we don't get trapped in superficial or imitation renewal.

Back to the Bible

It is absolutely vital that Christians always come back not only to the authority but also to the proper use of the Bible. In a world of twenty-four-hour television programmes and unreadable computer manuals, a world where the pace of life gets faster and faster, it is all too easy for Christians to be Bible believing in principle but Bible neglecting in practice.

When I was involved in publishing the NIV, one book bind-
ing company produced some sample leather editions in an
attempt to win business. One of those samples was bound in
top quality blue leather, with the edge of the pages beautifully
finished in gold. It was a book to grace any bookshelf. Only
when you opened it did you discover that anything was missing, for every page was blank. We have grown accustomed to
the fact that many people have an unread Bible tucked away
somewhere at home. My fear is that a growing number of
evangelical Christians today are biblically illiterate. Sometimes
it is the believers' Bibles that might as well have blank pages.

The sales of daily Bible reading notes have been steadily
declining for several years. If there was evidence that Christians have turned to different methods of regular Bible reading this would not be a cause for concern, but I know of no
such evidence. Perhaps partly in reaction against the old days
of believers carting round a big black Bible the size of a
doorstep, fewer Christians seem to be taking their Bibles to
Sunday services. What is more, in reaction against an old style
of dry-as-dust biblical exposition, the fashion has turned to a
style of preaching which is high in anecdote and personal
experience, but low in biblical content. The old saying
remains true: sermonettes make Christianettes. Such preaching is like a mediocre Chinese take-away, enjoyable at the
time, but not long after you find yourself hungry and dis-
satisfied. We need an urgent recovery of substantial and nutri-
tional biblical exposition, 'rightly dividing' the word of God
and applying it in wise and practical ways to daily living.

I have no hesitation in stating that turn-of-the-century
evangelicalism is at risk of drifting from its biblical moorings.
We need to understand afresh that without the Bible we
ultimately have nothing – no revelation of God to feed
upon, no saving truth to share. We need to reintroduce our

self-indulgent and biblically illiterate society to the Bible as God's definitive Word. But first we need to reform ourselves, as individuals, as churches and as a movement. It is time to get back to the Bible.

The centrality of the cross

In modern biographies, little space is usually given to someone's death, for most emphasis is given to the moments of greatest achievement. In each of the Gospels, however, about a third of the space is given over to the week leading up to Jesus' crucifixion. His death is not merely an inevitable ending, it is presented as the most important achievement of his life. The apostolic preaching, recorded in Acts, has the same emphasis as the Gospels, for the cross is at the very heart of their proclamation. Similarly, Paul advised the Corinthians that, despite the fact that he was fully aware of the offence of the cross in both Jewish and Gentile cultures, he was firmly resolved that the cross would always remain pivotal to his proclamation: 'For I resolved to know nothing while I was with you except Jesus Christ and him crucified' (1 Corinthians 2:2).

Had he been around at the time, a late 20th-century marketing consultant would surely have found it utterly incomprehensible that the first Christians even considered adopting the symbol of the cross. We can imagine such a style guru imploring the disciples to think again: 'Anything would be preferable to a symbol of ruthless execution by the state!' Given the enormity of the offence of the cross, would it not have been a wiser policy to play down or even quietly forget the way Jesus died? Such an approach was impossible, for the cross, far from being a distraction or an extraneous stumbling-block that needed to be removed, was seen to be irremovably at the very heart of the Christian message.

Because the cross is so central to the New Testament, we need to ensure that it always remains central to faith today. I am concerned that in some circles, we have come almost to take the cross for granted, with the result that little is heard of it any more. I am concerned that for some specialised Christian groups, their distinctive initiatives and concerns, however laudable, have begun to usurp the centrality of the cross. And I am concerned that much worship drifts away from the cross and resurrection, just as much preaching fails to return consistently and creatively to the cross.

A long-running series of adverts in Britain claims jokingly that only a certain kind of lager 'can do all this'. Why must the cross remain central to our faith, our worship, our Christian living and our proclamation? Because only the cross of Christ 'can do all this', making salvation possible and freely available in all its fullness. Whenever the church has lost the apostolic grasp of the centrality of the cross, we have inevitably lost our focus in faith and momentum in mission. Without the cross, we ultimately have nothing.

Imitation renewal

Every Christmas the streets fill with traders selling brand name products in fancy packaging at bargain prices. It is only when you get home that you discover you've bought a counterfeit. In the same way, many churches have introduced modern songs, developed a more intimate and informal style of worship, and experimented with dance and drama. But the packaging is not the product. The fact that the trappings of renewal have become trendy says nothing about whether the church is growing in the fruit of the Spirit and being clothed with power from on high.

In some churches, the leaders have taken the church into superficial renewal, but the leaders themselves cannot honestly say that they have been filled with the Spirit. In some churches the outward forms of renewal have been copied, but there is no clear teaching that every believer needs to be filled with the Holy Spirit. We see churches which are said to be 'in renewal', where long-established patterns of gossip, party spirit and backbiting still retain squatters' rights and have not been evicted, so the fruit of the Spirit are evidently not being well cultivated. We see churches where the gifts of the Spirit are accepted in principle, but the leaders wouldn't be seen dead exercising tongues or prophecy in a public meeting. They prefer to leave such risks to someone else. In short, we see churches that in theory are keen on immersion in the Spirit, but in practice never get beyond paddling.

Imitation renewal is a counterfeit. The packaging without the content may tart up a church, but it cannot make the people holy or empowered. The responsibility lies above all with church leaders. It is the leaders – not only ministers, but elders and deacons and PCC members – who need to be filled and know they are filled. They need to receive spiritual gifts and take the lead by using them publicly, showing bold faith and putting themselves in a risky and vulnerable position. They need to teach the need to be empowered and to grow in holiness, and they need to develop credible lives. A river will not rise above its source, and a church cannot go further into renewal than its leaders are prepared to advance.

All fads and fashions have their day, so imitation renewal will eventually bury itself in the sand. It is not enough to be theoretically in favour of the Holy Spirit and renewal, any more than it would be enough to be theoretically in favour of electricity, without getting round to having your house wired up and connected to the mains. It is a waste of time merely to tinker with externals and structures when what we need is the holy fire of the Spirit of Pentecost. Nothing less will do.

The power of the Holy Spirit is just as pivotal to New Testament Christianity as the authority of the word and the centrality of the cross. If we lose any one of these anchors we begin to drift from our moorings. Only when we embrace all three without reservation or hesitation can we enjoy the maximum benefit that each can bring. It is no good trying to bridge the gap to our surrounding culture unless we are absolutely confident that we are deep-rooted in these three. We can only be effective as God's ambassadorial new people in our mission to the world when we are first centred upon the cross, submitted to the word and keeping in step with the Holy Spirit. Only then can we begin to rediscover classical evangelicalism on fire, and explore its expression and development in ways that engage with the 21st century.

Embracing change

Many church leaders have been trained to approach change like chemotherapy. Should all else have failed, it can be tried, but only in the smallest possible dose. We need to face the fact that no growth is possible without change. Not only does growth inevitably bring change, but change is often required before we can begin to enjoy significant growth. We need to change in order to improve what we do already. More than that, we cannot make room for innovation and creativity without a preparedness to embrace change. Above all, there is no possibility of cultural engagement in the modern world without change. We cannot afford to suppose that all a church needs is a short, sharp shock of change in order to catch up once for all. The plain fact about our society is that constant change is here to stay. As a result, our task of bridging the gap rapidly begins to sound like the hare and the tortoise. Just as we begin to catch up with the post-war world, bringing the sound of popular music into the mainstream of our worship, we realise that our culture has entered a new era of video and computer driven multimedia communication, entertainment and information exchange.

Sir John Harvey-Jones, former chairman of ICI and a leading British management consultant, has a clear-sighted grasp of the attitude to change required by successful leaders. In one of his TV programmes he was advising a family firm where a new sales director had been taken on six months previously. When Harvey-Jones asked what the new man had achieved, the family owners explained that he had been settling in, getting his feet under the table and becoming accustomed to the style of the company. Harvey-Jones erupted in one of his familiar, derisory snorts and exclaimed that when you appoint someone to a senior leadership position, 'he should hit the ground running'. This family firm came from the same culture as those conventional church leaders who advise a minister arriving at a new church to change nothing for the first two years.

Sir John also gave some memorable advice at a televised seminar for business executives: 'The only habit of a lifetime you can afford today is a commitment to continuous change.' Here is a man who can be relied on to be forthright and blunt, but we need to hear him if we seriously aspire to apply the best contemporary insights into leadership and management skills to the development of local churches: 'Management in particular is not about the preservation of the status quo, it is about maintaining the highest rate of change that the organisation and the people within it can stand.'[1]

If this analysis holds good for businesses in the modern world it must also have relevance to churches. We simply have no choice but to operate in the same cultural context if we want to engage in effective mission. When those who are working to make a profit need to face up to the reality of an ever changing world, and adapt their management methods and organisational structures accordingly, how much more do we need to heed such insights and warnings? Our driving concern must be to bring the unchanging offer of life to a world that can no longer understand or identify with the churches of yesteryear.

Change is not only required from us by the modern world, it is also the result of openness to the Holy Spirit. The intention of the Spirit is to promote change in every believer, for he seeks to change us from glory into glory into the likeness of Christ (2 Corinthians 3:18). In a similar way, the book of Acts records that the Holy Spirit is for ever rocking the boat, breaking up comfortable and safe patterns of church life and stirring up believers for new advances in mission. Around 120 is a good size for a church – big enough for a wide range of skills to be present, but small enough to know everyone by name. Many churches have resisted further growth at around this size. After Jesus' ascension, around 120 believers met together in Jerusalem (Acts 1:15). Then the Holy Spirit came upon them in power. He took them into dimensions of worship they had never known before, then drove them out onto the streets in worship that flowed naturally into evangelism. By the time the Holy Spirit had finished that day, 120

---

[1] J. Harvey-Jones, *Making It Happen*, p. 14.

had been transformed into 3,000. Because the Holy Spirit is so willing to change church for the sake of mission, before they knew it their friendly little fellowship had become a mega-church!

In Acts 10 we read how the Holy Spirit shook Peter out of the lethargy that had overtaken the first believers. They were doing a great job of evangelism in Jerusalem and Judea, and after persecution their mission had extended to Samaria. But the Jewish Christians had not yet done anything to fulfil Jesus' command to take the gospel to the Gentiles. A reluctant Peter was obliged by the Spirit to go to the house of Cornelius, a Gentile in Caesarea. Once there, Peter rather grudgingly explained how unusual it was for a Jew to enter a Gentile's home, but then he began to preach. Poor Peter hadn't even reached the climax of his sermon when the Holy Spirit intervened again. Suddenly, Cornelius and his fellows interrupted Peter by beginning to praise God, speaking in tongues. Luke records the astonishment of Peter and his team: 'The gift of the Holy Spirit had been poured out even on the Gentiles' (Acts 10:45). Peter quickly concluded that water baptism must be in order, for these new believers had already been filled with the Spirit.

Once Peter returned to Jerusalem he was in trouble. The believers there were none too pleased at this revolutionary treatment of the Gentiles and Peter's abandonment of Jewish cultural traditions. In reply Peter explained that the decisive factor was the unquestionable demonstration that the Gentiles had received the Holy Spirit in equal measure to the Jewish believers: 'As I began to speak, the Holy Spirit came on them as he had come on us at the beginning' (Acts 11:15). Peter's explanation for his radical embrace of change as a vital ingredient in the mission strategy of the early church can be paraphrased in these terms: 'Don't blame me; blame the Holy Spirit!'

To sum up, present trends in society demand a radical and sustained high level of change in the church once we accept the priority of cultural engagement. What is more, the evidence from the early church is that the Holy Spirit is on the side of change, shaking churches out of our old accustomed ways to make us effective in mission to unreached people groups. Church leaders need to keep their eye on the ball, continually restating and imparting vision to the local church, so that all believers, some of whom may have a less than clear grasp of the larger and longer-term vision, are able to accept and cope with the continuing processes of change.

Bridging the gap

So what kind of church do we need to become in order to be mobilised and effective for the 21st century? To reclaim the dynamism of the first Christians, we need to become a people with vision, committed to worship and to one another, to apostolic teaching and prayer, and to mission to the world. We need to be mobilised into ministry as a high performance body. And we need to dare to declare the abolition of human religion as we live as God's royal priesthood and new temple. The 21st-century church needs to live under the authority of the Bible, for otherwise we can only offer opinions rather than revealed and absolute truth. The 21st-century church needs to be centred on the cross of Christ, for otherwise we cannot know or declare the hope of salvation. And the 21st-century church needs to be Spirit empowered, because otherwise we will not have the resources of God to reach a lost world. Only as we begin to apply these principles can we hope to see the multiplication of vibrant and growing, disciple-making churches, burning brightly with the gospel of Christ.

Above all, we have argued that the 21st-century church

urgently needs to learn to be culturally engaged, for otherwise we cannot hope to reach the vast majority who won't traditionalise in order to become Christians. If the church of the 21st century continues in the dismal course charted by the 20th-century church in the West, we will fail to be good news to our society, and we are doomed to remorseless decline. If we are prepared to return to our roots and find creative ways to bridge the cultural gap, we still have it within our grasp to embark upon the re-evangelisation of the West. Any hope for a decisive advance in mission demands that we begin with radical internal reform. If the modern world is to be reached with the gospel, the traditional Western church must first be born again. Cultural engagement is no optional extra. It is an absolute obligation for our future advance in mission. The church that is dedicated to the unchanging and life-transforming gospel of Christ has nothing to fear and everything to gain from making creative but uncompromised connections with the post-modern world.

In Rio de Janeiro I had the privilege of staying with a family where the parents' church had planted the daughter's church. The planting had been wise: the sending church was fairly traditional, but it gave the new church absolute freedom to explore church and mission in new ways. Even though both churches were Baptist, the parents gave me a wide-eyed description of the mysteries of the new church: their worship hardly ever contained any of the set components that always found a place in the traditional church service; the songs were nearly all new, and they sang them over and over again; no one knew when a service was going to end. It was a familiar story of two church cultures.

Later I spoke to the daughter. She explained that Rio had become such a dangerous place that she would move away tomorrow but for two factors: the new church was helping her grow so much as a believer, and they were reaching so many young people with the gospel. She went on to describe a recent meeting when the Holy Spirit came down upon them and they simply had to continue in worship, regardless of time. They were caught up in wonder, love and praise. Then she paused and said, 'You understand what I'm talking about, don't you?' With a growing sense of excitement I explained that very similar kinds of church are emerging today, both in Britain and around the world.

That day in Rio I began to realise the remarkable opportunities that arise from the emerging international culture, even though this culture is inevitably bringing about a major crisis in numerical attendance at many traditional churches, and is beginning to rock the boat of those newer churches which are beginning to look long in the tooth, trapped in modernity and culturally old fashioned. The apostles were able to take the gospel across the Roman Empire because the Empire provided a common language and relatively safe passage through the Middle East, North Africa and southern Europe. When the printing press was invented in medieval Europe, Christians used it to provide Bibles in the languages of the common people, together with many pamphlets and books. During the period of the European empires, the Western missionary movement was often able to travel on the coat tails of imperial expansion, travelling to previously inaccessible parts of the world. And now we have entered the post-modern condition of globalisation, with a common culture emerging worldwide, of which the universal language is English. We can afford to take heart from our history: at every previous stage of advance in transport and communication, the church has seized the day for a creative and momentous advance of the gospel.

With the Holy Spirit's help, we urgently need to pursue

effective cultural engagement. As we achieve this, new ways of being church that communicate clearly and persuasively in one part of the modern world will begin to provide us with an international currency of church planting and church growth for the 21st century. This could lead to an unparalleled capacity to plant churches across national boundaries. If we have the courage to reinvent the church in radical new forms, developing transferable principles that promote healthy and effective churches, while avoiding the inflexibility of dogmatic blueprints, the 21st-century church has a momentous opportunity to work towards a major and even global advance of the gospel. As the new millennium dawns, this vision is now within our grasp, not just upon a single continent but throughout the world.

Appendix

This vision statement is provided as a work in progress in order to encourage other churches to produce their own. If you dislike something in our vision statement, perhaps that will inspire you to produce something much better!

Kairos – *Church from Scratch*

Initial vision statement for a church that wants to stay relevant and keep growing in quality and in quantity.

What are we looking for?

- a Christ-centred approach in everything
- a word and Spirit church
- a church that is evangelical, charismatic, evangelising, believer baptising

- a church committed to excellence, but avoiding perfectionism
- a church for 21st-century generations
- a church for active service
- a church that gets real and stays real
- a church that seeks to avoid excesses (e.g. intensity, legalism, super-spirituality, negativity, cliques)
- a church for those who are bored or frustrated by traditional church
- a church that knows what must be changed and what must be kept unchanged
- a church that serves the poor
- a church that aspires to be large enough to make a regional impact for Christ as an interdenominational mission and resource centre
- a church that recognises that all other Christian churches are part of the kingdom of God
  - working in partnership with others in evangelism, social action and celebrations
  - appreciating other churches' strengths and not being threatened, suspicious or distant
  - freeing members to serve elsewhere
- a church that warmly appreciates those in 'back-room' tasks (e.g. finance, administration, stewarding)
- a worship style that is well prepared *and* welcomes the spontaneous, drawing on the diversity of contemporary worship, and giving space for youth styles
- a church that releases drama, dance and multimedia to communicate as effectively as possible in the digital age
- a church that is passionate about Jesus and the Great Commission
- a church that builds a strong sense of community and enjoys a good sense of humour

- a church that helps us keep growing as disciples in quality and quantity

What do we want to change about church in the UK today?

- too many demands on our time
- irrelevance
- unreality
- legalism
- negativity
- boredom
- triviality
- sectarianism
- majoring on minors
- lack of vision
- women marginalised
- authoritarianism
- too little gospel
- not enough evangelism and world mission
- failure to reach and keep teens and twenties

What God has joined together, let no one divide

- Jesus and Spirit
- Word and Spirit
- mind and heart
- worship and preaching
- evangelism and social action
- pastoral care, counselling and healing
- multi-generational – from children to elderly
- multi-ethnic – reflecting London as a world city
- single and married

- women and men
- Sunday and Monday to Saturday

Leadership style

We want to enjoy a liberating leadership team:

- the church will appoint leaders who will be liberated to lead
- the leaders will serve and remain accountable to the church, with a passion to liberate the full potential of every believer – drawing people in, including, encouraging, believing that everyone has a valuable part to play

We want to develop a leadership team of men and women that is:

- visionary, prophetic and pastoral
- rooted in the Bible, filled with the Spirit and in touch with the realities of life today
- servant hearted, accessible and always open to suggestions for improvements
- able to release others to follow their dreams and explore new ministries
- fallible, humble and accountable
- never autocratic, distant or self-appointing
- going for it, not cautious, taking wise risks, not safety first
- mutually accountable, protecting one another
- holding to their roles lightly, understanding that leadership is for a season, not a lifelong office
- nurturing new leaders: training, releasing, encouraging and supporting them
- willing to take the gospel very seriously, but keeping a modest view of themselves
- with lifestyles that seek to model our eight core values

Eight core values

As a result of Christ's cross and resurrection, once they had received the Great Commission and been filled with the Holy Spirit, the first Christians devoted themselves to four priorities (Acts 2:42):

1. Whole-life discipleship

'*They devoted themselves to the apostles' teaching.*'
We want to grow deeper as disciples.
Inspiring and practical Bible teaching applied to the real world of home and work, church and leisure – for abundant life.

2. Inclusive fellowship

'*They devoted themselves . . . to the fellowship.*'
We want to grow warmer as brothers and sisters.
Encouraging, forgiving, supportive relationships – for abundant love.

3. Breaking of bread

'*They devoted themselves . . . to the breaking of bread.*'
We want to grow closer to God.
Recovering the centrality of the breaking of bread – for abundant God awareness.

4. Impactful prayer

'*They devoted themselves . . . to prayer.*'
We want to grow stronger in God's resources.
Eager to pray for God to move in power with an imaginative exploration of Christian spirituality from every era – for abundant God dependence.

This fourfold dedication produced a lifestyle with four outstanding qualities (Acts 2:43–47):

5. *Active commitment*

'*They gave to anyone as he had need*' (*v.45*).
We want to grow more generous in service.
Releasing spiritual gifts, ministries and practical compassion to one another and the poor – for abundant participation and kindness.

6. *Vibrant worship*

'. . . *with glad and sincere hearts, praising God*' (*vv.46–47*).
We want to grow more open to God in worship.
Creative, participative worship – for abundant appreciation of God.

7. *Attractive lifestyle*

'. . . *enjoying the favour of all the people*' (*v.47*).
We want to grow more seeker friendly.
Pursuing the fruit of the Spirit and the positive holiness of Jesus – for abundant newcomers to be drawn to Christ.

8. *Fruitful witness*

'*And the Lord added to their number daily those who were being saved*' (*v.47*).
We want to grow more believers who are baptised and integrated into the church and the life of discipleship.
Relevant church and creative evangelism – for abundant conversions.

Selected Bibliography

R. Allen, *Missionary Methods – St Paul's or Ours?* (London, 1912).

R. Allen, *The Spontaneous Expansion of the Church* (London, 1927).

R. Anderson (ed.), *Theological Foundations for Ministry* (T & T Clark, 1979).

R. Bakke, *The Urban Christian* (Marc, 1987).

R. Banks, *Paul's Idea of Community* (Paternoster, 1980).

J. Bax, *The Good Wine – Spiritual Renewal in the Anglican Church* (CHP, 1986).

D. Bebbington, *Evangelicalism in Modern Britain* (Unwin Hyman, 1989).

H. Bettenson, *The Early Christian Fathers* (OUP, 1956).

H. Bettenson, *The Later Christian Fathers* (OUP, 1970).

D. Carson (ed.), *Biblical Interpretation of the Church* (Paternoster, 1984).

M. Cassidy and G. Osei-Mensah (eds), *Together in One Place* (Evangel (Kenya), 1976).

M. Cassidy and L. Verlinden (eds), *Facing New Challenges* (Evangel (Kenya), 1978).

V. Donovan, *Christianity Rediscovered* (SCM, 1978).

J. Drane, *Evangelism for a New Age* (Marshalls, 1994).

315

A. Dulles, *Models of the Church* (Gill & MacMillan, 1976).

J.G. Dunn, *Unity and Diversity in the New Testament* (SCM, 1977).

J.G. Dunn and J. Mackey, *New Testament Theology in Dialogue* (SPCK, 1987).

R. Ellis and R. Mitchell, *Radical Church Planting* (Crossway, 1992).

J. Ellul, *The Subversion of Christianity* (Eerdmans, 1986).

Kevin Ford, *Jesus for a New Generation* (Hodder, 1996).

R. Forster (ed.), *Ten New Churches* (Marc, 1986).

E. Gibbs, *I Believe in Church Growth* (Hodder, 1981).

A. Gilbert, *The Making of Post-Christian Britain* (Longman, 1980).

M. Green, *Freed to Serve* (Hodder, 1983).

W. Grudem, *The Gift of Prophecy* (Kingsway, 1988).

O. Guinness, *The Gravedigger File* (Hodder, 1983).

O. Guinness, *Fit Bodies, Fat Minds* (Hodder, 1995).

F. Hahn, *The Worship of the Early Church* (ET Fortress, 1973).

H. Harman, *The Century Gap* (Vermillion, 1993).

M. Harper, *Let My People Grow* (Hodder, 1977).

J. Harvey-Jones, *Making It Happen – Reflections on Leadership* (Collins, 1988).

J. Hayford, *The Church on the Way* (Zondervan, 1982).

D. Hilborn, *Picking up the Pieces* (Hodder, 1997).

D. Jackman, *Understanding the Church* (Christian Focus, 1996).

S. Jones, *Struggling to Belong* (IVP, 1998).

J.N.D. Kelly, *Commentary on the Pastoral Epistles* (A & C Black, 1963).

J.N.D. Kelly, *Early Christian Doctrines* (A & C Black, 1958).

C. Kraft, *Christianity in Culture* (Orbis, 1979).

H. Kung, *The Church* (Search Press, 1968).

A. McGrath, *Evangelicalism and the Future of Christianity* (Hodder, 1994).

T. Marshall, *Understanding Leadership* (Sovereign World, 1991).

R. Martin, *The Family and the Fellowship* (Paternoster, 1979).

I. Murray, *D. Martyn Lloyd-Jones* (2 volume biography): *The First*

Forty Years (Banner of Truth, 1982); *The Fight of Faith* (Banner of Truth, 1990).

S. Murray, *Church Planting* (Paternoster, 1998).

S. Neill, *A History of Christian Missions* (Penguin, 1964).

L. Newbigin, *The Gospel in a Pluralist Society* (SPCK, 1989).

H.R. Niebuhr, *The Social Sources of Denominationalism* (New American Library, 1929).

M. Noll, *The Scandal of the Evangelical Mind* (Eerdmans, 1994).

M. Noll, D. Bebbington, G. Rawlyk (eds), *Evangelicalism 1700–1990* (OUP, 1994).

C. Pinnock, *Flame of Love* (IVP, 1996).

R. Pointer, *How Do Churches Grow?* (Marc, 1984).

N. Postman, *Amusing Ourselves to Death* (Methuen, 1985).

M. Robinson and S. Christine, *Planting Tomorrow's Churches Today* (Marc, 1992).

R. Schnackenburg, *The Church in the New Testament* (Burns & Oates, 1974).

E. Schillebeecx, *The Church with a Human Face* (SCM, 1985).

C. Schwarz, *Natural Church Development Handbook* (BCGA, 1996).

C. Schwarz and C. Schalk, *Natural Church Development – Implementation Manual* (BCGA, 1998).

H. Snyder, *New Wineskins* (Marshalls, 1975).

H. Snyder, *The Radical Wesley* (IVP, 1980).

H. Snyder, *Liberating the Church* (Marshalls, 1983).

J. Stott, *One People* (Falcon, 1969).

J. Stott and R. Coote (eds), *Down to Earth – Studies in Christianity and Culture* (Hodder, 1981).

J. Stott, *The Contemporary Christian* (IVP, 1992).

H. Taylor, *Biography of J H Taylor* (Hodder, 1965).

D. Tidball, *Who Are the Evangelicals?* (Marshalls, 1994).

F. Tillapaugh, *Unleashing the Church* (Regal, 1982).

J. Tiller and M. Birchall, *The Gospel Community and Its Leadership* (Marshalls, 1987).

M. Tinker (ed.), *Restoring the Vision* (Kingsway, 1990).

A. Toffler, *Future Shock* (Pan, 1970).

D. Tomlinson, *The Post Evangelical* (SPCK, 1995).

WCC, *Baptism, Eucharist and Ministry* (WCC, 1982).

P. Wagner, *Strategies for Church Growth* (Marc, 1987).

M. Warkentin, *Ordination* (Eerdmans, 1982).

R. Warren, *The Purpose Driven Church* (Zondervan, 1995).

D. Watson, *I Believe in the Church* (Hodder, 1978).

D. Wells, *No Place for Truth* (Eerdmans, 1993).